International Real Estate Economics

International Real Estate Economics

PIYUSH TIWARI
University of Aberdeen

and

MICHAEL WHITE
Heriot-Watt University, Edinburgh

palgrave
macmillan

First published 2010 by
PALGRAVE MACMILLAN

Palgrave Macmillan in the UK is an imprint of Macmillan Publishers Limited, registered in England, company number 785998, of Houndmills, Basingstoke, Hampshire RG21 6XS.

Palgrave Macmillan in the US is a division of St Martin's Press LLC, 175 Fifth Avenue, New York, NY 10010.

Palgrave Macmillan is the global academic imprint of the above companies and has companies and representatives throughout the world.

Palgrave® and Macmillan® are registered trademarks in the United States, the United Kingdom, Europe and other countries.

ISBN: 978–0–230–50759–3 hardback
ISBN: 978–0–230–50758–6 paperback

This book is printed on paper suitable for recycling and made from fully managed and sustained forest sources. Logging, pulping and manufacturing processes are expected to conform to the environmental regulations of the country of origin.

A catalogue record for this book is available from the British Library.

A catalog record for this book is available from the Library of Congress.

10 9 8 7 6 5 4 3 2 1
19 18 17 16 15 14 13 12 11 10

Printed and bound in Great Britain by CPI Antony Rowe, Chippenham and Eastbourne

Contents

Figures

Tables

Acknowledgements

The authors would like to thank Geoff Keogh for his knowledge of the subject area and his contribution to the discussions on the initial structure of this book. We would also like to thank the production team at Palgrave Macmillan, especially Jaime Marshall for his enduring patience, and our students who over many years have listened to us discussing international real estate economics. Last, but not least, we would like to thank our families (Pushpa and Anushka, Irene and James) for their support.

Contextualising International Real Estate Markets

1.1 Introduction

The concept of an international real estate market is a relatively new phenomenon. Indeed, the idea of markets for certain commodities or services existing on an international, or global, scale is also relatively new, although in some sense it has existed in more or less limited ways since the beginning of economics itself as a distinct discipline. However, the past 30 years have witnessed the most significant growth in, or internationalisation of, the real estate industry. This is set within a wider context of global economic change and international economic integration. It is, therefore, also important that we begin by explicitly talking about economics, since this is the basis for the analysis that we will proceed to unfold in this text.

As an asset class, real estate has often been treated rather differently from other assets (see Hendershott and White, 2000). Real estate is usually an expensive asset due to its high unit value. It tends to be illiquid and heterogeneous, and consequently real estate markets display limited information, which can lead to inefficiency in resource allocation. Commercial real estate markets (offices, retail and industrial) are even less efficient than residential markets, since they display more pronounced high unit value and greater heterogeneity, and have even less information (many local markets may be 'thin'). In addition, even in well established and 'large' markets, problems created by these characteristics can still be significant. However, the market still tends to attempt to establish a reconciliation of demand for, and supply of, space. Thus the economics of the market has a crucial role to play in understanding the behaviour of real estate. Early applications of economics to international markets include those by Adam Smith and David Ricardo. Smith (1776) outlined key issues in international trade theory. These were refined and developed further by Ricardo (1817), who laid the foundation for the classical analysis of international trade based upon the theory of comparative advantage.

The internationalisation of trade and the creation of the modern global economy have beginnings as far back as the late fifteenth and early sixteenth centuries in Europe. Wealth creation was limited and income per head had been roughly unchanged since the 1100s. Industrialisation and technological change increased incomes and trade. World exports grew by 1,000 per cent in the 50 years after 1820, and by 3.4 per cent per annum from 1870 to 1913. Trade with colonial nations played a significant role in this period. Countries also imposed tariffs on certain imports to protect domestic industries from competition. The US, France, Germany and the UK all engaged in such policies. However, this period of 'spectacular growth in international economic integration was not accompanied by any significant institutionalisation of intergovernmental collaboration' (Ravenhill, 2005, p. 8). Governments tended to adopt bilateral trade agreements. They also adopted the gold standard (in which national currencies were linked to gold via a fixed exchange price that subsequently fixed their exchange rates against other currencies), which aided the development of international trade by essentially removing exchange rate risk.

There is no discussion in the literature of the period on the role of real estate. This is perhaps not surprising. Trade between countries was largely an exchange of manufactured goods for agricultural products. Trade in international services as they exist today had hardly begun. However, real estate had become an asset. Most residential real estate in the UK was not owned by the occupiers and provided an income stream to landlords. Indeed, some real estate firms that today provide services at an international scale already existed, although not in their current form (e.g., the modern CBRE originated as Richard Ellis).

After the growth of the international trade of the nineteenth and early twentieth centuries, the interwar period saw economic slowdown and then depression. As nations became concerned about the effect of competition from foreign imports on domestic industries, tariffs were increased and international trade declined significantly. It was only after 1945 that international economic integration gathered pace. This period also saw the establishment of international economic institutions, such as the World Bank and the International Monetary Fund.

The past 60 years have witnessed significant economic integration across the globe. After the depression of the interwar period and with the end of the Second World War, the setting up of the Bretton Woods system of fixed exchange rates sought to remove uncertainty and encourage trade between countries. Macroeconomic demand management policies throughout the 1950s and 1960s sought to maximise employment. Against this background international trade increased, developed economies increasingly became service sector-dominated, and economies that had previously been agricultural began to industrialise as overseas investment brought manufacturing industry and jobs. These changes created a resulting demand for real estate. Companies too, locating overseas, grew into multi-country organisations. Today, trade is dominated by multinational corporations with branches operating in many different countries, linking them into an increasingly globalised economic system.

The Bretton Woods system collapsed in 1972/3 and was replaced by various policies towards exchange rates, some floating in the market, some with a degree of floating permitted but with an element of government intervention. The turbulent economic environment of the period saw governments move away from Keynesian demand management to more liberal economic policies that favoured the reduction of the role of the state, arguing that the market was better at allocating resources. This school of thought argued for deregulation, and policymakers in the UK and the US in particular were among the earliest to adopt policies based upon this view of macroeconomics. Consequent policy changes, such as removal of exchange controls and further deregulation of the banking and finance sector, laid the foundation for many of the subsequent changes in the world economy. The impact on the real estate market has been substantial.

Since financial deregulation in the 1980s, international trade flows have come to be dominated by flows of international financial capital seeking the highest risk-adjusted return. As real incomes have grown and economies have developed, there has been an increasing demand for real estate assets across all property sectors: retail, office, industrial and residential. The real estate market itself has developed, reflecting user and investor demand on the one hand, and developer supply of space on the other. Real estate companies themselves have witnessed change in the range of services they provide and the range of markets to which those services are provided. It could be argued that within the last two decades a globalised international real estate market has been established.

However, significant differences across countries still exist. Countries vary in the extent to which they view property as an investment asset. In some countries, real estate is a distinct asset class competing for investment funds from other assets of bonds and equities. In others, it does not yet attract significant investment. In some countries most commercial real estate is owner-occupied; in others, occupiers rent space and investors receive an income and capital return. All countries are facing the same global challenges to attract investment in order to raise GDP and living standards. Consequently their real estate markets also attract attention from investors. Nations may, however, respond differently to similar challenges, providing the possibility for differentiation in outcomes across countries.

Not only is the real estate investment market becoming increasingly global, but in addition the real estate service providers themselves are increasingly becoming global operations. Many firms have moved beyond their home country base and have established overseas operations. Both 'push' and 'pull' factors have contributed to this change. Home markets may be relatively small or saturated, causing firms to look for new opportunities overseas. Also the firms' clients may be opening operations in other countries and require real estate service provision. The internationalisation of real estate companies has been facilitated by different strategies, including takeovers, mergers and strategic alliances. This process itself has been made easier by the removal or reduction of barriers to trade and a process of economic liberalisation that has characterised global economic development over the last 30 years.

Investors considering real estate as an investment class may consider different property sectors, including offices, retail, industrial and residential investment options. In different countries different sectors may take the lead (in terms of risk-adjusted returns) at different points in time. At any one time, differences in national economic structures may imply differential performance across the property sectors and hence determine which sector becomes the most attractive for investors.

However, even if property is performing well in an economy, this alone is insufficient to attract inward investment. Barriers preventing foreign investment, property rights issues, lack of transparency, and institutions operating within an economy may discourage or impede investment.

Economic uncertainty is another factor impeding investment. This is a general characteristic of market economies, and exists within national economies and also in the world economy. For an investor, the less is known about a market the greater the uncertainty, and hence overseas investment is often perceived as being more risky than domestic investment decisions. Periods of heightened uncertainty in one economy may or may not be correlated with uncertainty in other economies. The lower the intercountry correlation, the greater are the diversification opportunities afforded by international asset holdings.

Estimating the value of returns from overseas investments faces the additional complication of estimating expected future exchange rate movements. Exchange rate volatility can be a significant factor in affecting which countries provide the greatest return when converting to the home currency. Different time periods have witnessed varying responses to exchange rate volatility. The increase in international trade in the late nineteenth century occurred against a background of stable exchange rates founded on the gold standard with agreed rates of convertibility of currencies into gold. Some early attempts at monetary union were also in evidence, for example, between France, Italy, Belgium and Switzerland in 1865, and in 1873 between Sweden and Denmark, who were joined also by Norway in 1875. The First World War saw countries depart from the gold standard. During the interwar period it was reintroduced, but this was short-lived. The depression of the 1930s effectively ended the gold standard and the value of international transactions fell dramatically. It was only after 1945 that a new international monetary system emerged. Unlike the earlier period of the late nineteenth century, this period was notable for the establishment of new institutions such as the IMF and the World Bank, as mentioned above. However, it was similar in that a system of relatively fixed exchange rates was introduced. Against this background the world economy grew, and it is in this period that we begin to see the first real internationalisation of real estate markets. This Bretton Woods, system lasted until the economic turbulence of the early 1970s. Subsequent interventions in foreign exchange markets are discussed in the following chapters.

In this introductory chapter we outline the economic environment of international real estate, examine trends and cycles, and discuss challenges facing internationalisation with respect to different institutional environments, both formal and informal. We then proceed to discuss economic transmission mechanisms and the role of international real estate within these mechanisms before outlining how this book is organised.

1.2   Overview of international real estate markets

Estimating the value of real estate transactions is notoriously difficult. In terms of transactions volume, it is difficult to provide a complete picture across all real estate sectors of office, retail and industrial properties. Lack of accuracy in recording of transactions in some countries affects measurement. In addition, in many countries residential property is also a sizeable investment class. Global sales value across residential and commercial property in 2007 was estimated to be over US$1 trillion. Office transactions accounted for over 40 per cent of this total, followed by retail at around 17 per cent. Slightly more than 50 per cent of transactions occurred in North America, approximately 31 per cent in Europe and almost 15 per cent in Asia. Office transactions were more important in North America and Europe than in Asia.

Offices dominated the highest value transactions, and tended to be geographically concentrated in London and New York, with the second highest-value transaction taking place in Paris. Transactions by country for the top 12 are listed in Table 1.1 below.

The countries listed above accounted for 89 per cent of global real estate transactions in 2007. The countries map onto the global regions of North America, Europe, and South East Asia and Japan. The concentration of the highest-value

Table 1.1 Transaction values by country (2007)

Country	US$ Billion
United States	510.3
United Kingdom	104.4
Germany	60.8
China	59.6
Japan	38.1
France	37.3
Australia	29.6
Canada	19.7
Singapore	18.6
Sweden	16.9
Hong Kong	14.4
Spain	14.3

Source: Real Capital Analytics (2008)
Global Capital Trends, downloaded
from http://www.rcanalytics.com

transactions in the cities mentioned above indicates the unevenness of office location and concentrations. While the above figures provide an example for one year only, it is likely that the same cities would continue to be the location for future high-value transactions.

The growth of investment in real estate markets in the last decade has occurred against a background of real estate generally outperforming other asset classes. This growth has also taken place in a global economy characterised by increasing deregulation and relatively high and continued world economic growth. The end of 2007 and beginning of 2008, however, saw concerns over future economic growth, problems in the US sub-prime mortgage markets leading to lower income growth rates around the world, and increasing demand for commodities fuelling significant inflationary pressures. The period of high growth and low inflation experienced since the early 1990s seemed to be over. By 2009, the US economy, the UK economy and many others were in recession. Unlike the recession of the early 1990s, this one saw the problems in the financial sector restrict the availability of credit, and this affected the real economy. The consequent falling demand helped to reduce commodity price inflation, but the world economy was facing the most significant challenges to growth since the interwar period.

However, volatility is an inherent feature of market-based economic systems. In the postwar period, economic growth was experienced by Western economies between 1945 and 1973. While economies experienced some volatility and cyclical behaviour, fluctuations in the rate of change in GDP were comparatively small in comparison to either the 1970s and 1980s or the interwar period. Oil price rises, government macroeconomic policies and structural change impacted economies in the 1970s, leading to high inflation rates. The consequent rise of monetarism saw the introduction of restrictive monetary and fiscal policies as oil prices rose again in the early 1980s. Economies were faced with further structural change, and liberal market policies saw falling income tax rates, financial deregulation and removal of exchange controls. By the mid-1980s strong economic growth was occurring. However, inflationary pressures saw increases in interest rates in the late 1980s feeding into the recession of the early 1990s. Between 1992 and 2007 most Western economies experienced the longest period of sustained economic growth since before the first oil price shock took place in 1973. But 2008 saw slowing growth and recession. Recent changes in the world economy suggest that there may be a more volatile period ahead.

Since the late 1980s and early 1990s, real estate markets in general (and mature markets in particular) have experienced limited volatility and cycles with relatively low amplitude of fluctuation, certainly in more established markets. Nevertheless, rental value cycles have remained a feature of property markets across the world, with newer markets, for example in Bangkok and Shanghai, experiencing significant fluctuations. However, relative market volatility is not necessarily confined to newer office locations. London, which has a substantial direct real estate market, has exhibited more volatility than smaller markets in the UK since the 1970s, if not before.

These cycles themselves are not only due to endogenous fluctuations within the real estate sector but are also caused by exogenous influences, such as interest rate fluctuations and, in an international context, real interest rate differentials and differences between expected yields on property investment versus the cost of funds for leveraged investors. The ability to move funds internationally has raised the possibility of a disconnection developing between domestic user and investor markets on the demand side. This possibility is discussed more fully in later chapters.

In addition to the amplitude of fluctuation, the degree of synchronisation of cyclical fluctuations is an issue. It might reasonably be expected that the higher the degree of economic integration across countries, the higher would be the degree of real estate cycle synchronisation, as all countries are responding to the impact of similar economic shocks or events.

Furthermore, while there is variability in the amplitude of fluctuation and degree of synchronisation, real estate cycles also vary with respect to the impact they exert on the wider economy and, in the reverse causal direction, the degree to which changes in the economy affect real estate cycles. Dehesh and Pugh (2000, p. 2581) argue that 'in periods of domestic macroeconomic stability, property cycles tend to be endogenous – i.e. caused by disequilibria within the sector – and they are relatively subdued. In periods of domestic macroeconomic instability, property cycles tend to be exogenous – i.e. caused by various conditions in the macroeconomy – and sometimes feature exceptional fluctuations. The exceptional cycles, with heightened amplitudes and longer periodicity, exert [a] relatively deep and protracted impact on the wider economy.' Dehesh and Pugh proceed to argue that financial deregulation and economic integration across national economies have caused property cycles to be influenced by international economic events. They also imply that there is consequently an increased sensitivity in the causal relationship between the economy and the property market and vice versa.

In highlighting structural economic change internationally, Dehesh and Pugh focus on the role of the financial services sector. They suggest that this sector has impacted on property markets in specific cities across the globe where the sector is concentrated. The industry's requirements are seen to have affected new office development; occupiers desire large open floorspates, designed for holding modern communications technologies. Such a change in occupier requirements quickens obsolescence of older existing stock and increases demand for development. However, such structural changes within office markets may interact with, and occur contemporaneously with, fluctuations in both the macroeconomy and credit markets. The authors argue that: 'the interactions and interdependence can heighten inflation, cause financial collapse and then lead to recession in property sectors. More than this, cross-border interdependence of macroeconomic instabilities, via trade balances, and sometimes capital inflows and outflows, can generate international cyclicality in property' (op. cit., p. 2583).

Financial capital is now more mobile, and countries can experience significant inflows and outflows of funds. There has also been notable innovation in the availability and variety of financial products. More short and long-term financial instruments now exist in both debt and equity markets. This may exacerbate economic volatility by inducing excessive investment in growth phases and leaving an excessive debt burden and underinvestment in recessionary periods. The amplitude of the economic cycle is thus increased. 'All of this is more significant in post-1980 economies which are more volatile and exposed to international capital movements compared with the comparative stabilities of the Keynesian period' (ibid., pp. 2583–4) of macroeconomic management.

The exposure of the property sector to debt finance is a further problem. Although lessons were learnt from the last significant property cycle in the late 1980s and early 1990s, the subsequent financial innovation, incentives to market agents, integration of markets, and insufficient understanding of market product developments by regulatory authorities have led to problems in credit markets. These manifest themselves through reduced liquidity and particularly acute problems in relation to mortgage-backed securities. Since real estate is highly exposed to such financing sources, it is the most notably affected in comparison to other sectors of the economy.

Barras (1994) discusses the interlinkages between property and the economy and illustrates how a building boom is generated by the interaction of the business cycle, the credit cycle and the long cycle of development in the property market. Essentially focusing on the user market (and also implicitly assuming symmetry between the upswings and downswings), he describes the period leading up to the boom of the late 1980s in the London office market, this being the first boom that had occurred since international financial deregulation. A short-run economic upturn in the mid-1980s coincided with a relative shortage of space, leading to increases in rents and capital values, and falling yields. The development sector began construction of new space. At the same time interest rates fell in the macroeconomy, reinforcing economic growth. There was now a building boom but little new supply due to the time lag in constructing new buildings. In this situation, rising inflation now present in the economy leads to more restrictive monetary policy and interest rates begin to rise. The tightening of monetary policy moves the economy into the downswing of the macroeconomic cycle. New space is now supplied to the market as demand from occupiers and investors levels off or begins to fall. Rents and capital values fall. If there is a recession in the economy, absorption of space will continue to fall and development companies will go bankrupt. As the economy expands again, demand rises, but there will be no rise in rents and no new development, as vacant space will be absorbed.

This pattern is characteristic of the office markets in London from the late 1980s and into the 1990s. A similar pattern was also observed in the boom and bust property market of the 1970s. The most recent cyclical fluctuations in the London markets, from the mid-1990s until 2005/6, did not have the amplitude of fluctuation of the earlier periods, reflecting the lower volatility in the macroeconomy and also the increased importance of overseas investors. Thus the behaviour of the market did not seem to be adversely affected by the deregulated financial environment in which it had been operating. However, speculative development funded by financial institutions has been less of a feature in the last 15 years than in the late 1980s. Some commentators subsequently suggested that the finance sector had learned its lesson from the mistaken expectations of the past.

Recent events highlight another source of instability associated with the deregulated international financial market. On this occasion, it has been poor-quality sub-prime mortgage debt originating in the US. Mortgage defaults have reduced income returns from these assets. However, the ability to repackage and sell debt products internationally has meant that this problem in one country has become a global phenomenon. Similar repackaging of debt has been a feature in global financial centres. Financial institutions in many countries have become highly exposed and have been seen to have taken on too much risk in their investment decision-making. Governments have intervened in an attempt to prevent a collapse of the global financial system. In the UK, billions of pounds of taxpayers' money have been used to support banks, with the largest losses being seen at The Royal Bank of Scotland (RBS).

The global interlinkages within the financial system have spread these problems across countries. Financial institutions have begun to write off debt, losing considerable sums of money, and the increased uncertainty and risk in the financial market have left institutions less willing to lend, leading to a shortage of liquidity in the money markets. This has effectively resulted in an increase in the price of money, which has in practice become significantly higher than suggested by base rates set by central banks. In the property market there have been signs of significant falls in investment volumes in North America, Europe and Australia, with, globally, a 50 per cent reduction in the first two months of 2008 compared with the same period in 2007. North America and Australia saw property sales fall by over 70 per cent in the beginning of 2008 compared with 2007. In the UK there has been a 40 per cent fall from 2007 to 2008. Office properties seem to be the worst affected. Some financial institutions have been more exposed to commercial property than others. For example, RBS has been one major lender in commercial real estate.

The reliance in certain countries on commercial mortgage-backed securities (CMBS) as a financing source has been a key problem. The US and Japan are more reliant on these finance sources than other countries, although their importance has increased in Europe. This has affected the slowdown, and its lower impact in Europe means that it is expected to perform slightly less badly than North America in terms of market activity as the year progresses. In contrast, South America and Asia have seen increases in property sales, and equity finance availability was unaffected in mid-2008 by the 'credit crunch'. But, as the financial problems have impacted on real economies, there has been evidence that these regions are also experiencing reduced growth and recession.

Financial deregulation has permitted not only the unimpeded movement of international financial capital to where it can achieve the highest risk-adjusted return, but also a greater extent of contagion than would previously have been the case if bad debts had not been repackaged and sold throughout the world financial system, or if regulation had prevented such products from being developed.

These characteristics of the current international financial system may stem in part from poor regulatory control of a system itself developed from a desire for financial liberalisation on the premise of the invisible-hand ability of markets to allocate resources efficiently to where they are most needed. In a world of product (and service) complexity, self-interest-seeking behaviour and bounded rationality, it may have been too naïve to leave the invisible hand to its own devices. By 2009, the problems in the financial sector had led to recession or lower growth rates in countries around the world.

1.3   Challenges facing international real estate

Internationalisation of real estate companies began as a slow process starting in the 1950s. Internationalisation of real estate use (via multinational companies, for example) and investment was limited until the 1970s. In the immediate post-war period, real estate companies provided a limited range of services focusing on valuation. As the methods of valuation varied, UK firms' expansion opportunities were first and foremost in Commonwealth countries with similar laws and cultures of doing business. As multinational firms came to dominate trade and the global economy expanded, new opportunities for globalised real estate companies appeared. These firms could provide services to multinationals and offer investment-grade prime real estate in different countries.

However, many barriers to overseas expansion existed. Formal legal rules could prevent acquisition of property. Political instability and arbitrary expropriation hindered investment. In the qualitative dimension, different methods of conducting business existed (and still remain), and the culture of the real estate industry (if it existed) varied across countries. International real estate service providers faced competition from local real estate agents who had better local knowledge. Institutional differences could also prevent internationalisation. These institutional characteristics reflect societal preferences and may often act to constrain investment.

The professional standards to which real estate industries work in different countries may also vary. Legal mechanisms may mean that transactions may not involve real estate professionals such as surveyors. As the industry has changed and offers a greater range of services it has begun to employ a wider range of professionals, including economists, architects, lawyers and investment analysts, in addition to chartered surveyors. A dominant player within the UK industry is the Royal Institution of Chartered Surveyors (RICS), which has affected the way in which business is conducted. The absence of similar bodies from other countries does not necessarily imply a lack of professionalism, but it may signify that rules for conducting business differ and reflect the role of different professions in a specific society.

However, the internationalisation of business, and the dominance of multinational corporations in trade flows within trading blocs and across the world economy, have not only aided internationalisation of real estate companies (service providers) but also, more generally, globalised professional business service firms. Such firms are knowledge-intensive and service-focused. They use their professional expertise to provide services tailored to client needs. They add value through provision of bespoke knowledge-intensive services to meet their clients' requirements, and generally have an ongoing or close working relationship with their client base. They regard professional standards as important and may themselves have a relationship with professional bodies.

But such firms, given the above characteristics, may not need to be international or global in their coverage. Porter (1986) distinguishes between multidomestic and global industries. In a multidomestic industry, competition in one country is unrelated to competition in another country. In a global industry, 'a firm's competitive position in one country is significantly affected by its position in other countries or vice versa' (op. cit., p. 18).

Porter considers the 'value-chain' and separates upstream and downstream activities. Support activities, for example, would be considered upstream, while marketing and service would be characterised as downstream. He argues that 'downstream activities create competitive advantages that are largely country specific: a firm's reputation, brand name, and service network in a country grow largely out of a firm's activities in that country and create entry/mobility barriers largely in that country alone. [W]here downstream activities...are vital to competitive advantage, there tends to be a more multi-domestic pattern of international competition' (ibid., p. 23).

The internationalisation of real estate service providers could be considered as a specific case of professional business services. Real estate firms originating in, for example, the UK now usually have offices and operations in property markets in many different countries across the world. In internationalising they have had to adapt to different legal frameworks, institutional structures and cultural influences that have impacted on business practices. The lack of information in property markets is a significant factor in creating relative market inefficiency, and when going international this lack of information is acutely problematic, erecting, as it does, a significant barrier to entry and increasing costs of market penetration. In addition, as property transacting has specific national and, indeed, local characteristics, the ability of a new market entrant from overseas to be successful is significantly reduced. This, as we discuss later, has had an impact on the form which overseas expansion has taken.

Important for further integration of markets, and internationalisation of agreed professional service standards, is increased transparency of market practices. Currently there are still differences in valuation methods that make direct comparisons more difficult for investors. Leases, taxes, standards of accounting, information and market performance measurement also vary across countries. However, it is probably true to say that, for example, there is significantly more market information today than would have been available in the 1990s. This is true even of newer real estate markets (Shanghai, Beijing, Bangkok). Internationalisation of use, investment and development of real estate has also spurred harmonisation of practice. Furthermore, as information increases, transparency improves and international markets become more efficient. This is still an ongoing process and markets continue to vary with respect to the quantity and quality of information available.

As mentioned above, real estate service providers have internationalised against a background of national and local differences in the extent to which property is seen as an investment asset, and against various differences in market practices and institutional differences. While property markets are largely local in nature, there is pressure for local practices to respond to the needs of international economic forces.

International real estate service providers are often a catalyst for change in local markets, as they bring with them a particular set of attitudes, values and practices to the market exchange process. They themselves encourage internationalisation of professional standards of market exchange and their behaviour tends to raise information levels and encourages transparency in the markets they enter. D'Arcy *et al.* (1998) examine how the international real estate market has been affected by the internationalisation strategy of real estate service providers. They highlight the significant role played by UK and US firms in affecting the standards to which the industry operates at a global level. They also show how structural change in the industry has led to strategic alliances, mergers and acquisitions between firms as they endeavour to provide global real estate services to clients.

We discuss internationalisation strategies of real estate service providers further in the following chapters. The structure and range of provision are discussed, together with the impact that the firms' internationalisation strategies have had on the market exchange process (in relation to information availability, transparency and service quality).

1.4   Interlinkages between real estate and economic forces

We have alluded above to the interaction between economic change at a global scale and real estate market behaviour. We have discussed the factors affecting cyclical behaviour in real estate markets and how these might interact with the macroeconomy.

Recent economic history indicates that, when endogenous real estate forces interact with exogenous macroeconomic factors, real estate cyclical fluctuations can be significant in both amplitude and duration. In the UK context, significant cycles were observed in commercial property markets, particularly office markets, in the early 1970s and again in the late 1980s. The relatively small economic upturn around 1979 was not reflected in commercial property markets, as the excess supply constructed following the rent and capital value signals in the previous boom had still not been fully absorbed by the end of the decade. Cyclical behaviour has continued through the 1990s and into the first decade of the new millennium, but with less volatility.

Given the supply lags prevalent in the construction of commercial buildings, macroeconomic change does not immediately result in changes in supply at any given point in time. Recent problems with market liquidity have impacted on property yields, but supply already in the pipeline will still be delivered to the market, even though it is not clear what the level of demand will be when the space is ready for occupation. This is particularly problematic for speculative developments that have no identifiable occupier at the time construction is commenced.

In general, financial variables will respond first to economic change and embody an expectation of change that will occur in other sectors of the economy. The real economy is slower to adjust, and hence there is a tendency for financial variables to overshoot the new 'long-run' values, since all expected change is embodied in these variables first. The Barras (1994) description of the interaction between the real estate market and the economy has general applicability across all property markets in different countries. The added dimension is that real estate markets in different cities are linked by global economic factors. For example, the sub-prime mortgage market in the US has affected markets across the globe to a greater or lesser extent because of the exposure of these real estate markets to finance sourced from CMBS products. Excessive risk-taking by banks in many countries is also having adverse effects on liquidity.

Specific local factors will differentiate market behaviour. Differences in industrial structure and the spatial concentration of particular industries may lead to a degree of non-synchronisation in the timing of cycles, levels of absorption, and development activity. So, for example, office markets in cities in which the oil industry is a major employer may be less adversely affected by the 'credit crunch' than cities with high proportions of financial services, although they are not immune to market cycles. In 2006–8 markets affected by key commodities (such as oil) saw falling vacancy rates, rental growth and falling yields. They are located from Aberdeen, Scotland, to Edmonton, Canada. In other markets, where the main office occupiers are concentrated in the finance industry, such as New York and London, the current market situation will adversely impact on these property markets. Thus both local and global factors will impact on commercial real estate.

New building construction can be regarded as a form of new investment in the built stock. It can also be seen as part of the accelerator process that affects the economic cycle. As demand rises in the economy for goods and services, and assuming the existing stock has been absorbed (i.e., the vacancy rate is below the long-run average and rents and capital values are rising), there will be a resulting demand for new space. New construction creates new employment and expenditure, leading to a reinforcement of the multiplier effect. If there is little inflationary pressure, there will be no rise in interest rates and no weakening of occupier demand. Once the buildings are complete the occupiers take up the new space. If there is no extra demand for more space (when it arrives on the market) then the construction industry itself will contract, causing redundancies. This will weaken the multiplier effect in the economy and could lower the rate of economic growth.

The above scenario is similar to that described for the UK in the late 1980s, but without the excessive growth rate of the boom or the subsequent bust. Economies around the world face varying circumstances, variations in the strength of the economic growth phase, variations in the extent to which growth stokes up inflationary pressures, and variations in the depth and duration of recessions. Evidence suggests that economies in earlier phases of economic development have more volatile macroeconomic cycles. These also tend to be economies in which the construction sector contributes a larger proportion to GDP, and hence when macroeconomic and real estate cycles coincide there is the potential for significant volatility to be experienced. Financial liberalisation and openness to international economic forces tend to exacerbate volatility. This is particularly true when there are weak regulatory practices in the countries concerned, for example, Thailand in the latter part of the 1990s.

The fundamental driver lying behind the international real estate market activity is economic growth and development. This is a necessary condition for the growth of a commercial real estate market. However, it is not in and of itself sufficient for the development of an international real estate investment market. The latter requires legislation on ownership and use rights, and in general the appropriate institutional environment to encourage business (see Geurts and Jaffe, 1996, discussed in later chapters).

Economies move from being largely agricultural towards manufacturing and then to being service sector-dominated. Major developed economies today in North America, Europe and Japan have over 70 per cent of their workforces employed in the service sector. This tends to strengthen demand for offices relative to manufacturing units. But, as these economies have relatively high disposable income, there is also an increasing demand for retail. Developing economies have a relatively high proportion of their workforces in manufacturing, creating a demand for industrial property to house manufacturing equipment and workers. Typically it is cheaper to manufacture products in developing economies, where wages are lower. For example, the US, Western European and Japanese companies have largely moved their manufacturing to developing countries such as Mexico, Eastern Europe and South East Asia respectively. This move has caused relatively rapid economic growth in these regions. Higher value-added research jobs have tended to remain in the home economies, and higher value-added products often continue to be manufactured in home countries where the manufacturing jobs that remain may produce a higher added value than those shipped offshore. These moves also reflect the skills of the workforce and changes, over time, to skills embodied in the workforce.

A consequence of these long-term developments is a demand for real estate. This has been seen in South East Asia, particularly in Singapore, Kuala Lumpur and Bangkok. It is also evident in Eastern Europe, with development taking place initially in Poland, Hungary and the Czech Republic, and more recently with newer markets starting to develop in the Baltic states of Estonia, Latvia and Lithuania. In their infancy are markets in Romania and Bulgaria. Here there is only a limited amount of prime quality product available, and little in the way of an investment market, partly because few opportunities currently exist. For Poland, for example, this was the case a decade ago.

In developed economies, real estate investment markets exist in all major cities and in all sectors: retail, office and industrial. In developing economies, real estate investment markets may be focused solely on the capital city and on a few larger regional cities. Characteristics of the real estate market will also vary, so, for example, the industrial market in the UK consists largely of warehousing, whereas in developing economies it may reflect a greater proportion of manufacturing.

1.5   Aim and structure of the book

This book will provide a comprehensive analysis of international real estate markets. It will examine the rationale for their existence and development. This will be linked to the processes of economic change that have been experienced over the past 60 years, in particular following the economic deregulation of the 1980s. It will highlight the role of economic change, international financial diversification, institutional adaptation, and the role of, and changes in, business culture to provide an understanding of the behaviour of real estate markets. The book allows comparison of real estate markets in different countries, showing national differences in market characteristics. Moreover, the book shows how these characteristics have changed over time and how market development has been influenced by the entrance of international companies and the interaction between them on the one hand, and local agents and local institutions on the other.

The issues raised above are discussed more fully in the following chapters. Setting the theoretical context, and given that real estate services are internationally traded, Chapter 2 develops theories on international trade, from classical to more modern theories. From more general investment theory, models are applied to the real estate market, since real estate is also an investment asset. The chapter then proceeds to examine real estate service provision, setting real estate firms within the context of professional business services provision. This provides a management dimension to the discussion of real estate, as it is an asset that uniquely can be improved in terms of its quality and, hence, value. The chapter discusses internationalisation of capital flows in the form of foreign direct investment (FDI). It will discuss how this has itself internationalised, and highlight the characteristics of real estate services within this broader industry development.

Chapter 3 discusses financial theories, modern portfolio theory and the capital asset pricing model. These theories form the basis for understanding investment in securitised and unsecuritised property markets, which are then examined. The chapter finally proceeds to examine international institutional change, drawing upon new institutional economic theory. This is then specifically applied to the institutional environment of international real estate markets and real estate markets themselves, and the economies in which they operate are conceived of as institutions. Institutional theory provides an added layer of analysis to improve understanding and conceptualisation of property markets.

Chapter 4 examines the structure of real estate service provision, identifying changes in the range of services offered and trends in the mix of services provided. It examines the quality of services, the range of skills of firms' employees and how professional real estate services have been internationalised. It also highlights differences between the skill base for real estate in different countries.

International real estate market activity is discussed in Chapter 5. It draws out detail on international use (occupation), investment, and real estate development. Specifically, it analyses different real estate investment vehicles and the institutions that play a role in real estate investment. The chapter discusses issues of portfolio construction and diversification and the internationalisation of real estate investment. The structure of the development industry is outlined and sources of real estate finance are considered.

The third section of the book, Chapters 6 to 9, examines developments in international real estate markets around the world. The chapters analyse market performance in and between countries located in world regional trading blocs, measuring risk and return to international real estate investment, market trends and short-run volatility of market cycles. They consider market characteristics that affect market formation and exchange, including transparency issues, market maturity, professional formation, real estate and planning law. The chapters examine the extent to which there has been convergence or otherwise in market performance, the degree to which standardisation of market practice has occurred, market evolution, and the ways in which markets are becoming more efficient.

These broad issues listed above are discussed in relation to European real estate markets in Chapter 6, Asia-Pacific markets in Chapter 7, North American markets in Chapter 8 and markets outside the major trading blocs, for example South America, in Chapter 9.

The final chapter of the book synthesises the material. It shows how real estate markets have moved from simply being national to becoming international, highlighting the interlinkages across countries. The implications for real estate users, investors, developers and service providers themselves are discussed. Based upon current trends identified and an analysis of market developments, suggestions are then made for future directions in international real estate in terms of new markets attractive to investors in real estate, new challenges to internationalisation of real estate service providers, further developments in market information flows and levels of transparency, and increased integration of different economies with global economic forces.

Theorising International Real Estate 1

2.1 Introduction

With globalisation, cross-border property market activity in the use, asset and development markets has increased substantially. Some economic agents in the use market demand space, which is an input in their production of goods and services. Other economic agents own and supply space. Rent clears the market. Internationalisation of production of goods and services affects demand for space through two economic processes: (i) trade in goods and services; (ii) location of part of production by transnational corporations (TNCs). Trade in goods and services affects the production of these goods and services within the boundaries of a country. For example, if there were demand for goods produced in a country in international markets and the country could supply the goods at international price (assuming perfect market competition, numerous suppliers, and that the country is a price taker), the domestic production of these goods within the boundary of the country would increase. This in turn would imply that the space required to produce these goods would also increase. Precisely the reverse would happen if a country imported goods from other countries. The inference here is highly simplistic, and by no means suggests that trade is not advantageous if a country is a net importer. It will be demonstrated, when models of trade are discussed, that trade enhances welfare. The simple point that is being made here is that trade is one of the key determinants of demand for space in a country. TNCs locate part of their production processes in other countries, thereby contributing to the demand for use of space in these countries.

National allegiance of suppliers of space in the property use market could be domestic or foreign. Though property ownership in a country is largely dominated by domestic agents (individuals or private or public entities), in recent years the role of international economic agents in ownership of property and supply of space for use has increased.

In the asset market, investors invest in property in anticipation of realising returns. Property generates income (in the form of rent) and capital (in the form of change in capital values over time) returns for investors. Investors in the property asset market are both national and international. The nature of capital flows in property is of two types: (i) portfolio investment, where an investor resident in one country invests in stocks, bonds and other financial instruments related to property in the other country; and (ii) foreign direct investment (FDI), where an investor based in one country acquires property in the other country with the intention of managing it.

The development market is the market where developers combine land, material, capital and expertise to generate new space. Developers may be either national or international. In recent years, a number of international developers have been involved in development overseas. Many Hong Kong-based developers are active in development activities in China, Singapore-based developers are developing properties in Malaysia, India and other East Asian countries, Dubai-based developers are actively involved in development in India, and Germany-based developers are developing properties in Central and Eastern European countries.

There are three types of issues to consider: (i) internationalisation of economies through trade and foreign direct investment, which have implications for demand for real estate space; (ii) international capital flows in assets, including real estate; and (iii) internationalisation of real estate production processes and organisations. This chapter will explore various theoretical models that have been used in the economic literature to explain international trade in goods and services, capital and internationalisation of organisational structure.

2.2 International goods and capital flows

International trade in goods and capital flows are among the forms of transaction (other examples being trade in labour, technology, etc.) that take place between economic agents resident in different countries. Economic theory suggests that economic agents (consumers, producers, governments, etc.) can benefit from trade and exchanges. It is impossible for a country to be self-reliant without sacrificing its standard of living. There are three possible types of international transactions, as illustrated in Figure 2.1 (Krugman and Obstfeld, 2004).

Residents of different countries could trade goods and services for other goods and services, or they could trade goods and services for assets (that is for future goods and services), or they could trade assets for other assets. All three types of exchange lead to gains from trade.

It would be important to understand why trade happens and how trade between nations could be explained theoretically.

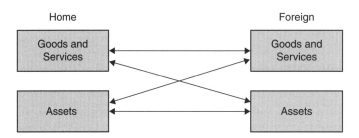

Figure 2.1   Types of international transactions
Source: Adapted from Krugman and Obstfeld (2004).

2.2.1   Reasons for trade

The five basic reasons why trade may take place between countries are summarised below:

Differences in technology

Advantageous trade can occur between countries if the countries differ in their technological abilities to produce goods and services. Technology refers to the techniques used to convert resources (labour, capital, land) into outputs. The basis for trade in the Ricardian Trade Model of Comparative Advantage is differences in technology.

Differences in resource endowments

Advantageous trade can occur between countries if the countries differ in their endowments of resources. Resource endowments refer to the skills and abilities of a country's workforce, the natural resources available within its borders (minerals, farmland, etc.), and the sophistication of its capital stock (machinery, infrastructure, communications systems). The basis for trade in the Pure Exchange model and the Heckscher–Ohlin Trade Model is differences in resource endowments.

Differences in demand

Advantageous trade can occur between countries if demands or preferences differ between countries. Individuals in different countries may have different preferences or demands for various products. The Chinese are likely to demand more rice than the British, even if facing the same price. Scots might demand more whisky, and the Japanese more fish, than Americans would, even if they all faced the same prices.

Existence of economies of scale in production

The existence of economies of scale in production is sufficient to generate advantageous trade between two countries. Economies of scale refer to a production process in which production costs fall as the scale of production rises. This feature of production is also known as 'increasing returns to scale'.

Existence of government policies

Government tax and subsidy programmes can be sufficient to generate advantages in production of certain products. In these circumstances, advantageous trade may arise solely due to differences in government policies across countries.

Differences in return on capital

Trade in capital may happen if the price of real return on capital across different countries varies. This may happen if demand for capital in present and future time periods differs among different countries.

The main reason for trade to take place is that countries find it advantageous to trade. As mentioned earlier, it is impossible for any country to be self-reliant without sacrificing its standard of living. This can be understood from the following simple illustration. Suppose that there is one good that the world produces and there is one good that the world consumes. This good can be produced by all countries; however, each country can decide whether to produce the good domestically or import it (partially or fully). Figure 2.2 presents the market equilibrium for the good under (i) no trade and (ii) trade scenarios.

In economics, the demand curve describes the quantity of a good that a household or a firm chooses to buy at a given price. Similarly, the supply curve describes the quantity of good that a household or firm would like to sell at a particular price. If demands of individual households in a country are aggregated, we can obtain an aggregate demand curve that tells us the total quantity of that good demanded at each price. Similarly, an aggregate supply curve would tell us the total good that would be supplied by a country at each price.

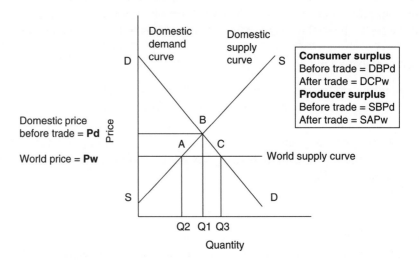

Figure 2.2 Demand, supply and market equilibrium

Consider first the case of a closed country (which means that this country does not engage in trade with foreign countries). Figure 2.2 plots the price on the vertical axis and quantity on the horizontal axis. The downward-sloping line DD is the aggregate domestic demand curve for the whole country and the upward-sloping line SS is the aggregate domestic supply curves. The point of intersection of demand and supply curve is the market equilibrium. This point determines the price that will be paid and accepted in the market. The point is labelled as B, for equilibrium, the corresponding price P_d is the equilibrium price and quantity Q_1 is the equilibrium quantity.

Now suppose the country which was closed to trade opens its borders (removes restrictions that were not permitting trade to happen. Restrictions in the real world could take many forms, such as import tariffs, export restriction or quantity quotas) so that trade in goods and services can take place. The supply curve that the country faces now is the horizontal world supply curve. The world supply curve is horizontal because competition would prevent prices rising above this level. If prices rose, producers around the world would take this opportunity to expand their market and increase their production, thereby bringing the equilibrium price to P_d.

The supply curve that the country faces is not the original upward-sloping curve but the horizontal world supply curve. The demand curve, which depends on domestic preferences, does not change. The new demand–supply equilibrium will be at point C. Note that at this point the equilibrium price of the good is Pw < Pd. Consumers demand quantity Q3. What happens to domestic producers? Does production shift abroad? The answer to this question is complicated by political economy of trade and the extent to which trade is protected by the country. However, in the above example, when there are no restrictions on trade after the opening up of the economy, the domestic producers could supply goods at world price up to a quantity Q2 because their marginal cost of production up to Q2 is less than or equal to the world price. Above Q2 the marginal cost of production would exceed the market price at which goods can be sold (= world price), so that producers would find it unprofitable to produce. The country with demand Q3 would produce Q2 domestically and import (= Q3−Q2) from the world market.

To understand the impact of trade on producers and consumers, let's use an economic concept called 'surplus'. Consumer surplus is the amount that consumers benefit by being able to purchase the good for a price that is less than they are willing to pay. For example, for all quantities supplied less than the equilibrium quantity, consumers are willing to pay higher than the equilibrium price. By paying equilibrium price, their surplus before trade is DBPd. The producer surplus is the amount by which producers benefit by selling at a market price mechanism that is higher than they would be willing to sell for. In the autarky (no trade) case, producer surplus is SBPd. Note that producer surplus flows through to owners of factors of production (labour, capital, land), unlike economic profit, which is zero under perfect competition. If market for labour and capital is also perfectly competitive, producer surplus ends up as economic rent to the owners of scarce resources like land.

Let us see how trade affects the welfare of consumers and producers. The trade has opened up opportunities to buy goods at a lower price. For domestic consumers, trade is welfare-enhancing. For domestic producers, however, the revenue has declined as they face price competition and find it unviable to produce more than Q2. Consumers' surplus, which was DBPd before trade, has increased to DCPw. Producers' surplus, however, has declined from SBPd to SAPw.

International trade is generally beneficial to nations; however, it is quite possible that trade may hurt some groups within the nation (in the above example, the welfare of producers has been affected). In other words, international trade has strong impact on the distribution of income. International trade can adversely affect owners of resources that are 'specific' to industries that compete with imports and cannot find alternative ways to redeploy these resources to alternative use (Krugman and Obstfeld, 2000; chapter 3). Trade could also affect the distribution of income between broad groups, between workers and owners of resources (Krugman and Obtsfeld, 2000; chapter 4).

2.3 Theoretical models of trade

Economic discussion suggesting that trade is advantageous dates back to Adam Smith's 'The Wealth of Nations'. In this early economics treatise, dating back to the eighteenth century, Adam Smith argues: 'If a foreign country can supply with a commodity cheaper than we ourselves can make it, better buy it of them with some part of the produce of our own industry, employed in a way in which we have some advantage.' The theory which Adam Smith proposed is based on the concept of **absolute advantage** in production. The idea here is simple and intuitive. If our country can produce some set of goods at lower cost than a foreign country, and if the foreign country can produce some other set of goods at a lower cost than we can produce them, then clearly it would be best for us to trade our relatively cheaper goods for their relatively cheaper goods. In this way both countries may gain from trade. However, if one country has absolute advantage in all goods, should other countries engage in trade with this country? The answer is not obvious from an absolute advantage model.

2.3.1 Comparative advantage theory

British economist David Ricardo proposed a comparative advantage theory in 1817 in his book 'On the Principles of Political Economy and Taxation'. The fundamental idea of the Ricardian model of comparative advantage is that the basis of trade is differences in technology. Ricardo demonstrated, using an example with two countries, two goods, and one country having productive advantage in both the goods, that the world output could be improved if each country specialised in the production of the good for which their opportunity cost was lowest. If appropriate terms of trade were then chosen, both countries could end up with more of both goods.

If there are two countries producing two goods and one country has productive advantage in both goods, to benefit from specialisation and free trade, the country with advantage in both goods should specialise and trade the good which it is 'most best' at producing, while the other should specialise and trade the good which it is 'least worse' at producing.

A simple way to demonstrate that countries can gain from trade is through a numerical example. Ricardo demonstrated, using a two-country two-goods example, that a country can gain from trade even if it has technological disadvantage in producing both goods. Let us assume that there are two countries: the UK and the US; two goods: Whisky and Computers; and one factor of production: labour. Suppose the UK has absolute advantage in production of both these goods. Suppose, in the UK, the labour requirement to produce one unit of Whisky is one and the labour requirement to produce one unit of Computer is two. The US can produce one unit of Whisky by employing six units of labour and one unit of computer by employing three units of labour. Total available labour in each of these countries is 24 units. By assumption, the UK is more efficient in producing both goods, as the labour required to produce one unit of Whisky in the UK is less than the labour required to produce one unit of Whisky in the US, and the labour required to produce one unit of Computer in the UK is less than the labour required to produce one unit of Computer in the US. In order to produce Whisky, the UK must produce fewer Computers. Economists use a term called opportunity cost to describe such trade-offs. The opportunity cost of Whisky in terms of Computers is the number of Computers that could have been produced with the resources used to produce given units of Whisky. The opportunity cost of Whisky in the UK is 0.5, as this is the number of units of Computer whose production is to be given up to produce one unit of Whisky in the UK. The opportunity cost of Computer in the UK is two units of Whisky. The opportunity cost of Whisky in the US is two units of Computers and the opportunity cost of Computer in the US is 0.5 units of Whisky. Table 2.1 summarises the discussion above.

Suppose that 24 labour units are available in both the UK and the US. The production possibility frontiers for both these countries are plotted in Figure 2.3. Production possibility frontier (PPF) is a graph that shows the different quantities of two goods that an economy could efficiently produce with limited productive resources. The PPF for the UK lies outside that for the US. Since the size of both economies is assumed to be same (both have 24 units of labour), the UK has absolute advantage over the US, because the UK can produce any possible combination of Whisky and Computer far more efficiently than the US. Levels of

Table 2.1 Summary of hypothetical inputs required for production

Goods	UK – Labour per unit	US – Labour per unit	Opportunity cost – UK	Opportunity cost – US
Whisky	1	6	0.5	2
Computer	2	3	2	0.5

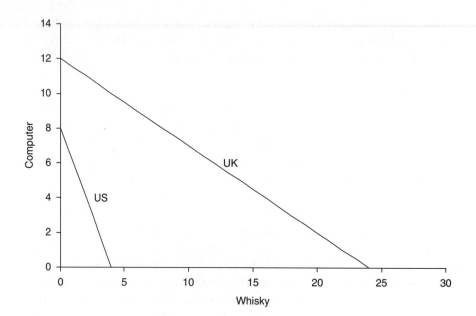

Figure 2.3
Production possibility frontier

production at points that will lie below the PPF make inefficient use of resources, and points above the PPF are infeasible. Points along the curve describe the trade-off between the two goods, that is, the opportunity cost. The opportunity cost of producing Whisky is lower in the UK than in the US. The UK has a comparative advantage in producing Whisky. Again, looking at Table 2.2, one can see that the opportunity cost of producing Computers is lower in the US than in the UK. This means that the US has a comparative advantage in producing Computers.

With full employment and efficient use of available technologies, production would occur at some point on the PPF. The level at which the economy would produce depends on the consumer demand for goods. Suppose the UK and the US do not engage in trade (a situation known in economics as 'Autarky'). Producers will produce at a level which consumers demand at prevailing prices. In autarky, this would mean that supply would equal demand. Let us assume that the consumption demand for Whisky in the UK is sixteen units and consumption demand for Computers is four units. This would be the point at which the UK would produce, and would be represented by a point on the PPF. Suppose the demand for Whisky in the US is three units and the demand for Computers is two units. Producers in the US would produce at these levels, and this would be represented as a point on the PPF for the US. In autarky, the total world output of Whisky is nineteen units and the output of Computers is six units. Table 2.2 presents the level of output in the UK and the US in autarky.

Suppose that the UK and the US each specialises in the commodity in which it has comparative advantage. The output levels are represented in Table 2.3.

Table 2.3 indicates that, if the UK and the US each specialises in a commodity in which it has comparative advantage, world output increases. The countries, however, would not benefit unless trade were permitted. These levels of

Table 2.2 Consumption and production in autarky

	Whisky	Computer
UK	16	4
US	3	2
World total	19	6

Table 2.3 Production with specialisation in the comparative advantage good

	Whisky	Computer
UK	24	0
US	0	8
World total	24	8

Table 2.4 Consumption and production after trade

	Whisky		Computer	
	Consumption	Production	Consumption*	Production
UK	18.5	24	5	0
US	5.5	0	3	8
World total	24	24	8	8

Note: * assuming that consumption of 0.5 Whisky is possible.

production were possible even in autarky, but countries were not producing at these levels because both goods were demanded by the residents of these countries. Production would match the consumption within a country if no trade were permitted.

Let us allow trade. There is a surplus Whisky production of five units and surplus Computer production of two units. If we allow this surplus to be split equally between the UK and the US, their consumption of goods will be at the levels shown in Table 2.4.

As can be seen from Table 2.4, consumption of goods in both countries has increased with trade rather than autarky. The above numerical example illustrates that even under circumstances where one country had absolute advantage in production of both the goods, if countries specialised in production of goods in which they had comparative advantage and trade, world output would increase. Both countries would gain from trade.

The above example demonstrates only one possible outcome of the model. The conclusions presented above are more likely possibilities rather than generalised results. It is quite possible that, with a different choice of production/consumption points in autarky, world output might not rise for both goods upon specialisation. This would mean that, even after trade, both countries might not gain. Moreover, in the above example we assumed a term of trade that generated the conclusion described above: that both countries benefit from trade. Under a very different assumption regarding terms of trade, the conclusion may be that only one country benefits from trade. Even if the country has more of both goods, the distribution of these may not be uniform across all consumers. Some consumers within a country may benefit, while others may not benefit at all.

These questions could be answered by describing the model more fully, which is beyond the scope of this present book (a detailed model is presented in Krugman and Obtsfeld, 2000, chapters 2 and 3); however, the conclusions that emerge from generalisation suggest that the proposition that trade is beneficial is 'unqualified'. The benefits from trade for a country could be thought of as an indirect method of production. Instead of producing a good for itself, the country could produce another good and trade with another country for the desired good. Whenever a good is imported, it is true that this indirect production requires less labour than when the good is produced domestically. Trade also enlarges the consumption possibilities of a country.

2.3.2 Heckscher–Ohlin trade model

The basis for trade in a comparative advantage model is the difference in efficiency in production of goods and services across countries. However, if, say, both countries had the same production efficiency, would trade still be possible? An answer to this question is provided by another important theory called the Heckscher–Ohlin (H-O) trade model, proposed by two Swedish economists. The rationale for trade in the H-O model is the difference in resources between countries. The H-O model emphasises the interplay between the proportions in which different factors of production are available in different countries and the proportions in which they are used in producing different goods. We develop the H-O model by using a simple example of two economies which can produce two goods using two factors of production, and we start with an autarky case, that is, these two economies do not trade. This is a convenient starting point, as it will be interesting to see what happens when the assumption regarding no-trade is lifted.

Assumptions:

In our simple model there are two countries (China and Portugal) which can produce two goods (Cloth and Wine). Production of goods requires two inputs (Labour measured in hours and Land measured in acres). China has a total labour stock of 500 hours and Portugal has a total labour stock of 200 hours. China has a land area of 1,000 acres and Portugal's land area is 600 acres.

China uses 0.5 acres to produce 1 metre of cloth

China uses 1 hour to produce 1 metre of cloth

China uses 2 acres to produce 1 gallon of wine

China uses 0.5 hours to produce 1 gallon of wine

Total supply of land in China = 1,000 acres

Total supply of labour in China = 500 hours

An important point to bear in mind here is the use of word 'uses' instead of 'requires' as in the Ricardian model. The reason for this change in the play of words is that in a two-factor economy there is a possibility of choice in the use of inputs. For example, Chinese cloth producers may be able to produce more cloth per acre of land by employing more labour. The factor combination choice that producers would make would depend on the relative cost of land and labour. If land rent is high and wages low, producers use less land and more labour per unit of output. If wages are high and land rents low, they use more land and less labour per unit of output. Assume that the costs in both countries are represented in US dollar terms rather than on their domestic currency basis. Suppose that the wage rate per hour of labour in China is $2 and land rent per acre in China is $4, and the input choices made above are dependent on the ratio of these two factor prices. The land rent to wage ratio is 2 (obtained by dividing $4/$2). There is a relation between Wage–Rental ratio and Land–Labour ratio, as shown in Figure 2.4. The curve for cloth lies to the left of the curve for wine, indicating that, at any given factor price, production of wine will always use a higher ratio of land than production of cloth. Wine is more land-intensive than cloth and cloth is more labour-intensive than wine.

To start with the autarky case, China and Portugal don't engage in trade and China will produce both commodities. Competition in each sector will ensure that the price of each good equals its cost of production (economic profit is zero under perfect competition). The cost of production depends on the factor prices. If land rent is higher, production cost of the good that is land-intensive will be higher. For a closed economy, if relative factor prices increase, the increase in the price of the commodity intensive in that factor is higher than the increase in the price of the other commodity, which does not use this factor as intensively in its production. There is a direct relationship between Wage–Rental ratio and Price of cloth (Pc) – Price of wine (Pw) ratio, shown by the upward-sloping curve in

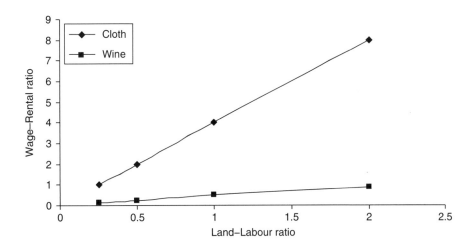

Figure 2.4 Factor prices and input choice in China

Figure 2.5. It is easy to draw this curve. For each Wage–Rental ratio, assume that the rents do not change and only the wage rate changes. Calculate wage rate for each level of Wage–Rent ratio by multiplying the ratio by rent. After calculating wage rate, production cost in each sector can be calculated by multiplying per unit of output by factor prices by respective factor inputs and by adding these factor costs per unit of output together. In a competitive market, production cost would equal price. For each Wage–Rental level, the ratio Pc/Pw can be obtained by dividing Price of cloth by Price of wine.

In our example, if the wage rate increased and the level of land rent remained the same, the price of cloth relative to the price of wine would increase more rapidly because cloth production requires more labour per unit of output than wine. Figure 2.4 and Figure 2.5 have a common axis and wage–rental ratio, and if we place these figures together (see Figure 2.6) an interesting relation between Price of cloth – Price of wine, Land–Labour ratio and Wage–Rental ratio emerges. If the relative price of cloth were to rise, this would also raise wages relative to land rent, as can be seen from the left figure. A rise in Wage–Rental ratio would cause

Figure 2.5   Factor prices and goods prices in China

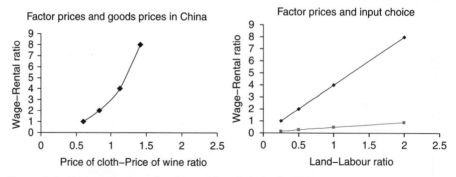

Figure 2.6   Factor price, goods price and input choice in China

an increase in Land–Labour ratio and both the sectors would shift their factor use towards land. Another important observation that could be made from the left figure is that an increase in Price of cloth – Price of wine ratio would lead to an increase in wages far larger than an increase in land rent.

Let us put together the story of two goods and two factors in the economy. Taking the relative price of cloth to wine as given, we can determine the Wage–Rental ratio which in turn would determine the Land–Labour ratio in the production of cloth and wine, as discussed earlier. The total factor endowments of labour and land in China are fixed and we assume that China would employ its supply of labour and land fully. Full employment of factors would determine the factor allocation across sectors.

The factor allocation across sectors could be shown using the box diagram, Figure 2.7. Figure 2.7 is a convenient representation of allocation of resources across two goods in a two-factor economy. Total labour supply in the economy is plotted as the horizontal axis and total land supply is plotted as the vertical axis. The resource allocation for cloth production is shown with its origin at Oc and the resource allocation for wine production is shown with its origin at Ow. The allocation of resources across the two sectors is represented by point E. At this equilibrium allocation, OcLc is the labour used in production of cloth and OcRc is the land used in the production of cloth. OwLw is the labour used in production of wine and OwRw is the land used in production of wine. The total endowment of labour in China: 500 = OwLw + OcLc and total endowment of land: 1000 = OwRw + OcRc. The point E has been determined from Figure 2.6 above. Given the cloth to wine prices, we can determine the rent to wage ratio in cloth

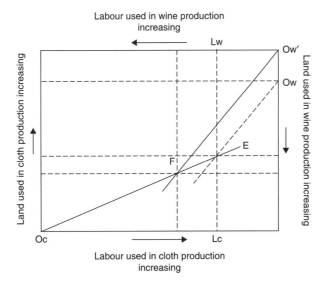

Figure 2.7 Resource allocation for production of two goods for the two countries
Source: Based on Krugman and Obstfeld (2000).

production on the left side of the figure. Projecting rent to wage ratio in cloth production to the right side of the figure gives the land–labour ratio for cloth production. A straight line drawn from Oc, in Figure 2.7, with the calculated land–labour ratio for cloth production as slope, is the line on which point E must lie. A similar straight line can be drawn from Ow once the slope of land–labour ratio in wine production is known. E is the point where these two lines intersect.

Suppose the land availability in China increases, holding both good prices and labour supply fixed. The increased supply of land makes the box taller. The origin for production of wine shifts from Ow to O_w. Again drawing the land–labour slope line originating at O_w, one can see that the equilibrium point has shifted from E to F. This has important implications because it suggests that the land and labour use in production of cloth has reduced. It also suggests that land and labour use in production of wine has increased. With increased land supply, the possibility of producing wine increases substantially and the economy shifts its production to wine production. An economy would tend to be relatively effective at producing goods that are intensive in the factors with which the country is relatively well endowed (Krugman and Obstfeld, 2000, chapter 4).

A similar description of the other two-factor economy, Portugal, can be offered. Suppose residents in China and Portugal have similar tastes and therefore these economies have identical demand for cloth and wine when faced with similar relative price of the two goods. Both these economies have similar technologies for producing wine and cloth. This means that the land–labour ratio to produce one unit of wine or cloth is the same in China and Portugal. Assumptions made above with regard to China and Portugal suggest that China is labour-abundant in comparison to Portugal, because the land–labour ratio is China is 2 while the land–labour ratio in Portugal is 3. Production of cloth is more labour-intensive than production of wine. The Chinese production possibility frontier relative to Portugal is shifted more in the direction of cloth than in the direction of wine. Other things being equal, China would have a higher ratio of cloth to wine.

With trade, the relative price of cloth in terms of wine would be the same across China and Portugal. Since China and Portugal differ in factor abundances, for any ratio of price of cloth to wine, Chinese production would be skewed towards cloth production. Portugal would specialise in the production of wine.

The Heckscher–Ohlin model suggests that the reason for trade is factor endowment. A country which is abundant in labour should specialise in production of goods that are labour-intensive, and a country which is capital-intensive should specialise in production of commodities that are capital-intensive. Both these countries would benefit from trade.

2.3.3 Intertemporal trade model

The exchange of goods and services is one of the ways in which economies trade. The other mode of trade is through the movement of capital. International capital transactions are quite substantial and take many forms through which economic agents in one country provide productive capital to agents in other countries. The mode of capital transfer is through financial transaction. For example, economic agents resident in the UK buy stocks of firms resident in Hong Kong. It is like saying that residents in the UK provide loans to residents in Hong Kong. Two points that need to be borne in mind in this example are: (i) the loan provided today would not be repaid until the next period and (ii) UK residents investing in Hong Kong dollars would be repaid in Hong Kong dollars. This means that they would have to exchange their domestic currency, pounds sterling, for Hong Kong dollars, and when they were repaid in the next period in Hong Kong dollars they would exchange these for pounds sterling and repatriate them to the UK. Expectations about exchange rate become an important part of international capital transfer decisions.

International borrowing and lending can be interpreted as a type of international trade – trade of present goods for goods in the future. Consider an economy that produces one good and exists for two periods – present and future. The economy faces a trade-off in the production of the consumption good between the present and future periods. The intertemporal production possibility frontier for the economy is shown in Figure 2.8.

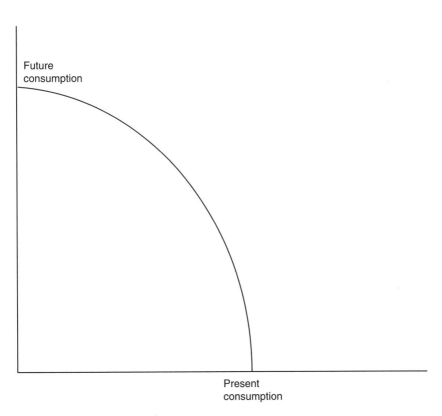

Figure 2.8 Intertemporal production possibility frontier
Source: Adapted from Krugman and Obstfled (2000).

The intertemporal production possibility curves of different countries would differ from each other. For some countries these would reflect production possibilities that are biased towards present output, and for others production possibilities that are biased towards future output. Suppose there are two countries, Home and Foreign, with different intertemporal production possibility frontiers. Home's production possibilities are biased towards present output and Foreign's are biased towards future output. In the absence of international borrowing and lending, the relative price of future consumption will be higher in Home than Foreign.

However, with trade, Home would export present consumption and import future consumption. The price of future consumption to present consumption is a function of real interest rate. Under the assumption that real interest rate is positive, the price of future consumption is lower than the price of present consumption. If trade in capital is permitted, the relative price of future consumption and world interest rate will be determined by the world relative supply and demand of future consumption (Krugman and Obstfeld, 2000, p. 169). A country that has comparative advantage in production of future consumption would have a lower production cost of future consumption. With trade in capital permitted, this country would offer a higher interest rate than the one where the production costs of future consumption are not as low. This would in turn mean that countries who borrow in the international market are those where opportunities exist.

2.3.4 International trade in capital and the role of international capital markets

Capital markets are markets where people, companies and governments with more funds than they need (because they save some of their income) transfer those funds to people, companies or governments who have a shortage of funds (because they spend more than their income). The two major capital markets are for stocks and bonds. Companies issue securities on the capital markets to raise capital for productive uses. Investors (savers – people, companies and governments) with surplus funds (savings) invest in these securities in anticipation of cash flows in the future. Recent developments in financial engineering have led to development and trading of a wide variety of financial and physical capital (assets) including stocks, bonds (government and corporate), bank deposits denominated in different currencies, commodities (such as petroleum, wheat, bauxite, gold, etc.), derivatives (forward contracts, futures contracts, swaps, options contracts, etc.), real estate and land, securities and derivatives backed by real estate assets (such as mortgage-backed securities, Real Estate Investment Trusts securities, etc.) and factories and equipment. The role of capital markets is to promote economic efficiency by channelling money from those who do not have an immediate use for it to those who do. The physical places where stocks, bonds and other derivatives are bought, sold and traded are called stock exchanges. Stock exchanges play a very important role in capital transfer, as they provide the regulation of company listings, a price-forming mechanism, the supervision of trading, authorisation of members, settlement of transactions and publication of trade data and price. Examples of major stock exchanges are the New York Stock Exchange (NYSE), NASDAQ (National Association of Securities Dealers Automated Quotations), the London Stock Exchange (LSE), the Tokyo Stock Exchange (TSE), the Hong Kong Stock Exchange, the Singapore Stock Exchange and stock exchanges in many other cities.

International capital markets are a group of markets (in New York, London, Tokyo, Singapore and many other financial cities) that trade different types of financial and physical assets. Though individual country capital markets are regulated by domestic regulatory authorities, there is increasing evidence of capital flows into foreign assets traded on foreign capital markets. During the 1980s and 1990s, it became quite common for multinational companies to seek a listing on several foreign stock exchanges. Reasons for listing on foreign stock exchanges could have been to attract wider investor interests or because local exchanges were small for the ambitions of the company. Multinational companies conduct their operations and businesses in local currency (different from their home currency) and, to hedge against currency risk, they often prefer to raise capital from local markets in local currency by listing on local stock exchanges. One of the consequences of these developments has been the expansion in primary issues and secondary market trading in non-domestic equities. Foreign listing requires compliance with foreign accounting and listing regulations. However, companies are willing to bear that risk because of the advantages associated with accessing larger capital markets. German automobile major Daimler–Benz accepted the US accounting rules, stricter than those in Germany, to be able to list on New York.

It may, however, be emphasised here that, though capital markets have become internationalised, there is no one single market. In essence, the international capital market is a number of closely integrated markets which conduct any transaction with an international dimension. Examples of assets traded on international capital markets are foreign exchange, internationally traded stocks and bonds (Eurobonds), American Depository Receipts (ADRs) or Global Depository Receipts (GDRs) issued by public enterprises in developing and transitional economies.

2.4   Dunning Eclectic Paradigm

Traditional trade models are able to explain international capital flows, but the explanation is only partial. Borrowing and lending, as envisaged in the intertemporal trade model described earlier, are only one of the ways through which capital movements occur. The World Trade Organisation (WTO) recognises two types of capital flows: (i) portfolio investment of the type described in the intertemporal trade model, where an investor resident in one country invests in stocks, bonds and other financial instruments in the other country; and (ii) foreign direct investment (FDI), where an investor based in one country acquires assets in the other country with the intention of managing them. FDI involves the transfer of much more than capital alone. Technological expertise, marketing and management skills, and other firm-specific resources are transferred to the host country as well. Each country has its own way of defining whether a particular investment should be classified as an FDI or a foreign portfolio investment. When measuring foreign investment flows, UNCTAD defines FDI as investments involving owner-ships of more than 10 per cent. Investments of less than 10 per cent are classified as portfolio investments. Portfolio investors, with a small minority holding in the investment, exercise very little, if any, control in the asset and thus are typically passive investors.

Traditional trade theories find it difficult to explain the ways in which FDI finances the production that is undertaken by transnational corporations (TNCs). Traditional trade theorists were less concerned with explanations of the compos-ition of goods and factors actually traded across boundaries than with theorising on what would happen in the real world if certain conditions were present. The Heckscher–Ohlin (H-O) model, discussed above, asserted that, provided certain conditions were met, countries would specialise in the production of goods which required relatively large inputs of resources with which they were comparatively well endowed, and would export these in exchange for others which required relatively large inputs of factors with which they were comparatively poorly endowed. Among the conditions were that countries had two homogeneous inputs, labour and capital, both of which were locationally immobile. Inputs were converted into outputs by the most efficient and internationally identical technologies. All enterprises were price-takers, there were no barriers to trade and no transactions costs. International tastes were similar. These assumptions and their implications have been criticised in literature. Under the conditions of factor immobility, identical technologies and perfect competition, the only possible form of international involvement is through international trade; pro-duction by one country's enterprises for a foreign market must be undertaken within the exporting country; and all enterprises have equal access to location-specific endowments.

One of the deductions of the H-O model is that trade will equalise factor prices. Replacing the assumption of factor immobility with that of immobility of goods, it may be shown that movement of factors also responds to resource endow-ments. This was used to explain the international (portfolio) capital movements in terms of relative prices or differential interest rates. For many years trade theory and capital theory paralleled each other, but eventually the two were for-mally integrated into the factor price equalisation theorem by Samuelson (1948) and Mundell (1957). Simply stated, the theorem says that when the prices of the output goods are equalised between countries as they move to free trade, then the prices of the factors (capital and labour) will also be equalised between countries. This implies that free trade will equalise the wages of workers and the rents earned on capital throughout the world. The theorem derives from the assumptions of the H-O model, the most critical of which is the assumption that the two countries share the same production technology and that markets are perfectly competitive. Over the last four decades, trade models introduced more realism to traditional trade theories in an attempt to explain observed trade flows (Dunning, 2000).

Another important development observed in international capital flows has been growth and composition of foreign direct investment (FDI) or production financed by such investment. Earlier explanations based on either location theory or investment theory did not quite convincingly explain the 'non-trade' nature of involvement of FDI flows. FDI flows have raised the 'non-trade' nature of international engagement of a country alongside trade, which needs to be explained. A country may engage economically with the outside world by letting economic agents (irrespective of their nationality) use resources located within its boundaries to produce goods and services for sale outside its boundaries, or may import resources or products based on those resources located in other countries. This has been the view of traditional trade theories. However, when we view the involvement of a country's economic agents in servicing foreign markets with goods and services, irrespective of where resources needed to do this are located or used, and the extent to which its own economic agents are supplied goods by foreign-owned firms, irrespective of where the production is undertaken, explanations based on geographical boundaries become insufficient. A country's economic space is perceived more in terms of the markets exploited by its institutions than its geographical boundaries. Economic involvement of one country's enterprises in another may be for the purposes of supplying both foreign and home markets. Production for a particular foreign market may be wholly or partly located in the home country, in the foreign market, in a third country or in a combination of the three. The capability of a home country's enterprise to supply either a foreign or domestic market from a foreign production base depends on its possessing certain resource endowments not available to, or not utilised by, another country's enterprises. These endowments include both tangible assets (such as natural resources, labour, capital) and intangible assets (such as knowledge, organisation and entrepreneurial skills, access to markets). Such endowments could be purely location-specific to the home country, in other words, they have to be used where they are located and are available to all firms, or they could be ownership-specific, that is, internal to the enterprise of the home country but capable of being used with other resources in the home country or elsewhere.

For some kinds of trade it is sufficient for the exporting countries to have a location endowment advantage over the importing country. Trade envisaged by the Ricardian or H-O trade model is of this type. Trade in highly skill-intensive or sophisticated consumer goods is based more on ownership advantages of exporting firms. This, however, presupposes that these advantages are better used in combination with location-specific endowments in the exporting country rather than in the importing (or a third) country. Where, however, location-specific endowments favour the importing (or a third) country, foreign production will replace trade. Foreign production, then, implies that location-specific endowments favour a foreign country, but ownership-specific endowments favour the home country's firms. Advantages associated with ownership-specific endowments are sufficient to overcome the cost of producing in a foreign environment.

John Dunning (1977) proposed an Eclectic Paradigm to explain international capital flows which take the form of FDI. The focus of the paradigm is to explain why firms choose the FDI route to participate in foreign markets rather than employing seemingly more convenient means of market participation such as strategic alliances, joint ventures or management contracts. Dunning argued that FDI is the most effective vehicle for serving foreign markets when the firm possesses an ordered series of advantages that arise under conditions of imperfect competition.

According to Dunning, to undertake production in foreign markets, the firm must first have some competitive advantages in its home market that are specific to the firm. These advantages arise out of inputs which an enterprise may create for itself – certain types of technology and organisation skills – or can purchase from other institutions, but over which, in doing so, it acquires some proprietary right of use. Such ownership-specific inputs may take the form of legally protected rights (such as patents, brand names, trade marks) or of a commercial monopoly through acquisition of a particular raw material essential to the production of the product or of exclusive control over particular market outlets, or there may be scale advantages. Firms that engage in production at international locations operate in different location-specific environments, from which they may derive additional ownership advantages – such as their ability to engage in international transfer pricing, to shift liquid assets between currency areas to hedge against exchange rate risk, and to reduce the impact of institutional risk in a country by operating parallel production capacity in other countries. Although the origin of ownership advantages may be linked to location-specific endowments, their use is not so defined. The ability of enterprises to acquire ownership endowments is clearly not unrelated to the endowment specific to the countries in which they operate, and particularly their country of origin. But, whatever the significance of the country of origin of such inputs, they are worth separating from those which are location-specific, because the enterprise possessing them can exploit them wherever it wishes, usually at a minimal transfer cost.

The possession of ownership advantages determines which firms will supply a particular foreign market, and the pattern of location endowments explains whether the firm will supply the market by exports or by local production. Whatever route the firm chooses, it could (i) supply the foreign market by selling or leasing its ownership advantages to a firm located in a foreign market or (ii) internalise its capital, technology and management skills within itself to produce goods. TNCs internalise the production of goods rather than externalising the use of ownership advantages by engaging in portfolio investment, licensing, management contracts, etc. Dunning (1977) argues that enterprises internalise their ownership endowments to avoid the disadvantages, or capitalise on the imperfections, of one or the other of the two main external mechanisms of resource allocation – the market and the public (government) system of resource allocation. Market imperfections arise wherever negotiation or transactions costs are high or information about a product is not fully available or is costly to acquire. Public intervention in the allocation of resources may also encourage firms to internalise their activities.

Based on this, Dunning proposed three sets of advantages (OLI advantages) that lead enterprises to locate part of their production process in a foreign market. These are:

Ownership (O-advantage): A firm's O-advantage must be unique to the firm, and it must be possible for those advantages to be transferred abroad. As discussed earlier, O-advantages largely take the form of common governance or the possession of intangible assets, such as specific know-how, proprietary technology, patents or brand loyalty, which are exclusive or specific to the firm possessing them. The greater the O-advantages of enterprises, the more incentive firms have to exploit those advantages in foreign markets.

Location (L-advantage): Location advantages are due to economic differences among countries and may take many forms. The host country may offer such features as low-cost labour, skilled labour, better access to raw materials or a large market. In addition, it may simply offer the opportunity for a firm to make a defensive investment to prevent its competitors from gaining a foothold. In the absence of L-advantages such as these, there would be no incentive for the firm to engage in FDI, and foreign markets would be best served entirely by exports.

Internalisation (I-advantage): When O and L advantages exist, internalisation advantages allow the firm to minimise transactions costs and other agency costs that would likely occur if the firm were to engage in some other form of market penetration strategy, such as a joint venture or strategic alliance. This would mean that the cost of directly managing and controlling all activities of the enterprise would be less than the cost of operating in any other manner. By direct entry, the cost of monitoring foreign partners, having information filtered through third parties, dealing with foreign financial institutions, etc., would be mitigated. If the firm had the ability to effectively exert control over its value chain, it would be more beneficial to the firm to utilise its I-advantages than to enter into leasing, franchising or other types of arrangements.

2.5 Porter's model of competitive advantage of nations

The reasons for trade among nations in Ricardo's comparative advantage model or the H-O model are differences in the following factor endowments: land, location, labour, natural resources and local population size. These factor endowments are largely inherited and difficult to influence. Traditional models, though interesting in understanding the rationale for trade, offer a rather passive view of national economic opportunity. Singapore has very little of these factor endowments, but is a very important global trade partner. Dubai has emerged as a global city without boasting many of the factor endowments necessary for comparative advantage.

Porter (1990) argues that competitiveness of nations and industrial growth can hardly be built on the abovementioned passive factors. According to him, the most important definition of the competitiveness of nations is 'national productivity' (Porter, 1990, p. 6). Porter proposed that the competitiveness of nations depends on four broad attributes (four diamonds) of the national location, namely, factor conditions; demand conditions; related and supporting industries and firms; strategy and rivalry.

Porter's factor conditions require that a nation has to have an appropriate supply of factors to be successful. These factors are land, labour and capital, but the interpretation of these is far more specific than suggested by comparative advantage or the H-O model. While interpreting factors, Porter looks at these at highly disaggregated levels. Distinctions are drawn between basic factors, such as climate and unskilled labour, and advanced factors, such as highly skilled labour and infrastructure. Basic factors are not sufficient for competitiveness, and the nation has to create advanced factors. Similarly, there is a distinction between generalised factors and specialised factors. Generalised factors can be deployed in a wide range of industries while specialised factors are industry-specific. Abundance of a factor supply does help in building competitive industry, as in the case of Denmark's success in furniture due to the availability of a pool of trained graduate furniture designers (Porter, 1990, p. 78; Davies and Ellis, 2000). The lack of availability of factors could also prove to be a boon in disguise by creating an environment for innovation if a nation wants to achieve competitiveness. Italy's high cost of capital and energy and shortages of basic raw materials led its steel producers to develop mini steel mill technology, in which Italy is the world leader (Porter, 1990, p. 82; Davies and Ellis, 2000).

Porter offers three demand conditions for a nation's competitiveness. He suggests that a country would be competitive in an industry which is more important at home than anywhere else. An example is Swedish industries, which are highly competitive in high voltage electricity distribution over long distances. The reason for their competitiveness is their experience in the home market in supplying electricity to distant and remote locations where energy-intensive paper and steel industries are located. The second condition is that demanding home consumers force companies to meet high standards. Americans' desire for convenience led to a fast food revolution, which has spread to other countries as well (Davies and Ellis, 2000). The third condition is that firms in the home market anticipate the needs of consumers in other countries. Japanese consumers and government forced firms to produce energy-saving products even before energy costs became important (Davies and Ellis, 2000). These three conditions are not necessarily dependent on the size of the domestic market, but force industries to innovate, giving them an edge over others in international competition; though a large domestic market which supported the above three demand conditions would be highly supportive of international competitiveness.

Porter argues that a nation's industries will be better able to compete in the international market if there are clusters of industries in the home economy, which are linked vertically and horizontally through demand, supply, technology, distribution and consumer networks. California has an IT and ITES cluster, which has helped firms located there become internationally competitive.

The fourth attribute for the competitiveness of nations proposed by Porter is concerned with the strategies and structures of domestic firms and the extent of rivalry between them. If the business environment favours family-run firms, the nation will specialise in industries that do not experience economies of scale, as in Italy. If the executives are dominated by engineers, the nation will have competitive advantage in those sectors that require high technology content, as in Germany. If the institutional structures for raising capital favour returns in the short term, the nation will be successful in industries which offer short-term returns. In addition to strategies and structures, Porter argues for the importance of rivalry of firms in domestic markets. This is important for innovation and leads to competitiveness internationally.

In addition to these four attributes, two other factors, chance and government, also play a very important role (Davies and Ellis, 2000). Chance refers to events, such as war, which offer opportunities to firms. Government plays a role through policies. Proactive government policies in Dubai have contributed to the business competitiveness of Dubai in the world market.

Another important feature of Porter's theory is that nations follow an evolutionary path of industrial development, moving from the factor-driven to the investment-driven to the innovation-driven and finally to the wealth-driven stage. For competitiveness, attributes have to be compatible with the stage of development (Porter, 1990). For prosperity to be reached and sustained, a nation must reach the innovation-driven stage of development (Davies and Ellis, 2000). This implies that comparative advantage in terms of factors is not sufficient for international success; a nation's industries must upgrade through innovation, product differentiation, branding and marketing. However, since Porter's model first appeared, a number of criticisms have also been voiced (see Davies and Ellis, 2000, for review). These authors argue that the suggestion in Porter's model that a strong four diamonds at home are necessary conditions for a nation's competitiveness has major drawbacks. This argument was attacked as inappropriate at a time when the world economy has become increasingly globalised and transnational corporations (TNCs[1]) are becoming increasingly important. Dunning (1993) argues that during the 1990s 'an increasing proportion of the assets of firms in a particular country are either acquired from or are located in, another country'. This in turn questions the importance of a strong four diamonds in the home base for the competitiveness of these firms. Porter's model is unable to explain the organisation structure of transnational corporations that locate their production processes in more than one country. Porter's model suggests that outward foreign direct investment (FDI[2]) is a sign of competitive strength in a nation's industry while inward FDI indicates that 'the process of competitive up-grading is not entirely healthy' (Davies and Ellis, 2000). Authors such as Lau (1994) argue that capital would flow to locations where it is highly productive, in which case inward FDI is a strength of competitiveness rather than a weakness. Chinese success can largely be attributed to inward FDI (Lin and Song, 1997). China has also used its comparative advantage in labour-oriented sectors for development rather than pursuing the 'up-grading' strategy of Porter (ibid.).

Traditional trade models and Porter's competitive advantage model are insufficient on their own to explain fully the reasons for some of the complex patterns of trade observed in capital and goods, such as FDI and the growth of TNCs. The pursuit of a better explanation has led to another interesting model (better referred to as a paradigm) used in international business literature, referred to as Dunning's eclectic paradigm, to explain the location of FDI and transnational corporations.

2.6 International real estate activity and trade models

Explaining international real estate activity is complex and requires explanation at the subsector level (use, investment and development). Real estate space is a local input in the production and supply of goods and services. Demand drivers in the user market are national and international but the supply drivers are largely local, though the national allegiance of suppliers could be international. Explanation of international activity in the user market requires an explanation of demand drivers, which are international in nature in this market. Increased exports lead to expansion of domestic production. Increased domestic production increases the demand for industrial space. Imports also have an impact on demand for real estate space. Goods imported need to be marketed and distributed, boosting the demand for retail space. Global trade has increased substantially over the last half-century (Figure 2.9). During 1950–2007, while the world GDP (in value terms) increased by around eight times, world exports of merchandise (in value terms) grew by 217 times. There are certain features of trade that need to be discussed. While world exports grew from US$5.6 trillion in 1997 to US$13.95 trillion in 2007, the profile of exporting nations/regions also changed dramatically during these 10 years. Three decades ago a large part of world trade took place within the triad of North America, Europe and Japan. However, the geography of trade has changed since then. Europe is still the largest exporter in the world, but its share in global exports decreased from 43 per cent in 1997 to 41 per cent in 2007. North America's share in world exports also declined from 18 per cent in 1997 to 13 per cent in 2007. Asia's share increased from 27 per cent to 29 per cent during the same period. The dominance of Japan as the sole exporting nation in Asia has been challenged by China and recently by Korea and India. Japan's share of exports in Asia declined from 27 per cent in 1997 to 17 per cent in 2007, while China's share increased from 12 per cent in 1997 to 29 per cent in 2007. Other regions, such as the Middle East Commonwealth of Independent Nations (CIS), have grown their exports substantially.

Regional trading blocs have played an important role in trade. A regional trade bloc is a type of intergovernmental agreement, often part of a regional intergovernmental organisation, where regional barriers to trade (tariffs and non-tariff barriers) are reduced or eliminated among the participating states (Schott, 1991). Trade liberalisation since 1980s has led to phenomenal growth in trade, but a large part of trade takes place within nations of various regional trading blocs. In

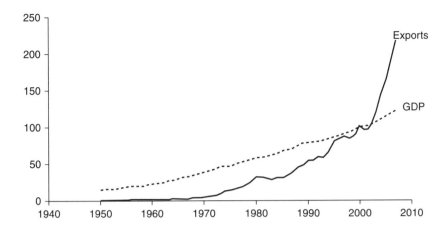

Figure 2.9 World merchandise exports and GDP (in value terms) (Index 2000 = 100)
Source: World Trade Data.

2007, nearly 68 per cent of exports from nations of the European Union (the EU comprises 27 countries: Austria, Belgium, Bulgaria, Cyprus, the Czech Republic, Denmark, Estonia, Finland, France, Germany, Greece, Hungary, Ireland, Italy, Latvia, Lithuania, Luxembourg, Malta, the Netherlands, Poland, Portugal, Romania, Slovakia, Slovenia, Spain, Sweden, the United Kingdom) were to countries within the EU, and around 64 per cent of imports by EU nations were of goods and services produced by nations in the EU. Nearly half of the exports and a third of imports from NAFTA countries (the US, Canada and Mexico) were to/from NAFTA countries. Another important regional trade bloc is ASEAN. However, ASEAN nations (Brunei Darussalam, Cambodia, Indonesia, Lao PDR, Malaysia, Myanmar, Philippines, Singapore, Thailand, and Vietnam) are less connected with each other in terms of trade than the EU and NAFTA. There are many other regional trade blocs (such as MERCOSUR or the Andean community) but the size of trade by these blocs is quite small. Among these regional trade blocs, EU nations have been by far the most connected, for the reason that the integration of nations within this bloc is wider than trade liberalisation. The formation of the European Union is based on convergence of governance (related to European community policies, foreign and security policies and justice and home affairs), the legal system (which is based on treaties among member nations). These treaties give power to set policy goals and establish institutions with the necessary legal power to implement them and the economy. Economic integration within the EU has led to the establishment of a single economic market across the territory of all its members. The single market allows free circulation of goods, capital, people and services across the Union. There is a common application of an external tariff on all goods entering the market. Many countries in the EU have adopted the Euro as their currency and have transferred the power to formulate monetary policies to the European Central Bank. Institutionally the EU has converged to a greater degree and this has led to increased internal trade within this bloc. Regional distribution and the nature of trade have a profound impact on the nature and location of real estate space required. Traditional trade theories are successful in explaining the reasons for trade between countries, but are rather weak in explaining the location of origination and destination of trade at subnational level and the role of institutions in determining trade flows.

Porter's model of competitive advantage of nations suggests that countries having four diamonds would grow economically. A corollary to this would be that these countries would have a higher demand for real estate space. Porter's model also discusses the role of government and chance in a nation's competitiveness. This argument could be extended further to argue the importance of facilitating institutional framework for economic growth. Real estate markets operate within a three-level hierarchy of institutions (Keogh and D'Arcy, 1999a). These institutions are: (i) at the top of the hierarchy, broader society level institutions such as legal, political, economic and social; (ii) in the middle, real estate market level institutions, which are far more local, such as legal and conventional aspects of property rights, legal and conventional aspects of land use and development, decentralised and informal institutions that affect real estate markets; and (iii) at the bottom of the hierarchy, an organisation of real estate markets itself, subgrouped according to bundling and unbundling of rights associated with real estate, such as use, investment, development and other services involved in this market, including real estate service providers, financial service providers, professional bodies, government and nongovernmental institutions. Real estate market institutions at the middle and bottom of the hierarchy are local, though operating within the top level of the hierarchy of institutions. These institutions could be influenced by government policies and other market forces at the local, regional and national levels.

Another important global economic trend is the growth of foreign direct investment (FDI). FDI inflows increased from US$55 billion dollars in 1980 to US$1,305 billion in 2006. As a percentage of world GDP, FDI inflows grew from around 0.75 per cent of GDP in 1980 to more than 3.5 per cent of GDP in 2006 (WIR, 2008). In recent years real estate companies have also been direct recipients of FDI. The geography of FDI has changed quite substantially over the last three decades. Up until the1980s, most of the FDI inflows were from and to developed economies (North America, developed Europe and Japan). The share of Asia minus Japan was less than 1 per cent in 1980. By 2006, the Asian region (Asia excluding Japan) was the destination for nearly 20 per cent of FDI inflows. The share of developed nations has declined to 66 per cent. Transitional economies have become a major destination for FDI inflows (Figure 2.10).

The inflow of FDI investment has an expansionary effect on the economic output and it also influences the organisation and management of the recipient industry. The share of the services sector as recipient of FDI has increased from 49 per cent in 1990 to 66 per cent in 2005 (UNCTAD, 2008). The impact of FDI on real estate space is in terms of expansion in demand as well as the nature of the space demanded, particularly since the international investor has management

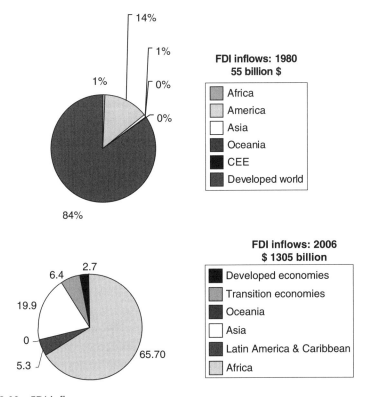

Figure 2.10   FDI inflows
Source: UNCTAD Development and Globalization: facts and figures (2008).

and organisational control which influences decisions related to the quality of space required.

Another important global trend in production of goods and services has been the growth of transnational corporations (TNCs) and their foreign affiliates. There were 78,000 TNCs and 780,000 foreign affiliates in 2005. Most large TNCs are headquartered in developed countries. According to the UNCTAD World Investment Report (2007), from 1990 to 2006 the value of assets of foreign affiliates increased five times (US$51 trillion in 2006), sales three times (US$25 trillion in 2006) and employment two times (US$73 million in 2006). Growth of TNCs and their foreign affiliates leads to increased integration of economic and business practices. This also generates demand for high-quality real estate space, occupation and management practices which are different from those of domestic firms. As discussed earlier, the organisation of the international production structure of TNCs is better explained by Dunning's eclectic paradigm. The global demands of TNCs and their foreign affiliates for real estate are better served by real estate firms that are global in nature. This has led to the emergence of real estate TNCs in the development sector and real estate services sector during the last 30 years. Chapter 5 will explain the internationalisation of real estate service providers in detail.

Real estate user demand generates interest for investment. The basic idea behind international investment in real estate could be explained by an intertemporal trade model. Evidence presented in Chapter 4 indicates that international investment in real estate has increased substantially. As discussed in Chapter 5, international real estate provides diversification benefits in mixed asset and real estate only portfolios. Real estate asset is like any other asset, but management of real estate requires a different focus from, say, stocks or bonds. Direct real estate has a long-term investment horizon while stocks or bonds have a short-term investment horizon. Management of direct real estate investment involves a host of integration and ongoing management issues (Tripathy, 2008). The skills required to manage a global real estate portfolio are diverse – ranging from managing information to managing investor relationships to managing multiple bank relationships to understanding of tax structures across different countries to understanding of components of real estate investment that enhance value (ibid.). Real estate investment requires local market knowledge – understanding of political, regulatory and tax structures – as well as understanding of global investors' needs for standardisation of processes and control, reporting standards and data standards. Management of real estate investment has led to the emergence of global asset managers with real estate capabilities. There are push and pull factors that have led to the globalisation of asset managers. Squeezing margins at home, competition and market saturation have caused domestic asset managers to look overseas. Internationalisation of investment clients, market expansion abroad, liberalisation of financial markets, maturity of investment culture, better governance and regulatory structures and so on have been pull factors for asset management firms to go overseas (EIU, 2007). Dunning's 'OLI' paradigm is well equipped to explain why global asset management firms establish part of their organisational functions abroad.

2.7 Conclusion

Explaining the internationalisation of property markets requires an understanding of the economic reasoning behind the internationalisation of market drivers, in this case the economy. The chapter briefly explains various trade models to explain why trade happens. An important aspect of this discussion is to review and present a critical evaluation of the potential of these models in explaining observed international economic trends.

Theorising International Real Estate 2

3.1 Introduction

In this chapter we examine theories of finance and investment. These were first applied to more general investment before being used in the field of real estate. We discuss modern portfolio theory and the capital asset pricing model. We then proceed to consider whether or not such diversification strategies are sufficient for internationalisation of real estate investment portfolios given the added costs attached to internationalisation, which are also discussed below. After this we examine research that focuses on real estate investment for both direct and indirect property assets and their potential role in both property-only and multi-asset portfolios. Finally the chapter discusses the institutional context within which real estate is traded and investment may occur. These 'institutions' can and do vary across countries. We analyse the role of institutions defined in different ways using new-institutional economics. While this field of economics has often been regarded as the poor relation to more empirically based economic approaches, it can not only provide a role in explaining events relating to the financial crisis, but also suggest potential remedies to avoid reoccurrence of such events.

3.2 Theories of finance and investment

Direct property investment can be expensive; it is a lumpy investment, and can therefore take up a large proportion of a portfolio. Investors are usually concerned with the risk and return combinations that their portfolio provides. In considering how much property, if any, to hold, we follow the work by Markowitz (1952, 1959), who laid the foundations for capital market theory. He developed the Modern Portfolio Theory (MPT), which considers how investors trade off risk and expected return from their investments. The theory considers the correlation in performance between assets held in a portfolio. Specifically, assets in a portfolio should at most have low correlations between them in terms of performance. This enables the investor to diversify away the risk attached to holding the assets. Essentially MPT argues that risk and returns on individual assets are not important in themselves, but only as they contribute to the risk and return of the portfolio. Following Hoesli and MacGregor (2000), the expected return on the portfolio equals the weighted average of expected returns:

$$E(R_P) = \sum w_i E(R_i) \tag{3.1}$$

where $E(R_P)$ is the expected return on the portfolio, w_i is the proportion of the portfolio given to asset i, and $E(R_i)$ is the expected return on asset i. The risk attached to the expected return performance of the portfolio, similar to the idea of variance, is given as:

$$\sigma_P = (\sum \sum w_i w_j \sigma_i \sigma_j \rho_{ij})^{1/2} \tag{3.2}$$

where σ_p is the risk attached to the portfolio, σ_i and σ_j are risks on assets i and j respectively, and ρ_{ij} measures the correlation between assets i and j. If asset returns are not perfectly correlated, portfolio risk is less than the weighted average of risks. This is the principle of diversification and influences the composition of the portfolio. The approach by Markowitz identifies the optimal proportion of a portfolio that should be allocated to a given asset. While it has traditionally been applied to the equity market, it can logically be extended to any risky asset class. Optimum combinations of risk and return produce an efficient frontier along which a higher expected return is associated with a greater risk. This is illustrated in the graph below. To find the risk and return trade-off an investor will choose his preferences, for risk and return must be considered. Some investors may be classed as risk-averse and will only accept greater risk for a significantly greater expected return. Alternatively, a risk-taking investor may be prepared to take on a lot more risk for a small increase in expected return.

The investor's preferences for risk and expected return are illustrated on the indifference curve. Along this curve an investor is indifferent between different combinations of risk and expected return, thus having constant utility. He or she would prefer higher expected returns for any given risk level and would therefore prefer to be on indifference curves above the one illustrated. Consequently, indifference curves below this one provide less utility. Given the portfolio of assets, the investor will be on the efficient frontier, and the optimal combination of risk and expected return occurs where this frontier is tangential to the indifference curve.

In practice, calculating the components of MPT makes its application very difficult. Not only do means and variances need to be calculated, but also covariance terms between pairs of assets. This becomes problematic as these terms increase

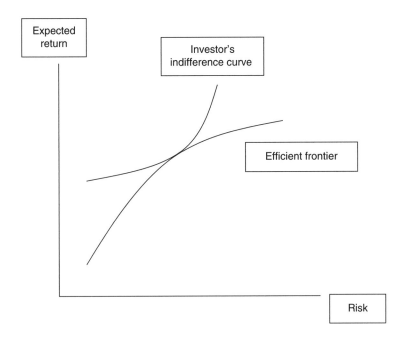

exponentially when more assets are added to the portfolio. In addition, investors are concerned with expectations of future asset performance, and data on historic returns will provide incomplete information upon which to base expectations.

However, if asset returns could be influenced by some common variable or variables, developing expectations would be easier. Sharpe (1964) developed what is termed the 'market model', which suggested that asset performance could be related to an index of business performance. This is the basis for the Capital Asset Pricing Model (CAPM), in which asset returns are determined by random factors and a common index:

$$E(R_{it}) = \alpha_i + \beta E(R_{mt}) \tag{3.3}$$

or

$$R_{it} = \alpha_i + \beta_i R_{mt} + \epsilon_{it} \tag{3.4}$$

where R is the return, i is the specific asset, m is the market and ε is the stochastic disturbance term. Extending the approach to portfolios, we can write:

$$R_{Pt} = \alpha_P + \beta_P R_{mt} + \epsilon_{Pt} \tag{3.5}$$

where the only change from (4) is that the terms relate to a portfolio, P, rather than an individual asset, i.

The assumptions upon which CAPM is built are developed from those for MPT and additionally assume the existence of a risk-free asset and free information, and that risk expectations are the same across investors. Investors can combine their optimal portfolio of assets with the risk-free asset. Key to CAPM, however, is that investors would be better off if they combined the risk-free asset with the market portfolio. 'The line which joins the risk-free rate to the market portfolio is known as the Capital Market Line (CML)' (Hoesli and MacGregor, 2000, p. 135).

In the graph below, the optimal position occurs where the efficient frontier is tangent to the capital market line at the market portfolio where risky assets are combined with the risk-free asset. If we only used the risk-free asset we would earn the risk-free return (RFR). Hoesli and MacGregor derive the equation for the capital market line as:

$$E(R_p) = RFR + \frac{[E(R_m) - RFR]\sigma_p}{\sigma_m} \tag{3.6}$$

For any investment we have:

$$E(R_i) = RFR + \frac{[E(R_m) - RFR]\text{cov}_{im}}{\sigma_m^2} \tag{3.7}$$

where the final term on the numerator is the covariance of asset returns. This expression can be rewritten as:

$$E(R_i) = (1 - \beta_i)RFR + \beta_i E(R_m) \tag{3.8}$$

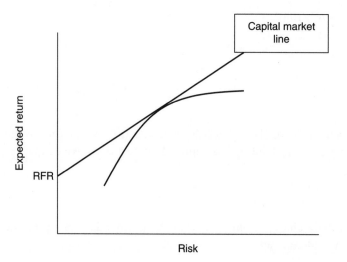

where $\beta_i = \text{cov}_{im}/\sigma_m^2$, and from (8) the expected return on the asset is related to the risk-free return and the expected return on the market. The beta (β) of an asset measures its volatility relative to the market. If $\beta < 1$ its expected return is less than the market's and it is called a defensive asset. If $\beta > 1$ its expected return is greater than the market's and it is termed an aggressive asset. The riskiness of the asset itself has two components. First, market (or systematic or non-diversifiable) risk and second, specific (or non-market or diversifiable) risk. Market risk cannot be removed from assets in a given market and the market element will impose some degree of correlation across the assets. Specific risks relate to an asset and can be reduced by portfolio diversification, holding assets that have low correlations in performance. In a direct property portfolio, investors would need to hold a number of properties before experiencing significant reductions in specific risk. This can be an expensive strategy given the high unit value of direct property investments.

A potential benefit of international investment is that it reduces market risk, since different countries have different economic circumstances and often have different currencies. Hence adding overseas assets to a portfolio will reduce portfolio risk, since the correlations between assets in different countries will be lower than the correlation between assets within one country. Investors will therefore be able to achieve a better risk-adjusted return on their portfolio. It may also be the case that substantially higher returns can be earned in overseas markets than would be available in the domestic market.

However, there are additional risks not encountered in domestic investment portfolios. Exchange rate risk is just one that could affect return performance. Home currency returns fall if the foreign currency depreciates. Interest rate differentials may also play a role. Lower interest rates in one country may encourage investors in that country to borrow in local currency to increase their investments. Theoretically we should expect interest rate parity, that is, real interest rates should be equal across countries. While this may be a long-run equilibrium condition, it may not hold in the short run and arbitrage opportunities will therefore be created.

Geurts and Jaffe (1996) suggest that the removal of market risk as a motivation of international investment is naïve and will not reduce risks sufficiently to encourage international investment. They suggest that investors will exhibit significant home asset bias, which they relate to possible institutional barriers to overseas investment in different countries, the transactions costs which overseas investment can incur, and taxation of income from investment assets. Investors may have imperfect information on institutional structure and hence on the behaviour of institutions in other countries. The cost of learning institutional behaviour may outweigh the reduction in unsystematic risk and hence the expected increased return of overseas diversification. Geurts and Jaffe suggest that there are a number of factors that investors must take into consideration. First they list risk assessment variables, including political, economic and credit risk, and financial risk ratings attached to countries. Second are property rights variables, including security, arbitrary expropriation, bribery and corruption, entrepreneurship and innovation, and intellectual property rights. Third are sociocultural factors including life expectancy, literacy, quality of life and home ownership. Finally, fourth are foreign investment variables covering the degrees of foreign control and treatment of foreigners. Stable economic policies aid the reduction of credit risk and improve a nation's financial risk rating. These are, furthermore, consistent with political stability, which also respects private property rights. Political instability is often positively correlated with arbitrary expropriation, corruption, lack of security of income streams from investments, and violation of intellectual property rights. These factors increase country risks and significantly discourage investment.

Investors have increasingly differentiated their portfolios internationally. Perhaps the strongest phase of internationalisation has been occurring since the financial deregulation of the early 1980s. Indeed, the scale of international financial flows dwarfs that of the flow of physical goods. More countries are becoming increasingly integrated into a global economy. Historically, Japan in the 1960s was a major manufacturer of electronic goods. As costs rose, manufacturing was increasingly undertaken by Japanese firms in South East Asian countries where labour costs were cheaper. This entailed the development of industrial property in these countries and a growth in their manufacturing sector. As the higher value-added jobs remained in Japan, the actual physical production jobs moved abroad. The development of manufacturing in South East Asian countries helped to move them from being dominated by agriculture as the labour force grew in the newer manufacturing sector. This in turn raised economic growth rates and furthered the development of a service sector. The new service sector itself expressed a demand for offices and created the basis for an office development market. Hence demand for property is a derived demand; it is used as a means to an end, for producing final manufactured goods or for facilitating the delivery of services to the final consumer.

Since 1997, following the Asian financial crisis, China has taken the lead in terms of economic growth rates. It has in many ways eclipsed South East Asia as the 'workshop of the world'. The growth of its manufacturing sector has fuelled economic growth, and higher real incomes have created a demand for services that in turn creates demand for offices.

However, economic growth does not necessarily lead to the same outcomes in relation to the establishment of a commercial property market containing use, investment and development sectors. Preferences in individual countries affect the establishment of these different sectors or functional divisions of the property market (Keogh, 1994). In some countries, legal systems discourage investors from reflecting a preference for property users. In such cases investment returns may be low and investors would not consider real estate as a viable or attractive alternative asset class. Other countries not only have institutional structures that favour the creation of an investment market in property, but also display the development of sophisticated financial products that permit a variety of ways to invest in real estate assets.

3.3   Explaining international financial flows

Securitised (indirect) and unsecuritised (direct) investment vehicles exist in real estate. Investment is dominated by institutional investors such as banks, insurance companies and pension funds. By the beginning of the new millennium, the international investment market across all assets was estimated to have a value of US$23 trillion. In real estate, the estimated total value of institutional investment in direct property was US$1.3 trillion. The indirect market in real estate securities was worth about US$265 billion, growing to almost US$300 billion by the end of 2002.

Within the direct market, it is likely that the size of the institutional investment-grade real estate stock is a lot bigger, ranging in value between US$3.5 trillion and US$6 trillion (Sirmans and Worzala, 2003a, p. 1081), leaving room for expansion of investment in this area.

Webb and O'Keefe (2002) suggested that property amounted to 10–20 per cent of total capitalised stocks, bonds and real estate in developed economies. They also suggest that most countries will need international property investment exposure, since their domestic markets are too small for it to be a unique asset class delivering diversification benefits.

Since the early 1990s there has also been substantial growth in investment vehicles. Baum (2002) finds over 100 funds in which to invest, most of which are high risk / high return ('opportunity') funds. As this market has increased in size, a substantial number of research studies have been undertaken to examine investment strategies and consequences.

As an alternative to direct investment, indirect vehicles can be used and may be preferred in an international context. Indirect real estate investment opportunities are unevenly distributed across the world, with the US accounting for almost 50 per cent of the market, Asia 25 per cent, the UK 10 per cent, and continental Europe 9 per cent. Indirect investors can more easily overcome information costs by working with local investors than would be the case with direct property assets. They may also avoid legalities relating to ownership issues that can arise with overseas direct investment.

As with direct investment, there has been growth in international indirect real estate investment, and research has examined the diversification benefits of overseas investment in both a multi-asset portfolio and a property-only portfolio context.

3.4   Direct real estate investment in multi-asset portfolios

A substantial number of studies have been undertaken to examine this issue. Key concerns surround whether or not there are international diversification benefits from holding unsecuritised real estate assets, and the role of currency fluctuations. The earliest studies date back to the 1980s after the first wave of financial deregulation liberated international financial flows. Marks (1986) examined stock and real estate returns for six countries from the perspective of investors in each country. For the period 1978–84 he found that real estate in the US outperformed the stock index in other countries, except Japan. He also highlighted the impact of currency fluctuations on investment risk and returns. Webb and Rubens (1989) use data from the UK and the US over a long time period, 1926–86, and compute efficient asset portfolios. They find that international real estate does not enter an efficient asset portfolio. Giliberto (1989), comparing US and UK real estate returns, suggests some benefits from overseas diversification, while Ziobrowski and Curcio (1991) find no diversification benefit when examining US and UK real estate data. Further, Ziobrowski and Boyd (1991) reach the same conclusion when leverage is present and hedging occurs to compensate for currency fluctuations when taking on local currency loans. Worzala (1992) and Worzala and Vandell (1995) examine mean returns and deviations from US and UK real estate and suggest that there are international diversification benefits from real estate, but less so when currency fluctuations are considered. They also suggest some instability in results over different time periods.

Newell and Webb (1996) examine real estate returns in the the US, the UK, Canada, Australia and New Zealand. They consider the possible impact of appraisal smoothing on the risk attached to real estate assets. Their findings are that risk is underestimated both due to smoothing and also when currency fluctuations are ignored. They also suggest some diversification benefits from the inclusion of international real estate in multi-asset portfolios. Stevenson (1998) examines 18 stock markets, five bond markets, US direct and indirect markets, and UK direct and indirect markets. In this research only non-property international financial assets are held in portfolios. His results suggest keeping real estate assets in a portfolio with international financial assets. Real estate is also present in a low risk / low return portfolio. Chua (1999) examines the US, the UK, France, Germany and Japan. Adjusting for appraisal smoothing, he finds that adding real estate improves risk-adjusted portfolio return performance in comparison to portfolios excluding real estate. Cheng *et al.* (1999) use data from the US, the UK and Japan. They design efficient portfolios and suggest that currency risk is significant but that international real estate can be included in portfolios for investors who are not too risk-averse. Hoesli *et al.* (2002) examine the US, the UK, Australia, France, the Netherlands, Sweden and Switzerland. They suggest that 15–25 per cent of an efficient portfolio should be devoted to real estate assets, both national and international. However, there is no analysis of the impact of currency movements.

3.5 Direct real estate investment in real estate-only portfolios

Most of the research conducted in this context does not consider currency movements, and this could perhaps qualify any inference from the results obtained. Again the earliest research dates back to the 1980s. Sweeney (1989) uses rental data for office markets and finds that there are diversification benefits from international real estate. Reid (1989), using similar data, provides similar findings. Gordon (1991) also finds concurring results, this time using real estate indices in the US and the UK. Worzala (1992) finds results consistent with the above, using the same US data as Gordon. In addition, she finds that when currency fluctuations are taken into account diversification benefits are reduced.

Eichholz *et al.* (1995) employ US and UK direct property indices and find that location has a greater impact than property type upon diversification benefits. They also suggest that the benefits of diversification will vary by country as well as by property type and region. Goetzmann and Wachter (1995) collect data on asking rents for office markets in 21 countries and examine return performance. They find a strong correlation with global economic cycles and office market performance, and therefore suggest that the diversification benefit of international real estate investment will be small. D'Arcy and Lee (1998) examine nine European countries covering industrial, office and retail sectors. They also examine markets in cities within these countries. Their findings suggest that a country's economic policy has the biggest impact on diversification benefits, followed by city-level effects. Some countries were more highly correlated in terms of performance than others. Addae-Dapaah and Yong (1998) examined countries in South East Asia, including Australia and New Zealand. Office rents and capital value data were used. Their findings suggest low cross-country correlations and only small increases in risk due to currency fluctuations.

Case *et al.* (1999) cover 22 markets and 21 countries, and suggest that property type is important when considering international diversification strategies in real estate. They find that office property offers the least, and industrial the greatest, diversification benefits. Henderson Investors (2000) found that an international property portfolio would provide higher risk-adjusted returns than property from an individual country. Whitaker (2001) examined IPD indices for the UK and Ireland, and the NCREIF series for the US. Portfolio benefits were found to exist for the US-based investor.

The issue of currency fluctuation, while not fully discussed in the works cited above, should not be considered insignificant. Direct property assets will have relatively high transactions costs in comparison to other assets and therefore tend to have relatively long holding periods. This in turn will increase the uncertainty of determining the final sale price of the asset. While hedging products can help reduce exchange rate risk for income returns, they are perhaps less helpful for the capital gain element, which is only realised on final sale, and thus this component will be more exposed to currency volatility.

3.6   Indirect real estate investment in multi-asset portfolios

Literature on international securitised real estate investment goes back to the early 1990s. Among the earliest of studies is that of Asabere *et al.* (1991), who examine equity returns of international real estate companies during the 1980s. They analyse returns, standard deviations and betas. They find a negative correlation between international real estate and US treasury bills and weak positive correlations with long-term government debt. They also find that the global real estate index outperforms domestic real estate but not global equities. Barry *et al.* (1996) examine emerging markets and find that risk-adjusted return performance improves as investment allocations to emergent markets increase. Eichholtz (1996), examining nine countries, finds that international real estate portfolio diversification improves portfolio performance. Mull and Soenen (1997), who adjust for the investor's home currency, argue that the addition of US indirect property provides limited portfolio improvement. Gordon *et al.* (1998) examine 14 countries and construct efficient frontiers. They find that inclusion of international real estate improves portfolio performance and that, as returns rise, real estate causes risk to fall.

Gordon and Canter (1999), using the same countries as above, examine correlations between stock markets and real estate securities. While they find that portfolios including international real estate assets outperform those that exclude real estate, they also find that correlations between asset classes vary substantially over time. Stevenson (1999) covers 16 countries and compares stock, bonds and real estate indices. Looking from the perspective of an Irish investor, he finds that UK real estate contributes only a small allocation of a mid-level risk-return portfolio. International real estate comes out of the portfolio when adjustment for currency is made. In a related paper, Stevenson (2000) finds that the diversification benefits of international real estate investment are eroded when currencies are considered. Interestingly, however, he suggests that strategies for hedging against currency risk could improve diversification benefits. Conover *et al.* (2002) analyse the UK, the US, Canada, Hong Kong, Japan and Singapore, constructing efficient frontiers. They suggest that portfolios containing international securitised real estate outperform those without it.

3.7   Indirect real estate investment in real estate-only portfolios

One of the earliest papers is Giliberto (1990), examining data from the 1980s across 11 countries. He computes portfolios where half is invested in the home country. He suggests that Western European property investments dominate the low risk/return portfolios and Japan dominates in portfolios with higher risk/return combinations. Addae-Dapaah and Boon Kion (1996) examine seven countries, including the UK, Canada, Japan, Australia, Hong Kong and Singapore, looking at mean returns and correlations. They find that correlations change over time and that diversification benefits are improved when currency adjustment is taken into consideration.

Wilson and Okunev (1996) examine the UK, the US and Australia. They apply co-integration analysis and construct efficient frontiers. They find that international investment is present in real estate-only efficient frontiers, although not at the highest risk/return levels. Pierzak (2001) examined 21 countries using mean returns and deviations. His findings suggest that there are diversification benefits from international indirect property investment. Bigman (2002) covers Europe, the US, Japan and South East Asia and finds that international diversification outperforms domestic-only portfolios.

Eichholtz *et al.* (1993) examine 12 countries across three continents. Using principal components analysis, they find a continental factor affecting performance and suggest that, in order to achieve diversification benefits, investment should be across the continents. Eichholtz *et al.* (1997) examine 30 countries and create domestic and international indices from their data. They suggest that domestic portfolios are preferred to international portfolios having preferable risk/return characteristics. Interestingly, they note a firm size effect that is also identified by Conover *et al.* (1998). Larger firms perform better than smaller firms.

Wilson and Okunev (1999) examine cycles in equity and real estate markets. They find weak co-movements that suggest there is room for diversification benefits with the inclusion of indirect property in portfolios.

3.8 International real estate returns

The above research highlights some contradictions in findings and sensitivity of results to time period covered, currency risk factors, firm size, and ability to provide diversification benefits. Bond *et al.* (2003) examine the risk and return characteristics of real estate shares from 14 countries from 1990 to 2001. They explore whether country-specific market risks are related to fundamental factors (such as book-to-market value, firm size) or economic risk factors (such as inflation rates, interest rates and default rates). They find variation in mean returns and standard deviations and that there is a global market risk component. However, country-specific market risk is still found to be significant, particularly in the Asia-Pacific region. They find that there are benefits from international real estate diversification, but these follow a more complex pattern than previously understood.

Glascock and Kelly (2007) examine the diversification benefits of international portfolio diversification. They use monthly data from January 1990 to July 2005 and separate out the influences of country and property type. Diversification across property types is found to account for only a small proportion of return variance, while country diversification produces significantly larger performance variation. This finding contrasts with studies examining diversification within countries, where property type diversification is often more important than diversifying across regions (Miles and McCue, 1982, 1984). However Glascock and Kelly also suggest that the relative importance of individual country impacts is diminishing. Their findings are consistent with those of Eichholtz (1997). They also show that correlations are higher between property types than between countries.

3.9 Institutional context

Transactions in real estate markets are often complex and time-consuming. The characteristics of exchange difference significantly from those assumed in neo-classical economic analysis: for example, instant equilibrium, full information, homogeneous product markets, and rational market behaviour. However, the property market in practice is highly inefficient, having limited and asymmetric information, no central trading place, infrequent trading, relative illiquidity and heterogeneous characteristics. Ball *et al.* (1998, p. 63) argue that for equilibrium to be feasible 'buyers and sellers must be able to use the full available information when making their decisions and operate according to the arguments of their demand and supply schedules. This may not occur, for example, if planning regu-lation freezes land supply or restrictive long leases severely distort demand.' Thus the speed with which equilibrium is achieved will depend on the institutional characteristics of the market.

Neoclassical economics has often been criticised by institutional economists because of what they perceive as its unrealistic assumptions. Van der Krabben and Lambooy (1993, p. 1384), for example, suggest that: 'Neoclassical economists assume that only rationally acting individual actors operate on the market. Price adjustments will automatically lead to an equilibrium.' However, these comments ignore recent developments in neoclassical theory (and its application), and Ball (1998) argues that neoclassical economics is often treated as a straw man, fash-ioned by its critics in a form that can be most easily demolished.

As Maclennan and Whitehead (1996) point out, neoclassical theory no longer rests on such assumptions as perfect competition, full information and instantan-eous equilibrium. According to Ball (2002), even rationality should be regarded as merely a working hypothesis or methodological standard. Rational market out-comes do not necessarily require rational behaviour by all actors. Ball *et al.* (1998) suggest that, although neoclassical economics shares many of the assumptions of equilibrium models, it seeks to explain actual behaviour in terms of rational expectations, transactions costs and asymmetric information.

This is a much broader view of neoclassical economics than that taken by crit-ics such as Hodgson (1999, p.102), who defines it as 'an approach which assumes rational, maximising behaviour by agents with given and stable preference functions, focuses on attained, or movements towards, equilibrium states, and excludes chronic information problems'. Critically, whereas Hodgson (1999) con-siders modern developments in mainstream economics, such as game theory, to be at the edge of or beyond neoclassicism, much of the rapidly expanding litera-ture on game theory is comfortably positioned within a neoclassical analytical framework (see, for example, Hargreaves-Heap and Varoufakis, 1995; Montet and Serra, 2003).

Although neoclassical economic models are abstractions that ignore many aspects of reality, Ball (2002) argues that the real test of their value lies in whether or not they explain market outcomes. According to Needham (1994), the quantitative advantages of neoclassical economic theory make it better able to explain some property market outcomes than such non-quantitative approaches as Marxist economics.

The last decade has seen a substantial development in the contribution of neo-classical economics to the analysis of property markets. It has travelled far from the point where, for example, neoclassical models of the development process could be criticised for their failure to distinguish between user and investor demand (Healey, 1991). Since then, Keogh (1994), DiPasquale and Wheaton (1996), and Colwell (2002) have each examined how the functional divisions of the property market relate to each other and have identified how the market signals linking the use, investment and development sectors.

The length of time taken to achieve market balance or equilibrium in real estate markets has been a key issue for researchers. Neoclassical economics does not consider market adjustment, since such adjustment was assumed to be instant. However, the real estate market is seen to adjust slowly, maybe taking a number of years to remove imbalances between supply and demand. The modelling of such adjustment processes is a key contribution that researchers have made to understanding the operation of property markets. The literature in this area is now substantial, for example, Wheaton *et al.* (1997), Hendershott *et al.* (2002a), Hendershott *et al.* (2002b), Mouzakis and Richards (2007). These authors either explicitly model rental adjustment in structural models or examine adjustment via an error correction mechanism in reduced form models. As Adams *et al.* (2005, p. 24) note, '...neo-classical analysis can be adapted to take into account information signalling, slow adjustment, spatial specificity and disequilibrium in property markets. .. The literature explicitly recognises the imperfections of property markets but seeks to analyse and accommodate them within a neo-classical framework'.

The relative inefficiency of the real estate market is one reason why neoclassical axioms are violated. Keogh and D'Arcy (1999b) consider an institutional dimension to the efficiency of property market operation. Institutions are often seen as the 'rules of the game'. Hamilton (1932, p. 84) describes an institution as: 'a way of thought or action of some prevalence, which is embedded in the habits of a group or the customs of people', suggesting that 'institutions fix the confines of and impose structure upon the activities of human beings.' Real estate markets can be considered similarly, as networks of rules, conventions and relationships (Keogh and D'Arcy, 1999b).

Institutions will reflect prevailing power and (dominant) interests within society. Yet, to be successful, institutions must be effective in generating 'workable mutuality' out of the formal and informal processes of conflict resolution from which they develop (Rutherford, 1994). In this context, what is legally or culturally feasible may deserve as much attention as what is technologically feasible (Keogh and D'Arcy, 1999b).

The most recent debates on the role of institutions in property markets are essentially based upon new institutional economics. Samuels (1995, p. 578) suggests that new institutional economics 'works largely within neoclassicism, and shares its rationality, maximisation, and market or market-like orientation and likewise tends to seek, though with less formalisation, the conventional determinate, optimal, equilibrium solutions to problems'.

New institutional economics can be divided into four main strands: transactions cost theory, property rights theory, public choice theory and game theory. Here we focus on the first, transactions cost theory. In this strand institutions develop in order to reduce the costs of exchange. It is high transactions costs that lead to inefficient outcomes. Adams *et al.* (2005, p. 43) state that: 'inefficiency rather than efficiency may well be embedded in the economic system as a result of uncertainty, individual risk aversion or moral hazard, all of which can be costly to reduce. New institutional economics thus calls on governments to consider instead how they might assign stronger rights of property to private decision-makers and create or support institutional arrangements designed to promote greater certainty within markets.'

One notable transactions cost in real estate, and in particular in international real estate, markets is the collection of information. Van der Krabben and Lambooy (1993) highlight the importance of uncertainty in explaining human behaviour and point out that, because the knowledge of decision-makers is severely limited (based upon incomplete and asymmetric information), people are boundedly rational and on occasion behave opportunistically.

The movement of real estate service providers into different countries around the globe has brought them into contact with various institutional arrangements that affect the existence, behaviour and operation of the property market, and especially whether an investment market in property can develop. Indeed, the real estate service providers themselves can be seen as institutions, just as the ways of doing business could be seen as the formal and informal rules of the game. The property market has to resolve demand from users and investors for a complex product/asset. The market will seek to adjust towards equilibrium between demand and supply. Its speed of adjustment will reflect information constraints, product heterogeneity and institutional behaviour influencing the property market. Thus an understanding of the operation of the property market will require an understanding of both neoclassical and institutional economics. While these represent different economic schools of thought, Ball (1998) suggests that even within neoclassicism there is recognition that institutions matter. Furthermore, as real estate service providers become international and interact with local institutions and service providers, institutional change may follow, and such evolution has been a core concern of institutional economics (Hodgson, 1989). However, it is not interpreted as a theory of everything because it does not ignore the local dimension to process of change, and locality is of specific importance in property market analysis. Also, whilst institutional analysis is more concerned with process than with outcomes, it is in agreement with neoclassical economics that developing theories of pricing is important in understanding market operation (op. cit., p. 169).

In neoclassical economics, property prices are determined by the interaction of demand and supply, and the operation of the price mechanism will return the market to equilibrium. Strictly, in accordance with neoclassical axioms, there is full information (the market is strong form efficient) and rational decision-making by market agents, market adjustment is instant, and (then) the price ruling in the market at any time is the equilibrium price. It is possible to think of the foreign exchange market as approximately meeting these strict conditions. For example, the price of sterling is determined in the global money markets, with one price set at any time balancing demand and supply side forces. Sterling will buy the same amount of foreign currencies in each market, and, if it did not, arbitrage opportunities would exist until such imbalances (or profit-making opportunities) were removed.

However, the characteristics of the property market move it far from the assumptions behind instant equilibrium. Limited information, heterogeneity, infrequent trading, transactions costs, and varying institutional structures that mediate demand and supply will increase the adjustment time needed to remove market imbalances. Barriers exist preventing the free movement of capital to where it can achieve the greatest risk-adjusted return. This is compounded in international real estate investment decisions due to the factors above. In addition, exchange rate risks (uncertainty) and limited information on institutional structures in overseas investment destinations add further transactions costs.

With such assumptions, neoclassical economics may seem inappropriate for analysis of property market behaviour, nationally or internationally. However, Maclennan and Whitehead (1996) argue that neoclassical economics is no longer dependent on assumptions of full information and instant equilibrium. Indeed, rationality is not required of all market actors (Ball, 2002); it is only required that a sufficient number of agents behave rationally. Furthermore, Ball *et al.* (1998) suggest that neoclassical economics can explain actual behaviour against a background of asymmetric information of the kind prevalent in property markets, and which affects decision-making in relation to international property investment.

Important for investment decision-making is the signalling role of rents, yields and capital values. These are made explicit by Keogh (1994), who provides a conceptualisation of the links between the functional divisions of property markets linking the user, investment and development markets. He discusses flexibility of adjustment to market signals in both short and long-run situations. Specifically, he highlights the institutional capacity to permit owner-occupiers to become investors in response to appropriate short-run pricing signals via separation of ownership and use rights. While this may seem obvious, legal systems that prevent such separation may undermine or weaken the establishment and/or growth of property investment markets. In the long run the development sector has time to deliver new product to the market if signals suggest. This in turn implies that the signal itself is clear enough for developers to respond appropriately. However, it has often been noted that such a response may produce new space when demand in the user market has changed. This was made evident, for example, in the London markets in the early 1990s and in the Shanghai market in the earlier part of the first decade of the new millennium. However inappropriately the property market responds, it nevertheless responds with the objective of matching demand and supply. While it cannot do this instantly, it still embodies the notion of market adjustment.

DiPasquale and Wheaton (1996) also discuss the linkages between use, investment and development. Their analysis is explicitly long-run in its focus, obviating discussion on short-run adjustment processes. They implicitly ignore any problems that might prevent smooth adjustment to long-run equilibrium positions. Colwell (2002) extends their discussion to make issues of protracted adjustment explicit. He also discusses the role of expectations in market behaviour.

These models, to a greater or lesser degree, apply what are essentially neoclassical principles to markets in which many of the basic axioms do not apply. In many cases the adjustment processes that are not debated in neoclassical economics (because they are not seen to be a problem, or they are in fact instantaneous) become the centre of attention.

In the context of the property market, which suffers from acute informational inefficiencies, market prices signals alone will therefore be insufficient to ensure an efficient allocation of real estate resources.

3.10 Conclusion

This chapter began by introducing theories of portfolio construction and diversification. It then examined the scale of international financial flows before examining direct and indirect investment in different portfolio contexts. The studies reviewed highlight the key factors affecting diversification benefits and whether sector or international location dominates the benefits from the inclusion of property in asset portfolios. Finally we discuss the institutional context. This discussion is rarely the focus of investment and financial performance analyses of real estate, but nevertheless it has a fundamental impact on real estate asset performance. The discussion proceeds to expand upon institutional economic theories and how these can be blended with more neoclassical approaches to enable a fuller understanding of property markets. This understanding is important in the context of international property investment markets, where different countries have different institutional characteristics that impact upon market performance.

Property Market Activity

4.1 | Introduction

In a market economy, market competition ensures efficient allocation of resources (goods, services, capital and labour) among the various users. Market forces of demand and supply interact to determine the market clearing price of the resources and to whom these resources are allocated. Property is both a consumption (use) and an investment good. In the market for use of property, property resources are allocated to various users – households, businesses and institutions. Users compete for physical location and space, and competition among them determines who gains the use of space and how much they must bid for its use. Capital for investment in property is allocated in the capital markets. Participants in the capital markets invest in stocks, bonds, mutual funds, private business enterprises, mortgage contracts, property and other opportunities with the expectation of receiving financial returns on their investments. Investment opportunities that yield the highest returns, considering risk, will attract a flow of capital. Property as an asset competes with a diverse set of investment opportunities to attract investment. Government affects property markets in a number of ways through planning, legal, taxation, subsidy and a host of other regulations. The value of the property is determined through the interaction of three sectors: the property use market, financial markets and government. Property values determined in this way become a guide to property developers. When market values exceed the cost of production of new properties, developers are inclined to build, thereby adding to the supply of space and simultaneously to the supply of investible property assets.

This chapter presents an overview of property market activity in an international context. To simplify the presentation, the market activity is discussed in the context of three property sub-markets: (i) use market, (ii) investment market and (iii) development. This chapter also presents an overview of the trends in financing property investment. The description in this chapter relies heavily on data information from various research reports published by real estate service providers such as CBRE (various years), Jones Lang LaSalle (various years),

RREEF (various years), PwC (various years), and other sources that are individually referenced.

Discussion of the international context is incomplete without discussing the motivation for internationalisation of property markets. Internationalisation of the use market is closely linked with globalisation of economic activities, evidenced through growth of Trans-National Corporations (TNCs) and substantial growth in foreign direct investment (FDI) and trade. All these lead to greater demand for space, and this demand shifts across national boundaries. Globalisation has also led to increased capital mobility for investment across countries. Property, as well as being one of the asset classes, is also a recipient of cross-border investment. Bardhan *et al.* (2008) describe two transmission mechanisms through which globalisation affects property rents and values. They argue that economic openness leads to higher local productivity and output, which increases the demand for non-tradeable goods such as property. Elasticity of supply in property markets is low, which causes rents and values to increase disproportionately. Another argument put forward by these authors is based on the Balassa–Samuelson Hypothesis, which states that increasing internationalisation leads to asymmetric increase in productivity of tradeable goods vis-à-vis non-tradeable goods. The impact of higher productivity is that wages in the tradeable sector rise, and, assuming that the labour within the economy is mobile between the tradeable and non-tradeable sectors, this raises wages in the entire economy. The relative price of property, a non-tradeable sector, will also rise.

If the markets are opaque, they offer opportunities for excess returns over risk-free rate for investors investing in property. With increasing international financial integration, the opportunity for excess returns will eventually reduce, thereby diminishing arbitrage opportunities, if they exist. Country and currency risk-adjusted returns will equalise across various property markets. Studies have been conducted to explain the forces that drive differences in property returns across countries/regions. Hamelink and Hoesli (2004), in their study on property security returns in 21 countries, find that country, scale and value/growth factors are important in explaining returns. Eichholz *et al.* (1998), Eichholz and Huisman (1999), Ling and Naranjo (2002) and Bond *et al.* (2003) find that country-specific variables play an important role in determining differences in property returns across countries.

If country-specific variables are an important determinant of property returns, could diversification benefits, in a mixed or single-asset portfolio context, be achieved through investing in international property? A number of studies have been conducted on the interrelationship between property markets across national boundaries, particularly from the point of view of examining the international property investment diversification potential. Conover *et al.* (2002) show that foreign property investment provides diversification benefits beyond those obtainable from foreign stocks. Liu and Mei (1998) find that inclusion of international property securities in a portfolio improves risk-adjusted returns, after accounting for currency risk. A similar result was found by Hoesli *et al.* (2002), who claim that portfolio diversification benefits are created by including property assets in a mixed-asset portfolio. A contrasting view, however, was given by Stevenson (2000), who found that the potential diversification benefits that could arise from investing in property securities are not generally statistically significant. A more detailed review of portfolio diversification by including property is presented in Chapter 3.

The research, as presented above and in Chapter 3, is inconclusive at one level but on the other hand raises an important aspect to be explored further – trends in international property investment and investor profile. In addition to the market activity, this chapter also presents changing trends in international property investment and investor profile.

4.2   Size of property market

Estimating the size of property markets is difficult due to the largely fragmented and private nature of the market. Various researchers have made attempts to estimate the size of the market (see, for example, ULI and PwC, 2007; Key and Law, 2005; PREI, 2003; DTZ, 2006/07, etc.). RREEF (2007a) estimated that the size of global property market (total[1] stock) was around US$26 trillion in December 2006. Due to data limitations, it is difficult to assess the composition of total stock by property type. RREEF (2008) reports the share of various property types with a caveat. Figure 4.1 presents the estimated size of global property market by property type as of 2007.

In markets for which data exists (in the form of a local index prepared by Investment Property Databank), such as the US or Europe, the majority of investment grade property is in retail (30–50 per cent, depending on the country) or offices (35–50 per cent, again a function of country). The share of industrial and other property types is small.

Of the total stock of nearly US$26 trillion, nearly US$10 trillion (invested stock) was owned by professional property investors such as funds, property managers, private investment vehicles, listed companies, institutions, etc. The rest was owner-occupied, termed investible because it may over time become owned by institutions. Most of the invested stock is located in the matured markets of

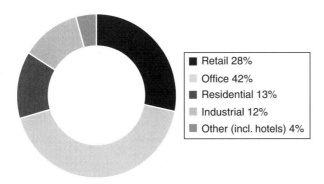

Figure 4.1   Size of global property market by property type, 2007
Source: ING Real Estate (2008), Global Vision (2008).

America and Europe. Of the total stock of US$9.5 trillion in America, nearly US$4.7 trillion is already invested (RREEF, 2007a). In Europe, US$3.2 trillion worth of stock out of a total of US$9.2 trillion is already invested (ibid.). Asia has the smallest proportion of the total stock that is invested. Of the total US$5.9 trillion worth of property, only US$1.9 trillion worth of stock is invested. The size of the 10 largest property markets is presented in Figure 4.2.

The US dominates the global invested property market with a share of 48 per cent of the total. Europe and Asia follow the US, with a share of 33 per cent and 19 per cent respectively. Within Europe, the Western countries dominate, with the four largest markets of Germany, UK, France and Italy representing nearly 70 per cent of the total. In Asia, the more mature economies of Japan, Australia, Hong Kong and Singapore account for 80 per cent of the total (RREEF, 2007a).

Emerging markets in Europe and Asia have a small, but the fastest growing, share in invested property. Central and Eastern Europe accounts for 5 per cent of the value of the European property stock. In Asia, China and India have grown dramatically in recent years and their invested stock represents around 10 per cent of the regional total.

Besides the differences in the size of the market, these markets differ in the share taken by different property types. Highly mature markets like the US, the UK and Australia have a high share of retail property space, reflecting the maturity and concentration of retail industry in these countries. RREEF (2007a) estimates that nearly 56 per cent of invested stock in Australia by the end of 2006 was in retail. The share of retail in total invested stock in the UK and the US was around 47 per cent and 20 per cent respectively by the end of 2006.

In the mature economies of Western Europe (e.g., Germany, France and Scandinavian countries) and Asia (e.g., Japan), office markets tend to dominate the invested market. This reflects the importance of the service economy

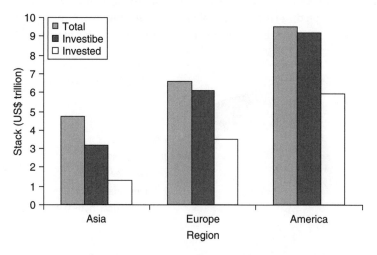

Figure 4.2 Region-wise size of real estate markets (as of December 2006)
Source: RREEF (2007a). The future size of the global real estate market.

in these countries and the relative immaturity of retail and logistics markets. Emerging economies, on the other hand, display a relatively high share of retail and logistics in their total invested stock (though the overall level of stock is very small), reflecting the export orientation and manufacturing-dominated economic structure.

4.3 | Use market

The use market for commercial property mirrors the economic picture of the city. Evidence of property use market activity can be seen from indicators such as rental levels, the market's position on rental cycles and vacancy levels. As discussed earlier, most of the investment-grade commercial property stock is located in matured economies. The emerging markets' share is fairly small, but is becoming increasingly important as rapid economic growth is driving demand for space from domestic and international users.

For users in the property market, space is cost. The position of a property market on a rental cycle vis-à-vis other markets reflects both the opportunity and the challenges for users. Businesses evaluate the cost of space in their decision to locate offices.

Rental evidence as of May 2008 for key office markets is presented in Table 4.1. Some interesting observations can be drawn from the above table:

1. It is obvious that the rents (occupancy cost) differ substantially across different markets. However, the more important message that comes out of the table is that it is not necessarily the matured markets that are expensive. Neither are they located in the same geographical region. Among the top five most expensive markets, three are in Asia and two in Europe. From the standpoint of market maturity, Moscow and Mumbai are classified as emerging, while Tokyo is mature and London is a highly mature market (JLL, 2008; Real Estate Transparency Index).

    a. Another point to note from the above table is the growth in rents. Markets like Moscow, Ho Chi Minh City and Singapore have seen a change in rental to the extent of around 100 per cent over May 2007. Markets in the UK have seen rental growth in single digits, and rents in London City have in fact declined over the last year.

    b. The third point that emerges from the above table is the differences in lease term and rent-free period across markets. Lease terms vary from 25 years in Dublin to two years in Ho Chi Minh City. A general observation that could be made is that matured markets usually have longer leases, with the exception of Singapore in Table 4.1, which is a matured market but has a lease term of three years. Rent-free period depends on the market conditions. In a weak market, landlords offer incentives in the form of rent-free periods, and in a strong market precisely the reverse would happen.

Table 4.1 Rents and vacancy levels in key office markets

Market	Rent (US$/SF/ annum)	% change over 12 months	Typical lease term (years)	Typical rent-free period (months)
London (West End), UK	299.54	24.2	10–15	9
Moscow, Russia	232.37	92.7	7	6
Tokyo (Inner city), Japan	220.25	35.9	5	1
Mumbai, India	210.97	52.4	3+3+3	1
Tokyo (Outer central), Japan	175.35	22.2	5	1
London (City), UK	164.18	−0.9	10	15–18
New Delhi, India	145.16	24.9	3+3+3	1
Paris, France	141.98	27.1	3/6/9	3–6
Singapore	139.31	105	3	1
Dubai, UAE	128.49	43.4	3–5	1
Hong Kong	126.79	30.4	3 or 6	2–3
Dublin, Ireland	126.60	18.9	25	3
New York, Midtown, US	103.43	22.7		
Paris La Defense, France	103.20	39.3	3/6/9	3–6
Birmingham, UK	100.38	15.0	10	15
Oslo, Norway	97.30	89.3	5–10	0
Madrid, Spain	96.64	23.3	3–5	1–2
Zurich, Switzerland	92.99	37.3	5+5	1–3
Luxembourg	92.78	34.6	3/6/9	12
Edinburgh, UK	92.43	4.2	10	12
Manchester, UK	87.46	2.5	10	12
Stockholm, Sweden	86.69	38.3	3–5	2–3
Ho Chi Minh City, Vietnam	85.84	94.4	2	1
Milan, Italy	85.41	25.3	6+6	6
Abu Dhabi, UAE	84.14	10.3	3+	1
Frankfurt am Main, Germany	82.63	35.9	5+5	3–5
Bristol, UK	81.49	18.7	10	12
Glasgow, UK	80.50	2.6	10	12
Geneva, Switzerland	78.43	32.1	5	0–3
Warsaw, Poland	76.55	57.4	3–5	1–6
Leeds, UK	76.53	2.7	10/15	18
Rio de Janeiro, Brazil	74.60	35.6	5	1–2
Athens, Greece	73.79	40.0	12	0–2
Aberdeen, UK	72.55	7.2	10+5	9
Sao Paulo, Brazil	71.41	44.0	5	3
Seoul, South Korea	71.40	−0.4	2–3	1–2
Rome, Italy	71.18	41.3	6+6	6
Sydney (Core), Australia	68.52	13.9	8	9.9
Shanghai (Pudong), China	68.45	25.5	2–3	1–2
Munich, Germany	67.55	22.9	5+5	3–6

Continued

Table 4.1   Continued

Market	Rent (US$/SF/ annum)	% change over 12 months	Typical lease term (years)	Typical rent-free period (months)
Perth, Australia	66.58	48.9	5	0.0
Calgary, Canada	66.27	19.5		
Brussels, Belgium	64.77	16.2	3/6/9	12
Liverpool, UK	64.60	31.8	5/10	15
Barcelona, Spain	64.43	30.0	3+2	2
Brisbane, Australia	63.32	35.2	5	1.0
Toronto, Canada	62.44	19.5		
Los Angeles, US	62.06	18.6		
Jersey, UK	61.46	1.4	15	18
Shanghai (Puxi), China	61.26	25.0	2–3	1–2

Source: CBRE (2008) Global market rents May 2008: Office rents and occupancy costs worldwide.

Table 4.2   Typical lease lengths of European retail and office properties

	Retail	Office
Netherlands	5 years	5–10 years
Belgium	9 years	3–9 years
France	9–12 years	6–12 years
Germany	10 years	5–10 years
Spain	10–15 years	3–5 years
UK	10–15 years	10–15 years
Sweden	3–5 years	3–5 years

Source: ING (2008), Global retail markets.

It is also important to note that the currency units for rental values presented in above table are in US$. Rents are paid in the local market in local currencies. Though it is convenient to show rents in US$ here, growth rates in local currency would be very different from the growth rates in US$ terms.

The differences across markets are further compounded when one makes comparisons across various property types. As an example, in many markets the lease terms for retail and office markets differ substantially (Table 4.2). Lease terms for retail and industrial properties are usually longer than for office property.

4.3.1   Cycles in the use market

At a given point in time different markets face different conditions regarding rental growth. Property consultants depict the position of a market using a diagrammatic representation (called the property clock by JLL and the property cycle by RREEF) of the markets with an indicative position of the market at a

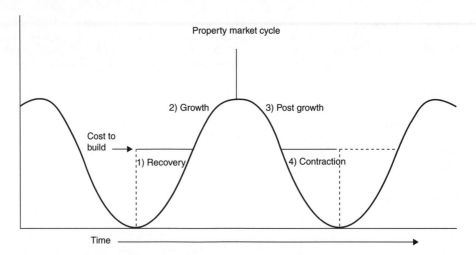

Figure 4.3   Property market rental cycle
Source: RREEF(2006a) Asia-Pacific property cycle monitor November 2006.

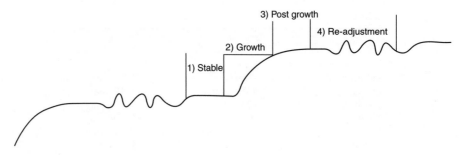

Figure 4.4   Retail property market rental cycle in Europe
Source: RREEF(2006b) European property cycle monitor, December.

particular point in time. Though these diagrams do not indicate either the level of growth in rental values or the peak and amplitude of the property cycle, these are useful ways of presenting the direction in which future rents are expected to move. Figure 4.3 is the representation of a property cycle. General conditions for the recovery phase are high but show declining vacancy rates and stable to rising rents. The growth phase is characterised by low and declining vacancy rates, and rising rents that support construction of new space. The post-growth phase is characterised by low but increasing vacancy rates and rising/flattening rents. The contraction phase witnesses high or increasing vacancy levels and declining rents.

The retail market also has cycles (the underlying driver of retails is consumer demand, which is affected by the economy), but these are not as pronounced as the office market cycles. A representation of the retail cycle is shown in Figure 4.4 (RREEF, 2006b). Stage 1 is characterised by stable rents and an upturn in

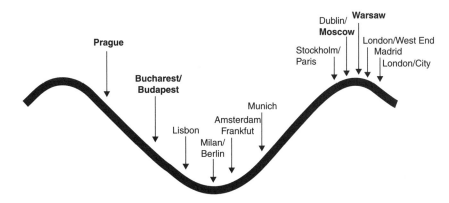

Figure 4.5 European office rental cycle (October 2007)

Note: Cities marked in bold represent the Central and Eastern European markets.

Source: RREEF (2007a), RREEF Global real estate insights 2007, October.

consumer spending. Stage 2 is the growth phase when rents are rising and there is strong consumer spending and/or retailer demand. During Stage 3, rents start to stabilise and consumption growth also slows down. Stage 4 is the readjustment phase. During this stage rents are stable or start declining. Consumer spending is also slow or declining.

The position of various European markets on the office market cycle as of October 2007 is presented in Figure 4.5.

Figure 4.5 illustrates the office market conditions that these cities are facing. For example, the rents in Milan (Italy) and Berlin (Germany) have bottomed out, and rents in these markets should start recovering. Budapest (Hungary) and Lisbon (Portugal) are still witnessing declining rents. Warsaw (Poland), Moscow (Russia), Dublin (Ireland), Stockholm (Sweden) and Paris (France) have reached/almost reached the peak on rental cycle. Rents in London (UK) and Madrid (Spain) have started to decline.

Figure 4.6 presents a rental cycle for industrial property in Europe. An important observation that could be made here is that the positions on the property cycle for different asset types do not necessarily coincide. For example, the office market in Munich is in the recovery phase, but the industrial property market is in the post-growth stage. Even though the main driver for all property types is growth in the economy, market microstructures (such as supply conditions, economic competition from other markets and economic structural changes) also play an important role.

The European retail property cycle as of October 2007 is presented in Figure 4.7. The position of a market in the retail rental cycle is a function of economy and market microstructure. According to RREEF (2007a), Western Europe witnessed strong economic growth during the first half of 2007, which led to good performance from European shopping centre markets. Strong retailer demand and lack of good-quality shopping centre space had created a positive rental environment for retail, with some exceptions, most particularly in the UK and the Netherlands.

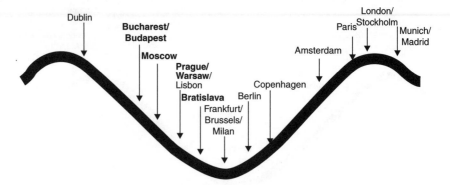

Figure 4.6 European industrial property rental cycle (October 2007)
Note: Cities marked in bold represent the Central and Eastern European markets.
Source: RREEF (2007a), RREEF Global real estate insights 2007, October.

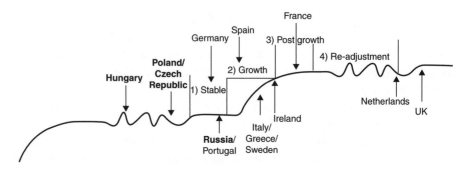

Figure 4.7 European retail property rental cycle (October 2007)
Note: Cities marked in bold represent the Central and Eastern European markets.
Source: RREEF (2007b), RREEF Global real estate insights 2007, October.

The UK retail market had been experiencing rising interest rates, falling house prices, weakening consumer spending and an increase in new supply. Slowing rental growth reflected these conditions. The retail market in the Netherlands had been wavering between readjustment and stability due to an ample amount of new supply and retail price deflation. Greece, Spain, Sweden and Ireland were at an attractive stage of their growth cycles. Ireland and Spain were benefiting from rapidly expanding economies in recent years. Retail property rents benefited from rapid expansion of foreign retailers. A shortage of good quality of supply in France and the improving economic outlook in Germany boosted the retail market performance in both countries.

European rental cycles differ in amplitude and timing from those of Asia-Pacific. Rental cycles have been quite pronounced in the cities of Asia-Pacific, where economic conditions have changed quite dramatically in the past. During the financial crisis of 1997, many of the Asia-Pacific economies suffered. Following 1997, rents in the office market had declined to around a third

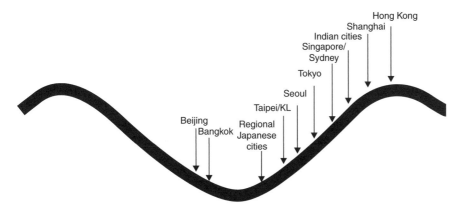

Figure 4.8 Asian office property rental cycle (October 2007)
Source: RREEF (2007b), RREEF Global real estate insights 2007, October.

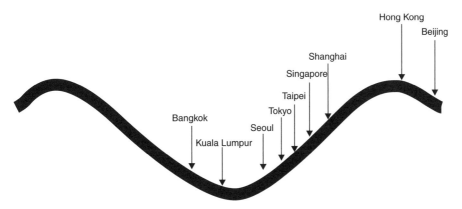

Figure 4.9 Retail property rental cycle in Asia-Pacific (October 2007)
Source: RREEF (2007b), RREEF Global real estate insights 2007, October.

by 1999 in the central business district (CBD) of Beijing. By 1999, Hong Kong had also seen a fall in office property rents to a third of its 1995 peak rent levels. Though rental levels have recovered since then, they have not reached the peak levels that were witnessed during the first half of the 1990s. Office property rental levels in Tokyo (Japan) remained subdued since 1996. Rents in Tokyo started to increase after 2004 in response to the recovery in the Japanese economy. Rents in the Singapore office market softened after the 1997 financial crisis. However, the market started to recover by the end of 1999. By 2001 rents had increased by nearly 20 per cent from their levels in 1999. The cycle was repeated with the SARS outbreak, which affected Singaporean economy quite badly, and rents fell sharply. The rental cycle for the office market in Asia-Pacific is shown in Figure 4.8. Asian office markets have experienced a strong growth cycle. The economic fundamentals are strong, as Asian economies have been growing rapidly, and this is attracting external capital into property in this

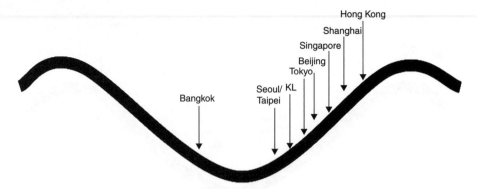

Figure 4.10 Asia-Pacific industrial property rental cycle
Source: RREEF (2007b), RREEF Global real estate insights 2007, October.

region. There is also a huge pipeline of new supply in markets such as Australia, India, Singapore and Hong Kong, which should soften the rental values in the near future. Beijing (China) and Bangkok (Thailand) are in the contraction phase.

Economic growth and rising level of affluence are driving retail demand in Asia-Pacific. This is reflected in the retail rental cycle (Figure 4.9). Most markets, except Bangkok (Thailand) and Kuala Lumpur (Malaysia), are in the growth phase of the cycle.

Figure 4.10 presents an industrial property rental cycle in Asia-Pacific. The economic structure of the region is manufacturing-based and exports-oriented. There is a shortage of good-quality industrial property, as this sector is in its stage of emergence in most parts of the Asia-Pacific region.

4.4 | Investment market

In recent years, property investment activity has increased substantially (Figure 4.11). During 2007, capital flow in global property markets amounted to US$795 billion (RREEF, 2008). However, a large proportion of this activity is concentrated in the US (around half) and Europe (around a third). The size of the property investment market in Asia-Pacific is small but increasing in importance, particularly in the listed property investment market, where Asia-Pacific leads the way. Nearly 15 per cent of the Asia-Pacific investment market is in listed securities compared with the global average of 9 per cent.

The US and Continental Europe have had a long tradition of property investment, with highly developed direct and indirect property markets. The diversity of investors includes institutional investors, private national buyers and foreign investors. The active investment market in Asia-Pacific only emerged from the mid-1980s (Walker and Flanagan, 1991). A large part of the real assets in Asia-Pacific is owner-occupied, but the direct property investment market is growing

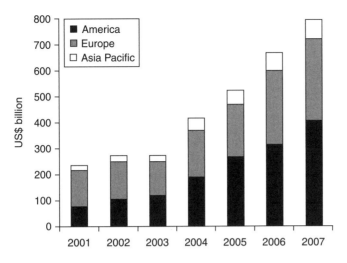

Figure 4.11   Property investment market activity

Source: RREEF (2008) Global real estate investment and performance 2007 and 2008.

rapidly. This region has witnessed far more activity in listed property investment market than the US or Europe since the 1980s. In the earlier phase, the listed securities market was dominated by real estate developers. The property market collapse in many Asia-Pacific countries during the Asian financial crisis of 1997, and the dominance of developers, made the listed property market volatile. However, since 2002, Japan, Singapore and several other countries introduced Real Estate Investment Trusts (REITs), which has helped in stabilising the listed securities market.

Property investment activity has become global, and the share of cross-border investment has increased more than fourfold since 2001 (Figure 4.12), amounting to nearly 28 per cent of the total investment. Europe witnesses a large share of cross-border investment activity within EU countries. The share of cross-border investment activity is also increasing in the US and Asia-Pacific. In 2007 the share of cross-border investment in the US was 21 per cent and in Asia Pacific 12 per cent. Investment behaviour has changed substantially over the last 10 years. Literature has long argued that in a mixed asset portfolio context it is possible to diversify risk by investing in international real assets because individual country returns are less than perfectly correlated (Hoesli and Macgregor, 2000). However, studies such as Geurts and Jaffe (1996) did not find much evidence of international diversification, and they attributed the lack of international diversification to investors' home asset bias. Investors understand their home market well but face formal and informal barriers when they invest abroad. These barriers in turn discourage cross-border investment. In recent years, due to globalisation of economic activities, convergence of political and economic structures (for example, due to the enlargement of the European Union), convergence in property market practices and increased market transparency, cross-border activity has increased. Capital from the US and the UK was at the forefront of cross-border investment in

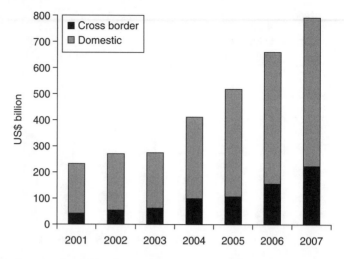

Figure 4.12 Property investment by origin

Source: RREEF (2008) Global real estate investment and performance 2007 and 2008.

Table 4.3 Cross-continental investment activity 2007, US$ billion

Sources of capital	Destination of activity		
	America	Europe	Asia-Pacific
America		46.1	12.6
Europe	21.0		1.3
Asia-Pacific	14.0	7.7	
Total cross-continent	35.0	53.9	13.9
Total cross-border	48.1	150.5	25.8
Total transaction	410.0	307.5	75.6

Source: RREEF (2008) Global real estate investment and performance 2007 and 2008.

2007 (RREEF, 2008), amounting to nearly 40 per cent of total global cross-border investment. With better understanding, increased confidence and development of diverse property investment products across the globe, a large proportion of investment has become cross-continental (Table 4.3). The destination of capital flows depends on investors' risk and return preferences. While a large proportion of the American capital has flown into emerging markets, the UK capital has been largely concentrated on mature markets in Asia and Europe.

Overall, the performance of property markets had been quite robust until the first half of 2007, though there had been variations across different markets. Huge capital inflows in property have led to declining cap rates (Figure 4.13) and the trend in movement of cap rates in all regions has been southwards.

There have been variations at the individual market level, as shown in Figure 4.14; some markets, like Seoul (South Korea), have seen far greater compression than other markets (like Tokyo, Japan) located in the same region. Cap rates in Hong Kong have in fact moved outwards.

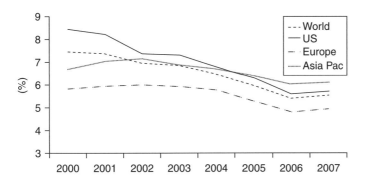

Figure 4.13 Global office cap rate trends

Note: Aggregate weighted average performance based on twenty four global markets – 10 in US, 10 in Europe and 4 in Asia-Pacific.

Source: RREEF (2008) Global real estate investment and performance 2007 and 2008.

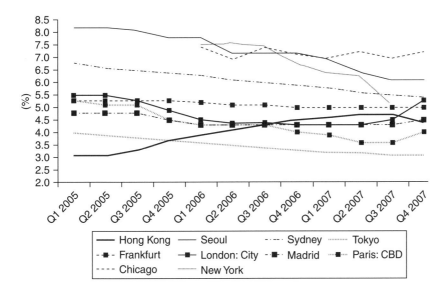

Figure 4.14 Cap rate movement across major office markets

Source: RREEF (2008) Global real estate investment and performance 2007 and 2008.

Property investment has delivered better returns than other asset classes, with far lower volatility over the last 10 years in all markets (Table 4.4).

Property securities have outperformed direct real estate returns. Caution must, however, be exercised in interpreting these numbers, as the averages conceal marked variations over time and from market to market. Japan, for example, has seen negative performance in the late 1990s (RREEF, 2007b).

Region-wise direct property returns are shown in Figure 4.15. The total property return during 2005 and 2006 was around 16–17 per cent, though this level of return is unlikely to be achieved during 2007 and 2008.

Table 4.4 Risk and return for various asset classes

		Direct property	Equities	Property securities	Bonds
Europe					
	Return	9.5%	10.1%	19.0%	5.9%
	Risk	1.8%	21.4%	16.7%	4.7%
	Return/Risk	5.3	0.5	1.1	1.3
North America					
	Return	12.7%	8.3%	14.9%	6.1%
	Risk	4.3%	20.1%	19.0%	5.3%
	Return/Risk	3.0	0.4	0.8	1.2
Asia-Pacific					
	Return	4.3%	3.8%	12.7%	
	Risk	8.6%	24.0%	21.8%	
	Return/Risk	0.49	0.16	0.58	

Note: Europe: All property total returns is a weighted average of Germany, France, Spain, Ireland, Italy, the Netherlands and the UK.

North America: All property total returns is a weighted average of Canada and the US.

Asia-Pacific: All property total returns is a weighted average of Australia, South Korea, China, Japan, Singapore, New Zealand and Hong Kong.

Source: RREEF (2007b), Global real estate insights 2007.

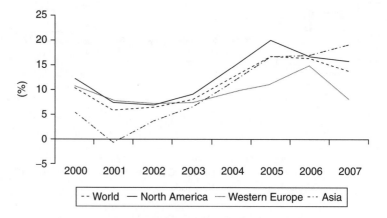

Figure 4.15 Direct all property total returns
Source: RREEF (2008) Global real estate investment and performance 2007 and 2008.

Total return has two components: income returns and growth in values. During recent years the share of value growth in total returns has increased substantially, as evidenced from the cap rate compression in Figure 4.11. Value growth in the US, France, Spain and Sweden has averaged 60 per cent of returns. High share of value growth in total returns has increased investment risk and has shifted the risk towards the end of the holding period.

Indirect public and private property investment markets have developed and grown substantially around the world. As demonstrated by Figure 4.14, until the first half of 2007 property securities returns across major markets were

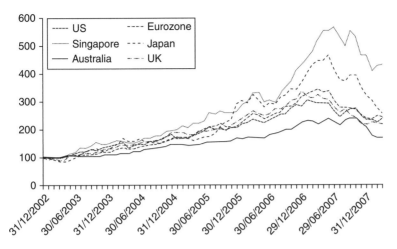

Figure 4.16 Property securities returns across major markets

Note: Real estate securities returns indexed to end 2002 = 100 in local currencies.

Source: RREEF (2008) Global real estate investment and performance 2007 and 2008.

phenomenal. During the latter half of 2007, capital flows in property declined due to the credit crunch, leading to a decline in property securities returns. An interesting observation from Figure 4.16 is the simultaneity of the movement of property returns across various markets located in Asia, Europe and America.

4.5   Investor profile

Nearly 93 per cent of global commercial property is privately owned, though there are some regional differences – for example, Hong Kong and Australia have 10–12 per cent public ownership. A number of public and private investment vehicles have emerged that have facilitated investment in property. There are differences between public and private vehicles for investment in property. Public vehicles have the advantage of being highly liquid, diversifiable and gearable, and have limited liability. There are disadvantages as well; since they are traded on stock markets, they tend to have high correlation with equity markets. Usually the cost of valuation of publicly traded property is high. Private vehicles offer higher leverage and have limited liability for investors and potential for stock market diversification. Their disadvantage is that they are less liquid.

During the last two decades, public vehicles have gained popularity because of their liquidity. These vehicles have provided mechanisms for institutions and individuals to get exposure to property quickly and in a cost-effective way. Some investors, such as institutional investors, prefer continuous pricing of their assets, and public vehicles provide that feature as they are traded on stock markets.

One of the reasons for the strong performance of property from 2001 until recently has been due to phenomenal investor interest in this asset class from a range of investors including pension funds, REITs, leveraged buyers and retail investors (RREEF, 2008). Property as an asset has become an important component of a mixed-asset portfolio for both individual and institutional investors. Figure 4.17 presents the current and target allocation of investment to property by pension funds in select countries.

In most countries, the allocation of funds by pension funds for property is expected to grow. Substantial growth is expected in countries like Japan, where investors are seeking to allocate as much as 8 per cent to property.

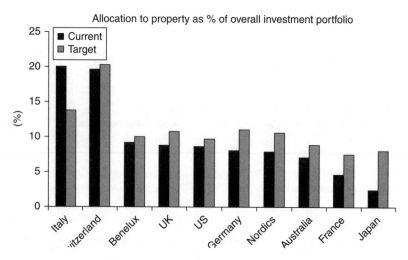

Figure 4.17 Pension funds allocation for property asset
Source: RREEF (2008) Global real estate investment and performance 2007 and 2008.

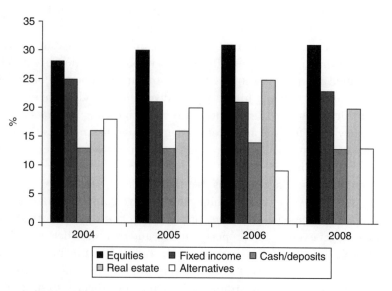

Figure 4.18 Middle eastern HNWIs asset allocation 2004–8
Source: RREEF (2008) Global real estate investment and performance 2007 and 2008.

Besides institutional investors, two other groups of investors that have been active in the property investment market are Sovereign Wealth Funds (SWFs) and equity-rich individuals (high net worth individuals, HNWIs). SWFs control huge sums of capital and at the moment have low or no allocation to property. However, as reported by RREEF (2008), this is changing and there is a significant potential for a share of these funds to be invested in property. HNWIs comprise a diverse group – retail-driven investors in German Open End Funds and Australian wholesale funds, HNWIs from the Middle East, Asia and Eastern Europe. As indicated by Figure 4.18, their allocation for property (an example of asset allocation of Middle Eastern HNWIs) has been increasing.

With the increasing diversity of investors interested in property, the profile of investors has also changed (Figure 4.19). The change in profile, however, differs from market to market and is a function of local conditions. The New York office market (Figure 4.19) has witnessed an increase in the share of private investors

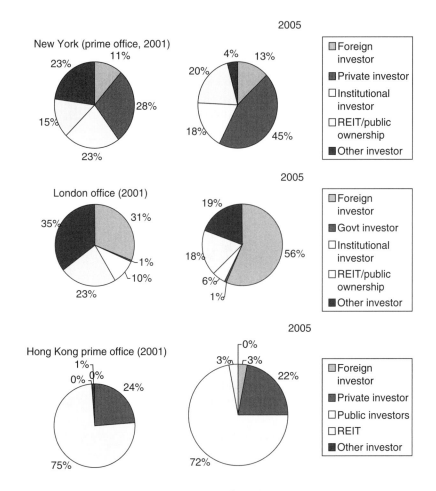

Figure 4.19 Share of investors in total invested stock

Source: CBRE (2006) Who is buying the world?

in 2005 compared with 2001. The increased share of private investors has been due to repricing of risk by investors following September 2001, which led to an increase in the share of local buyers, and national buyers such as institutional investors moved to other locations. The London office market has witnessed a substantial increase in the share of investment in office stock by foreign investors. American, Irish, German and Middle Eastern investors have increased their activity in this market. Hong Kong office stock is largely under public ownership. However, the trend indicates that the share of REITs and foreign investor ownership is increasing.

4.6   Development

Development activity is triggered by current and expected use and investment market activities. The prevailing regulatory and planning regime, the availability of construction finance and other resources constrain development activity. Figure 4.20 presents the completion of office stock in eight metro areas (Kelly, 2002).

An immediate observation from Figure 4.20 is the length of time series information, illustrating that it is difficult to obtain information on completions from published sources. While availability of information on other property market indicators, such as rental growth, total return and yields, has become easier as

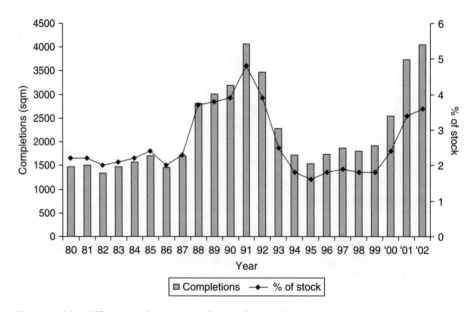

Figure 4.20 Office completions in eight North West European cities

Note: The eight cities are Edinburgh, Dublin, London, Brussels, Paris, Ramstadt, Dusseldorf, and Frankfurt.

Source: Kelly (2002).

real estate service providers and property data agencies like IPD have started to compile them and publish them, development pipeline and completions for various markets are still not reported for easy access as are other indicators. The other important observation from Figure 4.20 is the cyclical nature of development activity. Barras (1994) present a conceptual model for building cycles. He argues that building booms and busts are generated by the interaction of the business cycle, the credit cycle and the long cycle of development in the property market. Figure 4.21 presents the evolution of shopping centre stock in five matured property markets.

The five countries covered in Figure 4.21 house over 3,000 shopping centres with a gross lettable area of 64 million square metres (62 per cent of all shopping centres in Europe). As discussed earlier, the economy is also a driver for shopping centres, but rental cycles are not as pronounced as for office or logistic property. As shown in Table 4.2, retail leases are either longer than or similar to office leases. Moreover, shopping centres are less volatile than other commercial property sectors (Figure 4.22). These factors have led to significant interest in retail sectors from investors and developers. Planning restrictions have influenced the supply of new shopping centres in the last decade in the UK and France. In these countries, out-of-town centres were restricted in order to regenerate town centre retailing through extensions or redevelopments. Barcelona in Spain has imposed a moratorium on new shopping centre development. Despite these measures, new stock has continued to increase.

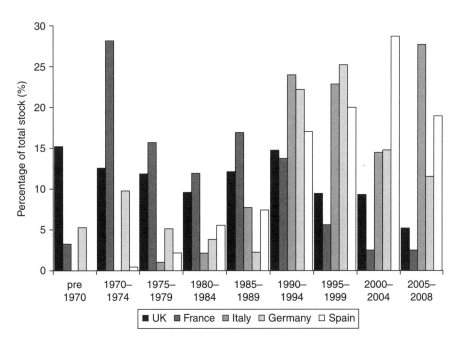

Figure 4.21 New shopping centre completions as percentage of total stock
Source: JLL (2008), The Big Five: Shopping centre investment in core Western Europe.

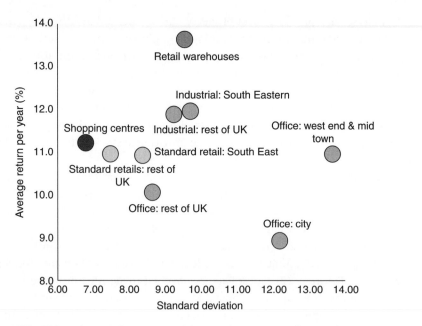

Figure 4.22 Risk and return for commercial property sectors in the UK (1981–2007)
Source: JLL (2008), The Big Five: Shopping centre investment in core Western Europe.

The specialist nature of the retail sector has led to the appearance of sector specialists, though generic investors and institutions are also actively involved. The ownership structure differs from country to country. While the UK market has seen a diverse range of owners (mainly REITs), France, Italy and Spain have seen a large proportion of retail assets owned by sector specialists.

An important trend in the development sector has been the internationalisation of property developers. There are a number of property developers who have entered foreign markets. HongKong Land has developed properties in Singapore, Thailand, Macau, Indonesia and Vietnam as well as its home market of Hong Kong. British Land has undertaken major development projects in Spain, though their main focus is the UK market. The American developer Hines has expanded far beyond the US market to China, Spain, Germany, Brazil, etc. Another developer, Goodman, has developed properties in Europe and Asia-Pacific. Globalisation and market integration have opened opportunities beyond the home market. The demand for high-specification buildings has also led developers with domain knowledge to export to other markets. Saturation and competition in the domestic market also push developers overseas.

4.7   Financing of property

Globally, the institutional property industry has been transformed substantially over the last five decades. The changing needs of capital users and providers, regulatory shifts, advances in financial engineering and risk management meth-odologies, and new opportunities created by cyclical and secular changes have led to a wide array of investment vehicles and strategies (Conner and Liang, 2003). Institutional investment in property started with mortgages and direct property, then gradually expanded into public securities (like REITs and shares of listed companies) and opportunistic and value-added investments (ibid.). Developments in risk management tools and the sustained performance of property markets have attracted institutional investors to private equity investments in real estate companies.

Figure 4.20 presents four buckets of capital sources for commercial real estate. The columns represent public or private market and the rows represent equity and debt. Four combinations emerge, based on the market and nature of funding – private equity, private debt, public equity and public debt. These combinations represent four buckets, as mentioned earlier. Whole mortgages are private mort-gage investments (debt) typically provided by banks and financial institutions to property developers or investors in real estate. Mortgages are non-recourse loans which stay on the balance sheet of lenders for the full term or until repayment. A number of structured debt instruments have been developed which provide depth to simple mortgages and exploit the risk–return characteristics of property investments. Structured debt investments, such as commercial mortgage-backed securities, synthetic mortgages and hybrid vehicles, etc., are categorised under public and private markets. Innovation in risk measurement, which has allowed structuring of investments according to risk–return profile, has permitted the structured debt market to create fundamentally different instruments that appeal to different investors. Public securities include REITs, stocks of listed property companies, and, in select international markets, publicly listed property unit trusts. Traditionally, private equity in real estate used to be direct investment in

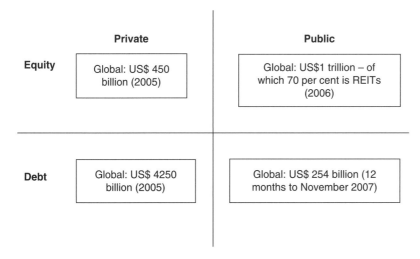

Figure 4.23   Capital sources for real estate
Source: RREEF (August 2006); ING Real Estate (2008), Global Vision 2008.

properties. Private equity as mentioned in Figure 4.23 has the traditional meaning. This definition, however, is different from private equity investment outside the real estate industry, where private equity means entity-level investment. Later in this chapter, private equity refers to this definition and private equity means entity-level investments in real estate companies.

Figure 4.23 also presents the volume of capital flows in each of the four categories. The global trend indicates that, though private debt is the major source of investment in property, the public capital markets also contribute nearly US$1 trillion. Private equity has emerged as an important source of capital for property investment. The scope of private equity that has been raised during the last two to three years goes beyond the traditional definition of private equity and includes various forms of capital markets arbitrage between different segments (public, private, equity, debt) of the property's capital base.

Public sources of capital (debt and equity) have also become an important source of finance for property investment. The public debt market, comprising corporate bonds and commercial mortgage-backed securities (CMBS), is an important source of capital. Figure 4.24 presents the volume of global CMBS

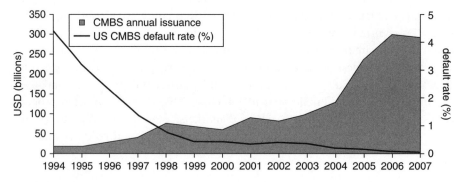

Figure 4.24 Global CMBS issuance and default rate
Source: ING Real Estate (2008) Global Vision.

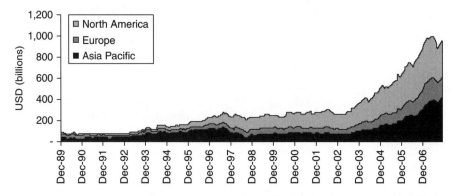

Figure 4.25 Market capitalisation of listed property globally
Source: ING Real Estate (2008) Global Vision.

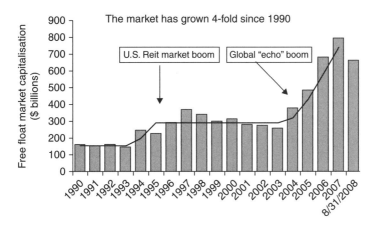

Figure 4.26 Global REITs market capitalisation
Source: CBRE (2008) Global REIT market trends and outlook.

issuance. From nearly no CMBS issuance during early 1990s, the volume of global CMBS issuance had grown to US$254 billion during January–November 2007. Of this total volume, nearly 75 per cent is attributable to the US. Other markets, though small, are becoming increasingly important. According to ING Real Estate (2008), during the 12 months to November 2007, US$30.8 billion of collateral based in the UK and another US$47.6 billion in Continental Europe had been securitised through CMBS, while Japan (US$7.8 billion), Canada (US$4.1 billion) and Australia (US$2.6 billion) were the other significant CMBS markets. The default rate on CMBS has been low (Figure 4.24) and this has contributed to the growth of the market for these securities.

Public equity has emerged as an important source of finance for property investment, and the market for listed property has grown substantially since the early 1990s (Figure 4.25), as an increasing number of countries are adopting REITs or REITs-like structures. By December 2006 the market capitalisation of listed property stood at around US$1 trillion, of which REITs accounted for nearly 70 per cent (Figure 4.26).

4.8 | Conclusions

The overview presented in this chapter of property use, investment, finance and development markets indicates that substantial internationalisation has happened. Globalisation of economic activities has generated a demand for space that shifts across national boundaries. Globalisation of economies has also led to international capital flows in assets, including property. A number of debt or equity-based instruments have emerged, which have facilitated investment in commercial properties. Though property is still largely financed by private debt and equity, the role of public markets as a provider of debt and equity has increased substantially. Among the regions, most of the invested commercial properties are located in North America and Europe. Asia, despite strong economic growth, has a relatively low proportion of invested commercial properties. Internationalisation of property markets is leading to convergence of market practices, as evidenced by aligning of lease terms. The availability of market data and information differs from market to market. Market maturity plays an important role in shaping the landscape of the geography of property investment. This topic will be dealt with in detail in Chapters 6 to 9.

Institutions in Real Estate Service Provision

5.1 | Introduction

International firms have become the main end users of prime commercial property. Their demand is global and today coincides with a deregulated and liberalised financial market. Strong user demand across different countries has been correlated with investor demand for property as an income-producing asset. While these 'quantitative' changes have been apparent, what is less apparent, but equally important, are the qualitative changes that have affected real estate service provision. This raises issues of the extent to which local market practices and structures need to adapt to the requirements of international property interests and the extent to which real estate companies adapt and change to different institutional contexts in which they operate during the process of internationalisation.

This raises the importance of institutions in the property market covering the production and trading of space, the legal framework, investment and planning practices and cultural attitudes to ownership and transactions in property.

This chapter considers institutions that affect the behaviour and performance of real estate markets. There are three key institutional characteristics of real estate markets that are worth attention. Firstly, there are the formal rules that frame transactions, which may be directly or indirectly determined by wider institutions outside the property sector. Secondly, there are informal conventions or the unwritten 'rules of the game'. Thirdly, there are networks of relationships between market participants and issues surrounding the development of trust and the creation of other forms of social capital within the marketplace.

Institutions were briefly discussed in Section 3.8. Here we provide a more comprehensive analysis. 'Lawson (1997) applies the term institution to those systems, or structured processes of interaction (collecting together rules, relations and positions as well as habits and other practices) that are relatively enduring and can be identified as such' (Adams *et al.*, 2005, p. 39). Keogh and D'Arcy (1999a) consider the real estate market to be characterised by interlinking networks between market actors, and set institutions in property markets within broader institutions in an economy that themselves reflect prevailing cultural and power influences in society. This itself is not necessarily seen as fixed and unchanging, but, rather, can be dynamic.

The market itself may be seen as a social institution. However, disaggregation is important, as markets for different products or services may behave differently, having their own procedures and routines set within particular institutional contexts. Markets then depend upon, and are affected by, their wider cultural and institutional contexts. Firms within markets may themselves be seen as institutions. They transact using formal and informal rules in the market and generate networks of market agents/participants. Their behaviour will reflect cultural and economic forces, both of which may change, the latter perhaps more quickly than the former.

The structure of real estate service providers (RESPs) today is, in many ways, substantially different from those of 50 years ago. Across the world, these companies have changed in different ways. However, what is apparent today is the presence of large international RESPs that have operations in many different countries in the world's three key trading blocs of Europe, South East Asia, and North America. In this chapter we discuss RESPs as institutions, how they have changed, and the globalisation of such firms. The relationship with the markets that they enter is also discussed.

5.2   New institutional economics

Rutherford (1994) argues that most work within new institutional economics is an extension of neoclassical economics. Ball (1998) also places new institutional economics within a mainstream economic analysis of real estate markets. As mentioned in Chapter 3, there are four main strands within new institutional economic theory: transactions cost theory, property rights theory, public choice theory, and game theory. Coase (1937, 1960) considers the importance of transactions costs. Firms can be seen to exist in order to minimise transactions costs of market exchange. He links market failure to the presence of high transactions costs, which are especially relevant for real estate markets, where such costs are high relative to other commodities. Such market failure may also be reduced by government intervention that strengthens the system of private property rights. For example, in this context, it is possible to think of the impact of disputes over property rights affecting the spatial distribution of new development in some Eastern European cities where issues of restitution have existed.

Van der Krabben and Lambooy (1993) highlight the (transactions) cost of gathering what in the property market is often limited information. They also point out that this may lead to opportunistic behaviour on the part of those with more information than others. When such advantage is collected it may be used to reinforce and maintain the status quo. Even though sharing of information may improve market efficiency and increase values in the long run as resources are allocated more efficiently, there may still be significant obstructions to change as particular parties expect to lose out. The institutional structure will then exert a considerable impact on how the market develops and, contrary to the rapid adjustment assumed in neoclassical economics, change may be slow or completely prevented due to the power that vested interest groups may be able to exert upon policy and decision-makers.

One of the key insights from the debate on institutions is that the economy is broader than the concept of the market (Samuels, 1995). Thus, 'it is important not to restrict economics to the study of market systems but [also] to investigate the whole range of institutions that determine the form and operation of markets. This approach regards the economy as fundamentally "processual" with emphasis placed not on the achievement of [an] ultimate equilibrium but on the means by which it evolves from one state of existence to the next' (Adams *et al.*, 2005, p. 44). Thus institutions may change not only because of economic signals but also because of changes to social norms and values. Furthermore, any discussion of institutions affecting real estate markets also needs to consider processes or events leading to institutional change.

At 'ground level', networks of relationships between market actors mediating information exchange can have an impact on market efficiency. Realisation of the benefits that better resource allocation can bring might in turn lead to institutional change to facilitate easier attainment of such benefits. This creates a role for the development of institutions that themselves might improve information availability in terms of both quantity and quality. In the UK, for example, the Investment Property Databank (IPD) is a major source of market information, and it has extended its operations to many other European countries. This feeds directly into the transparency of different property markets discussed in earlier chapters, and transparency has also been found to increase flows of investment funds. In addition, the presence of the RICS may also be seen to lead to improvements in the accuracy and thus quality of data reporting as well as to the standardisation of market practices, a further key component in market transparency that reduces investment risk.

Real estate market performance is also affected by formal rules and regulations. Legal frameworks can favour landlords or tenants. In the case of the latter, it becomes difficult for landlords to respond to changes in demand and replace existing tenants with higher-value occupiers who would generate a higher rent and increase the landlord's income return (and probably capital return too if there is a general rise in demand across a specific location). However, tenants would benefit from effective security of tenure. Such policy and institutional choices reflect societal preferences, in this case for stability and (greater) certainty for one particular group. The cost is extra earnings foregone for the landlord. Legal changes can affect the balance of power between these groups. Keogh and D'Arcy (1999a) discuss changes in commercial leases in Spain that gave greater power to landlords and effectively underpinned the development of an investment market in commercial real estate as discussed in Chapter 3 above.

The property market also exhibits informal customs and conventions. In relation to information exchange, for example, this may be informal, through the network of relationships outlined above. The industry is one in which face-to-face contact is an important means of exchange and building long-term client relationships. Thus the nature of doing business might engender greater informal information flows.

Building long-term client relationships, improving information quality and quantity via networks of relationships, reinforced by institutional change can facilitate the creation of trust between market actors. This will be particularly important in complex transactions conducted against a background of product heterogeneity and limited and asymmetric information.

While firms can be seen as institutions, prevailing culture sets policy preferences, and these are reflected in macro-level institutions such as the legal system and government bodies that may have some regulatory influence, active or passive, on the property market. Authorities adopt approaches that can sometimes favour self-regulation over direct legislative change. How effective such voluntary schemes are is a matter of debate. Key institutional and regulatory failures at different levels could be argued to be responsible for the liquidity shortage. In some senses, the most threatening beggar-my-neighbour policy of the last two or three decades has been (overly) light regulation that has failed to keep pace with financial product innovation and has left both public and private bodies unable to accurately understand the potential downside risks of new financial products. The impact on the real estate sector has been particularly severe.

Such experiences build up pressure for new regulation and raise the possibility of regime shifts occurring where former relationships can no longer hold. Extreme events can, therefore, cause relatively rapid changes in institutional characteristics that affect formal and informal rules as well as the parameters under which networks of relationships can operate. Such change may be thought necessary to re-establish trust, which in very practical terms translates into lower lending rates and re-establishes flows of finance.

5.3   Professional business services

RESPs are really a subset of a larger category of professional business service firms (PBSFs). As economies grow and mature, a clear pattern of production emerges where there is a movement from agriculture to manufacturing and then to services. In the latter stages, services come to dominate the economy, and within this PBSFs begin to grow and develop. Certainly in Western economies, it has been knowledge-based service industries that have seen the fastest growth over the past 20 years and have made the greatest contribution to the economy. This trend has mirrored changes in the workforce, where human capital investment has increased the skill base and the productivity of the labour force, and it has been productivity growth that has been the main source of economic growth for developed economies.

Often specialised knowledge-intensive services have been (out)sourced from firms with specific expertise, as this has been found to be more cost-effective than maintaining in-house teams. Thus knowledge intensity generally varies within and between firms. This leads on to the question of what identifies a professional business service or a PBSF. Selling packages of services to potential clients without considering the appropriateness of the package for the clients' specific needs would not constitute a professional service. Løwendahl (2000) defines a PBSF as a firm that is 'highly knowledge-intensive and service oriented, ... [making] a commitment to the delivery of client-tailored services based on a careful and ethically sound professional judgment' (p. 144).

Such firms employ highly educated individuals who are able to provide high-value knowledge-intensive services that are tailored to the clients' needs. The employees may be members of professional organisations (although this is not essential) and will be involved in building working relationships with clients. These exchanges build ongoing working relationships, which are necessary to establish trust and to meet client needs, and convey often complex information needed for the provision of tailored or bespoke knowledge-intensive services.

A discussion of professions raises questions of how someone can enter those professions, and also of entry barriers. If certain types of knowledge-intensive services are provided by specific professions who hold or have access to asymmetric information that is costly for other economic actors to collect, then members of the profession could charge monopoly fees for provision of that information. This in itself would be a barrier to efficient market operation. If the elasticity of demand for the service is low, the profession can make more fee income by keeping its charges high.

In some cases information asymmetry is very large, and organisations such as the RICS are in a position to ensure standards of quality of information provision. In many countries where the RICS does not exist or has only a small presence, other professional bodies may exist, or highly educated employees may work to professional norms to provide knowledge-intensive services in the best interests of the client. Thus, 'firms which fundamentally base their organisation, their strategy, their hiring practices, and their managerial hierarchies on professional standards, and which deliver professional services (almost) all the time, rather than just occasionally, may rightfully be called professional service firms' (op. cit., p. 147).

Today PBSFs are located in many different countries, and many firms are themselves international, having world headquarters in one of the major world trading blocs: North America, Europe, or Japan and South East Asia. World regional headquarters are then found in key cities in the other trading blocs. Thus, for example, a US firm may have its world headquarters in New York, its European (regional) headquarters in London, and its Asian (regional) headquarters in Singapore.

International firms may find themselves in multi-domestic or global industries according to Porter's (1986) definition. In the former, competition in a country is independent of competition in other countries in which the firm has a presence. In the latter, '...a firm's competitive position in one country is signifi-cantly affected by its position in other countries or vice versa' (ibid., p. 148). Thus competition between firms is on a worldwide basis.

Porter suggests that global markets have been more common in manufactured goods than in services, although our focus in this book is on the latter in relation to real estate service provision. While it may be difficult to determine whether international RESPs are multi-domestic or truly global industries, internation-alisation strategies have been key components in the development and change experienced by a significant number of real estate companies. This internation-alisation has been driven in part by the growth of multinational corporations themselves, who have required real estate services in the countries in which they have opened new operations. Such global clients required a consistent stand-ard of service throughout the global reach of their interests. The costs of pro-viding this service in-house might have been more than the cost of employing higher-value specific real estate services, and hence this would in turn generate a rationale for RESPs' international expansion strategies. While this may be seen as a 'pull' factor, there are also possible 'push' factors. For example, saturation of the domestic market may have reduced opportunities for growth and may have undermined profitability. Smaller markets where push factors may have been important include The Netherlands and Sweden.

This process of internationalisation has very much been associated with the economic growth of the post-war period. Early internationalisation strategies by UK RESPs had involved Commonwealth countries, where barriers to entry were low and institutional characteristics, such as legal systems and approaches to doing business, were similar to those of the UK. By the 1980s and 1990s, RESPs were entering markets outside the Commonwealth and interacting with differ-ent legal systems and cultural attitudes to business and to the role of real estate as an asset class. RESPs have opened offices in developing and developed coun-tries and have experienced varying barriers to entry. For example, entering the US has proved difficult. In response there have been mergers and strategic alli-ances between firms. For example, Jones Lang Wootton (from the UK) merged with LaSalle Investment (from the US) to become Jones Lang LaSalle, one of the largest international RESPs. Healey and Baker (UK) merged with Cushman and Wakefield (US), but have now been submerged into Cushman and Wakefield, and hence their brand name has disappeared.

In Europe, many UK firms have a presence in most other European countries. As the EU has expanded, such firms have also expanded the list of countries in which they operate. Thus many are now present in the new real estate markets in former Eastern Bloc countries, including the Baltic States, Poland, Hungary, the Czech Republic, Slovakia, and more recently Romania and Bulgaria.

In South East Asia, key hub locations for RESPs have been Hong Kong and Singapore. As countries have experienced inward investment and economic growth, RESPs have opened in Malaysia, South Korea, Thailand, and the Philippines. More recently, economic growth and change have seen expansion of RESPs into China and Vietnam.

As institutions themselves, RESPs embody approaches to doing business that may be inappropriate to the new markets they enter. To be successful (profitable) they need to consider how to adapt to the cultures they encounter as they globalise. Further, the firms themselves may reflect different cultural influences, depending upon their countries of origin.

5.4   Real estate service providers and business cultures

D'Arcy *et al*. (1999) suggest that UK and US RESPs could be seen as representing something approximating to 'a global badge of quality' in the real estate industry. While these firms have also been experiencing internal institutional/organisational change, they have played a substantial role in internationalisation of real estate services. D'Arcy *et al*. (2000) suggest that '[it] seems reasonable to hypothesise that there might be a distinctive cultural "flavour" associated with particular societies, particular industries, and particular firms. Indeed, from the perspective of economic performance the literature suggests that "successful" national cultures might be an important, even exportable, source of competitive advantage (Casson 1991, Dunning and Bensal 1997, Porter 1990) and that corporate cultures can be "managed" to enhance the productivity and profitability of firms' (p. 6).

However, as Hofstede (1991) suggests, it is difficult to associate national and corporate identities. Further, drawing such conclusions is predicated on identifying historical examples, but history itself also shows that what may be considered as successful cultures may not remain so.

Di Maggio (1994) examines the interrelationship between culture and business. He suggests that corporate culture is a response to external pressures and forces, perhaps within a given industry or economy. Thus business environment more generally may mould the culture of the firm, which may then partly explain 'herd' mentality of behaviour within given industries. He also suggests that different cultures, with different priorities and rituals, may operate within an organisation. Different groups within a managerial hierarchy may behave differently. Di Maggio also notes that specific organisational cultures do not have a direct impact on a firm's productive efficiency, although they may impact on the firm's reputation.

Using an institutional economics approach, if culture can be seen as a 'subset of institutions' (D'Arcy *et al*., 2000), cultures will reflect attitudes and values possessed by a society. This may, in the case of real estate, be reflected in the attitude to private property, which would then be reflected in the legal system. There may also be attitudes to adaption to change or a preference for stability (either economic or political or for particular ruling elites) that would impact on the real estate industry. This in turn has implications for occupiers, investors and developers in real estate.

Culture will also affect how different actors within real estate relate to and interact with each other: '...there are overlapping cultural environments relating on the one hand to business practices in real estate and on the other to business practices in advisory services' (op. cit., p. 11). Whilst in the past RESPs drew their income from a narrow, clearly defined and well understood range of services, changes in the industry now mean that the range of services provided is much broader and focused on the individual client. As a consequence of this, RESPs now employ individuals from a much wider range of professions and skill groups. This in turn means that they employ a range of business-related cultures that to some extent changes the culture of business that they would have had in the past.

Figure 5.1 below is a diagrammatic representation of the relevant institutional levels. 'This distinguishes between the broad institutional environment within which RES provision and other real estate activity occurs (the economic, social,

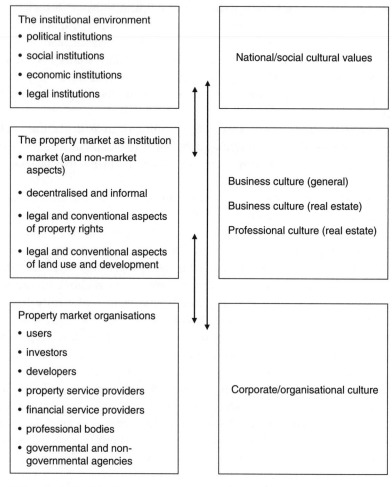

Figure 5.1 The institutional/cultural hierarchy of real estate markets
Source: D'Arcy *et al.* (2000).

political and legal parameters), the status of the real estate market as an institution, and the formation of organisations or actors within the real estate market (including, of course, RES firms). It is a hierarchy in the sense of progressing from the broad to the narrow, with an implication that the more micro aspects are nested within the more macro' (ibid., p. 9). The arrows indicate possible interactions between different levels and suggest how the whole system can possibly respond to change.

As RESPs have internationalised they have encountered varying approaches to transacting in real estate. Most of the major international RESPs have their world headquarters in the UK or the US. While consideration of the internationalisation strategies of these firms may assume that the US and the UK are very similar in terms of their cultural approach to doing business and have thus focused on the more different cultures into which they have come into contact during the process of internationalisation, they have differences of approach between themselves.

D'Arcy *et al.* (2000) describe the UK as a 'high to medium trust' society, and this in turn affects the institutional characteristics that frame transactions processes (Casson, 1993). Business culture in the UK is described by Trompenaars and Hampden-Turner (1997) as somewhat person-oriented, and is neither flat nor very hierarchical. Culture has shifted towards a task-centred rather than a person-centred approach. This may also point to a decline in paternalism in business, which would be consistent with the greater pace of economic change experienced in recent decades.

As indicated above, RESPs have expanded overseas and the range of services they provide has also widened. Thus they, like MNCs, have become exposed to a wide variety of cultures and approaches to doing business. As clients have required new services, RESPs have moved away from their earlier concentration on valuation services to provide, for example, investment advice for clients with existing or new holdings of real estate assets in different countries. As part of this, there has been a growth of research departments within firms. In many cases these will also be fee-earning, but still providing advice on market performance and forecasting key growth areas (by both sector and region/country) for investment clients. Thus the increased range of services provides further opportunities for provision of high value-added bespoke services. These may also generate more income than the possibly narrow range of services previously provided.

Interestingly, the wider range of services and new professionals now within real estate may have weakened the previous business culture, which was based upon chartered surveying. However, their skill base failed to respond to clients, who saw real estate as another financial asset to aid portfolio diversification nationally and internationally. As external pressures caused the real estate industry to change, the firms have embraced other business cultures brought in by economists, accountants, investment analysts, etc. The RESPs have become closer to the model of PBSFs. In real estate firms, the emphasis now is on ability to meet clients' needs rather than membership of specific professional bodies. This is even truer outside the UK, where the RICS may have only a small presence, or none at all.

Business culture for real estate faced its most significant change during the 1980s and thereafter: a widening service base and internationalisation into countries which were different from those entered during earlier expansion in the 1970s (mainly Commonwealth countries with shared cultures and practices). Expansion into European markets, and subsequently in Asia, brought firms into contact with significant barriers in terms of language, legal institutions, professions and professional approaches to business, plus general cultural factors. 'As the RES firms extended their operations they had to introduce management structures which would enable them to preserve the identity and reputation of the organisation, guarantee service standards, but also incorporate knowledge and business practice relevant to the new markets in which they were operating' (ibid., p. 17).

The most expensive internationalisation strategy adopted by firms was to establish branches or subsidiaries in other countries. This has been referred to as direct corporate expansion. A less expensive alternative has been expansion through the creation of a network of alliances with companies in other countries. This is referred to as indirect corporate expansion. While direct expansion benefits from ensuring a consistent quality of service provision, indirect expansion does not, and this could impact negatively on the firm's reputation. Direct expansion also brings UK or US managers into other business cultures and opens up an arena for exchange of business practices associated with different cultures. As firms have become more established overseas, management positions have been increasingly filled by nationals, who, while not being chartered surveyors, bring a wide range of related professional skills to real estate firms. Potentially this can obviate the 'bandwagon' effect that can dominate the industry when service providers are overwhelmingly drawn from one profession and the hubris that can overtake the industry. Newer professions within the industry have perhaps weakened the core values that would have been associated with the industry when it was more dominated by its historically narrower skill base.

Table 5.1 below shows the changes over time from 1950 in British real estate service companies, examining cultural influences, organisational structure, and agents for change. The changes listed to some extent reinforce the point made earlier by Di Maggio (1994) that corporate culture changes may be due to changes in external factors impacting on the firm or industry. Culture, then, may not be a driver of change, but change happens due to economic forces that may require firms to adapt in order to survive and grow. The response to this challenge will then make the firm different, which in turn affects corporate culture. An internationalisation strategy, then, can be thought of as part of a response to changing circumstances, and this itself can lead to further changes in the business culture of the firm.

US real estate firms have also experienced change, and, while similar to the UK, their business strategies have been task-oriented for a longer time period than in the UK case. Business culture in the US is also regarded as egalitarian, having

Table 5.1　The changing corporate culture of British RESPs

	Corporate culture		Change agents	
	Principal cultural influence	**Organisational characteristics**	**Principal change influence**	**Secondary change influences**
1950 ↓	domination of professional culture ↓	hierarchical + person ↓	changes in the domestic economy ↓	domestic expansion ↓
↓ ↓	↓	↓	↓	↓
1960 ↓	↓ ↓	↓ ↓	↓ ↓	domestic expansion + internationalisation
↓ ↓	↓ ↓	↓ ↓	↓ ↓	↓ ↓
1970 ↓	↓ ↓	hierarchical + person/task ↓	↓ ↓	domestic merger activity + internationalisation
↓ ↓	↓ ↓	↓ ↓	↓ ↓	↓ ↓
1980 ↓ ↓	joint influence of professional and managerial cultures ↓	hierarchical + task ↓ ↓ ↓	changes in real estate asset market + internationalisation ↓	domestic merger activity + service provider competition ↓
1990 ↓ ↓	domination of managerial culture ↓	hierarchical/ egalitarian + task ↓	international merger activity ↓	globalisation of financial markets + information economy
↓ 2000 ↓	↓ ↓ ↓	↓ ↓ ↓	↓ ↓ ↓	↓ ↓ ↓

Source: Adapted from D'Arcy *et al.* (2000), categories based on Hofstede (1991).

relatively flat management structures that focus on product (service) delivery. US institutions have created formal transparent ethical rules to serve business in a highly individualistic and litigious culture.

Specifically in relation to the real estate sector, US firms have also expanded. This expansion has taken place to establish a national presence in their domestic market, growing from local or regional players. This expansion did not, therefore, face the same cultural variations as those experienced by UK firms when entering European markets. However the expansion reflected similar competitive pressures to those experienced by UK firms in terms of needing to provide a wider range of bespoke higher value-added services to clients. The prevailing business culture may have made this easier to achieve in the US, since it was more clearly focused on tasks and service delivery.

Interestingly, in contrast to the UK, there is no equivalent body to the RICS in the US. The business culture of the real estate industry may not, therefore, have been closely aligned to the values and practices of any single profession. It may also reflect differences in the characteristics of transacting in real estate, particularly in the user market for commercial space. Thus there may not have been the combinations of circumstances present to require the creation of a similar type of body. Professional bodies do exist, for example, the Appraisal Institute, but its role has not been the same as the RICS and its members have not come to dominate the real estate sector in the same way as the RICS has done in the UK. The US experience has shown an industry that is effective as a professional business service provider incorporating a range of professions without the need for specific recognition of such employees by a particular professional body.

The educational background of US and UK real estate actors has also been somewhat different. The US has been faster to embrace links with finance and economics. In the UK, this link has been acknowledged only slowly, although valuation as a subject area has clear linkages with, and is based upon, economic theory. However, professionals in economics or finance may not be members of professional bodies such as the RICS. As firms in the UK have moved towards a more task-based approach, there has been an increasing need to include a wider range of professions. In the US, there has perhaps been a more rapid and flexible approach, given a corporate culture that embraces different business professions with or without a particular professional label.

However, one interesting feature of the UK real estate industry is how the RICS itself has changed, and, while remaining the dominant professional body in the UK, has an increasing number of members from a wider range of educational backgrounds. The adaptability of the professional body is in itself a positive benefit to the industry, as it indicates that pressures for change are recognised by the profession itself, and it will itself adapt and change its professional composition. This obviously has further implications for the future development of the RICS itself. It could be argued that, by embracing change and understanding the forces bringing change, the RICS will be able to remain a key feature of the UK industry in the future. Furthermore, as the industry has changed in ways that have made it more exportable, the RICS too may become exportable, so that its business and professional culture can be disseminated to other countries.

In contrast to the UK, the US corporate culture could be regarded as more managerial and less professional. 'Scientific management' has been an important influence on US corporations, as it attempted to monitor and control workers in an environment where there was perhaps less trust or loyalty between firms and their workforces. But corporate culture in US RESPs has remained independent of the culture of any one profession.

US firms began internationalising in the 1990s to realise the potential financial benefits that this could bring. The main strategy adopted has been the purchase of existing firms in other countries and constructing networks of alliances to enable provision of professional business services to international clients. Such expansion has on occasion brought US and UK firms into collaboration via network alliances, or has resulted in mergers and/or takeovers. US internationalisation processes also involved management consultancies that incorporate real estate services as part of a broader range of business services. This strategy shows the role that can be provided by other professions outside real estate that can be brought into the sector to add value for clients. Table 5.2 below summarises the changes to corporate culture in US RESPs.

According to D'Arcy *et al.* (2000), culture as reflected in shared values and norms of (market) behaviour may influence the behaviour of RESPs. Thus they can impact on market processes and outcomes. The international expansion of real estate firms has also affected their business culture in different ways relating to the mix of professions employed and the national cultural influences with which they have come to interact. However, the question still remains as to the impact of culture on economic performance or, indeed, the impact of economic performance on culture. They may be simultaneously determined, or causation may indeed start with one and end with the other, with lesser feedback loops present. Economic change may also be faster than cultural change (or vice versa), in which case pressures for change arise. Such change may be reflected in national

Table 5.2 The changing corporate culture of American RES firms

	Corporate culture*		Change agents	
	Principal cultural influence	**Organisational characteristics**	**Principal change influence**	**Secondary change influences**
1950 ↓	domination of managerial culture	hierarchical/ egalitarian + person/task	changes in the domestic economy	domestic expansion ↓
↓ ↓	↓ ↓	↓ ↓	↓ ↓	↓ ↓
1960 ↓ ↓	↓ ↓ ↓	↓ ↓ ↓	↓ ↓ ↓	domestic expansion + service provider competition
↓ 1970	↓ ↓	↓ egalitarian + person/task	↓ ↓	↓ ↓
↓ ↓ ↓	↓ ↓ ↓	↓ ↓ ↓	↓ ↓ ↓	↓ ↓ ↓
1980 ↓	↓ ↓	egalitarian + task ↓	changes in real estate asset markets	domestic expansion + internationalisation
↓ ↓	↓ ↓	↓ ↓	↓ ↓	↓ ↓
1990 ↓ ↓	↓ ↓ ↓	↓ ↓ ↓	internationalisation + international merger activity	globalisation of financial markets + information economy
↓ 2000 ↓	↓ ↓ ↓	↓ ↓ ↓	↓ ↓ ↓	↓ ↓ ↓

Source: Adapted from D'Arcy *et al.* (2000), categories based on Hofstede (1991).

institutional change, or lower-level behavioural changes that impact on decision-making and ultimately change institutions themselves.

5.5 Relationships between local markets and international real estate companies

As RESPs have internationalised, they have carried particular cultural approaches to business with them into new markets where approaches to business may be very different. This has been the experience of property companies from the UK expanding into continental Europe. In some European countries, business culture may be 'closer' to that of the UK than in others. For example, those countries high on the transparency index may have similar approaches to business as the UK, which has the highest transparency score in Europe. Other countries will have (more) different approaches.

De Magalhães (2001) examines UK real estate companies as they constructed a transnational European service provision, opening branches in major cities in different countries. His study focuses specifically on British property companies moving into Madrid and Milan, and he considers the relationship between the foreign firms and the new business environments they enter, including the institutional context in which they would then operate.

In relation to institutional economic theory, real estate companies can be seen to reduce transactions costs for property users and investors who operate in different institutional and cultural environments across the globe. They play a key role in the delivery of property services to a demand that is international. Aharoni (1993) argues that having an international presence is increasingly seen as essential for real estate firms. International firms have become the main end users of prime commercial property. Their demand is global and now coincides with a deregulated and liberalised financial market. Hence they provide a strong incentive for the internationalisation of RESPs.

As commercial real estate is often spatially concentrated at key urban hubs, economic growth in these regions has been particularly important. A literature on city competitiveness has emerged in which there is a key role for the contribution of real estate to revitalisation and regeneration of urban areas that have experienced significant economic change as developed economies have moved from manufacturing to service-based industries. Also, as higher-cost countries have moved production activities to less expensive countries and locations, their behaviour has helped to generate economic growth in other countries and produced a demand for commercial real estate.

The development of commercial real estate in different countries in response to demand changes is itself affected by the institutional environment. For example, leasehold investment property may not be the outcome of this demand. Instead, institutional factors may be in favour of owner-occupied commercial property. Leases may contain upward-only rent reviews, or rents may be based upon turnover. These differences drive differences in expectations about future income growth prospects, which can impact on yield differences when property is looked at from an investment perspective.

The office market has attracted particular attention from international investors, as has retail. Industrial markets tend to have been less attractive from an international investment perspective. This may have been due to weaker capital growth prospects than in the other sectors.

One key institutional change witnessed over almost the last 30 years has been the process of globalisation. Many countries have experienced economic change that has been amplified by an adoption of more liberal economic policies. Such adoption may reflect cultural change within nations as they wanted to participate in and benefit from economic growth and change. As preferences changed, these were embodied and reflected in institutional change that permitted stronger linkages with global economic forces. Few, if any, countries today remain completely isolated from the often uncertain and usually cyclical world economy.

Institutional change that permitted economic liberalisation and increasing pressures for globalisation does not necessarily mean that everyone benefits. But pressure to reverse institutional change may be weak as long as those who benefit are greater in power and/or number than those who lose. It is against this deregulated and integrated world economy that RESPs have internationalised in the last 30 years.

Investor demand for income-producing assets that aid their diversification strategies has been important in the internationalisation and opening up of overseas commercial real estate markets. Newer markets have been characterised by relative high risk and higher expected returns to compensate investors for the risk exposure. As these markets have become more established, their commercial markets have grown in size and value, and the risk of investing has fallen. As property companies and other investors have moved into these markets, they learn about market processes and practices and the institutional characteristics of the market, and this in turn increases market information and helps to reduce uncertainty and, hence, risk.

But the process is also one where the new market entrants can have an impact on local business culture and institutional change. In many property markets there is 'a need to adapt market practices and structures to the requirements of transnational property interests' (de Magalhães, 2001, p. 100). Thus there is a 'local dimension of the internationalisation process, with the formation of a global market place for property happening simultaneously and intertwined with structural changes at the local level' (op. cit., p. 100).

Structures and structural change relate to market practices and associated institutions in real estate transactions and the overarching legal framework that affects property rights and finance. Alongside these are planning policies, investment decision-making practices and attitudes to ownership and transaction in real estate that reflect prevailing cultural attitudes and that would be reflected in national institutional structures and feed into the model of operation and the extensiveness of networks of relationships between property market participants.

The interrelationship between internationalising RESPs and the markets they enter in different countries has meant change affecting both parties. The business culture of UK and US real estate companies, focusing on tasks and the availability of information and its use in providing advice to clients, has had an impact on the amount of information made available in newer (less mature or transparent) markets.

Over the last 20 years, these markets have not only seen an increase in investment but have also experienced change in their own business cultures. For example, there is more information available and exchanged. Commercial real estate has become more open to investors, and a larger proportion of transactions are conducted through agents. The real estate industry has become more professionalised and offers a professional business service to clients. But the RESPs, too, have changed. They embody a wider range of professionals, many without a particular badge or professional body. However, locally specific characteristics interact with global trends. Thus, outcomes of global economic change are translated into local outcomes via locally specific customs and business practices. Therefore, in terms of how individual markets in various countries develop, 'an institutional approach to [understanding] market maturity [should consider the] complex interplay of global economic forces and the social, economic, institutional and cultural structures framing each market, rather than a linear and universal evolutionary process' (ibid., p. 101).

Thus, while the arrival of international RESPs may impact on local markets, there remain specific local characteristics that affect processes and ultimately outcomes for commercial real estate. The behaviour of domestic real estate companies may also impact on the extent to which new international firms affect local market business cultures.

As an institution, the real estate industry takes on different structures in different countries. For example, in the UK context, and somewhat similarly in the US, the industry could be characterised as being dominated by a relatively small number of large firms that have a presence throughout the country. The largest firms include Jones Lang LaSalle, DTZ, CBRE, Cushman and Wakefield, GVA Grimley, Drivers Jonas, Knight Frank, and Colliers CRE. In contrast is the real estate industry in Italy, which consists of a large number of relatively small firms. Business culture is also clearly different, with a distinct lack of information availability in Italy.

Thus it seems that the institutional characteristics of the industry itself can have an impact on the success of internationalisation strategies in addition to wider corporate cultural and national institutional characteristics. However, RESPs have been flexible enough to adapt to changes brought about through their own internationalisation strategies. They have also been involved in mergers and acquisitions of local firms that have helped them penetrate newer and more opaque markets.

5.6 | Conclusions

This chapter has provided a discussion of the key institutions affecting the real estate industry. We see that broad national cultural factors have influenced the behaviour of industry in general, which has affected real estate. The market, then, can be seen as a social institution mediating exchange, and is more than the invisible hand of the price-signalling mechanism allocating resources. Real estate companies themselves can be seen as institutions, perhaps minimising transactions costs but also experiencing internal change as the nature of business has changed. Client relationships have changed over time, not simply with respect to the services they demand, but also in relation to the bespoke nature of services, which opens up an opportunity to create value. This has led RESPs to broaden their range of services and skill base. This in turn has changed the corporate culture of the firms themselves.

The internationalised firms must then interact with local markets, local business cultures and institutions regulating market behaviour. US and UK firms are the ones that have internationalised, and most of the large RESPs have their home headquarters in the US or the UK. In some senses, there has been an exporting of the business cultures of these two countries, as embodied in their real estate sector, which has interacted with local property markets in other countries.

Both the US and the UK are regarded as highly transparent markets. This contrasts with the markets into which they have moved. However, they have acted as agents for change in more opaque markets, and this has been one of their contributions to the growth of an investment market in commercial real estate in other countries. Such growth has also enabled economic change, or at least facilitated economic change, as, for example, in the case of the Spanish market, where legal institutional changes affected the creation of an investment market in real estate. More recently we have seen the development of investment markets in Eastern Europe, most notably in Hungary, Poland and the Czech Republic. This has also been contingent with economic and institutional change.

However, as suggested above, there is no necessary linear path in terms of the future trends in the structure of the real estate industry. National and local institutional characteristics may cause market processes and outcomes to differ (even if there were no differences in economic circumstances) and the behaviour and structure of the real estate industry may remain different. Today, however, there are global real estate companies, many of which are built upon US or UK companies and inherit their corporate approaches to business. Is this the dominant business model? It is a model that seems to have been successfully exported, and, while there is variation within it, many countries have adopted at least some institutional elements that seem to have aided its success.

European Real Estate Markets

6.1   Introduction

The past 30 years have seen significant economic and political change in the continent of Europe. They have witnessed a growth in the size of the European Union, the opening up of Eastern Europe to the market economic system, significant change in economic structure, and increasing economic integration of different countries. In an increasingly integrated and global economic system, countries and cities compete for international businesses. The economic base of many of Europe's cities is increasingly related to the global economy. Key global resources of money and knowledge are attracted to some cities more than others. The successful cities develop into centres for the information economy, with an emphasis on knowledge-related activities. This has an impact on the commercial property market, which is highly concentrated by value in key commercial locations. The productivity and competitiveness of cities and regions will be determined by their ability to combine informational capacity, quality of life, and connectivity to the network of major metropolitan centres at national and international levels. The challenge facing cities is to articulate globally oriented economic functions at the local level.

Reflecting the changes in national and local economies, commercial real estate markets have experienced rapid development in the past 30 years. Countries have started from different bases with varying degrees of exposure to real estate as an investment class. Institutional structures have varied widely. In 1980 many had little or no real estate investment markets, due to institutional structures and/or lack of market information. In Eastern Europe, the command economy operated in Poland, Hungary, Czechoslovakia (as was), Romania, Bulgaria and the Baltic States. Today this is no longer the case. Within Western Europe a variety of approaches to the role of real estate in the economy had also developed, with some more open to investment than others, again reflecting institutional approaches to property that themselves reflected the preferences of the societies (or at least the preferences of the ruling elites in the societies) in which they operated.

All of these countries experienced significant change over the last 30 years. Economic restructuring during the 1980s changed the economic landscape of many countries and most, particularly in Western Europe, saw a shift towards service sector employment. Concurrent with these changes was the adoption of more liberal economic policies giving greater role to the operation of market forces. Part of this approach saw the removal of exchange controls in the UK and then across other countries. This permitted capital to flow to where it could achieve the greatest risk-adjusted return.

At the same time, the European Economic Community (EEC) expanded. Today most countries in Europe are members of the European Union (EU). Some notable exceptions include Norway and Switzerland. As a consequence of this expansion, perceived risk attached to international investment has somewhat diminished. This is not because of any guarantee of economic stability in new member states, but because of the expectation that they will honour legally defined private property rights which previously may not have existed. In fact, while the EU has harmonisation policies implicit in the objectives of the Treaty of Rome, it is in the areas where such objectives have been less explicit that the most important changes have occurred, at least from the perspective of international property investors. Such changes have been related to the institutional context within different nation states.

Many countries within the EU have adopted the Euro to replace their individual currencies. Currently these countries are Austria, Belgium, Finland, France, Germany, Greece, Ireland, Italy, Luxembourg, the Netherlands, Portugal, Slovenia and Spain. Denmark, Sweden and the UK have retained their individual currencies and have also, therefore, retained monetary policy, which the member countries of the Eurozone have given to the European Central Bank (ECB). The policy of monetary union has been a long-held objective, and it has permitted price transparency across markets in addition to removing exchange rate risk between countries within the monetary zone. Classical economic theory suggests that such (enhanced) price transparency will make resource allocation more efficient and will thus act to encourage investment and identification of the highest risk-adjusted returns. While monetary union does not yet extend to most Eastern European member states within the EU, many have monetary union as an explicit policy objective. Hence they will also relinquish national monetary policy to the ECB. However, the behaviour of the ECB since the introduction of the Euro has focused on controlling inflationary pressures, as is the case with other central banks. Thus the ECB has created monetary policy credibility, and this has been reflected in the performance of the Euro in international foreign exchange markets, where it has seen appreciation in value. Currently the ECB faces challenges similar to other monetary zones with respect to reacting to liquidity problems in financial markets, and to balancing inflationary pressures due to commodity price rises against the risk of recession due to falling real incomes and weakening economic activity, which also itself in part reflects the stronger Euro.

In this chapter we examine the development of real estate markets in European countries. We show how investment flows have increased across countries over time, and discuss the barriers to the development of a real estate investment market and how these can be overcome or removed. We also highlight the continuing volatile nature of the real estate market, the non-synchronisation of market behaviour between countries, and the interaction between the real estate sector and national economies. The increasing interlinkage between European economies and the role of real estate within them is also discussed. In covering all of the above we compare market performance and market characteristics, and cross-border activity and its impact on standardisation of market practice and institutional development.

6.2 | Current market performance

Table 6.1 above provides a snapshot of key data for offices, retail units and warehouses across many of the key markets in Europe. The first thing to note is the number of cities covered for which market information exists. Thirty years ago there would have been no data for Budapest, Moscow, Prague or Warsaw. Limited information would have made finding comparable data difficult for Barcelona, Lisbon, Madrid and Milan. Some cities are still not recorded, particularly Athens, Bucharest and Sofia, where the real estate investment market is still in its infancy.

Second, it is clear from the table that there exists substantial variation in rents within each property sector. In the office sector, London and Moscow have the highest rents, substantially above all other cities and in excess of rents in Paris, which is the third most expensive office location. While office rents may currently be similar in London and Moscow, this similarity does not imply that market characteristics are similar across the two locations. The London market is highly transparent, with significant information flows and research activity, has a culture of information sharing, and is highly professionalised, with standardisation of market practices. Many of these characteristics are absent from Russian property markets. Also the rents recorded for the last quarter of 2007 do not imply similar rental growth rates in future, and thus the performance of London and Moscow (in terms of rent levels) may diverge.

Retail rents also display significant variation across cities. Moscow appears as the most expensive retail location, followed by Paris and then Dublin. Significant rental growth from 2006 to 2007 pushed Moscow into the category of the most expensive office and retail locations. Such rental growth has been higher than other locations. It will be important to distinguish between trend and cyclical influences in forecasting future relative rental performance across cities.

Smaller variations in rents are observed in the warehouse sector, where yields are also highest on average. The newer markets of Eastern Europe seem to perform well, as indicated by yields that are not dissimilar from those in more established markets, indicating that the risks that were initially attached to such investment locations have fallen. While all of these cities have experienced positive economic growth over the last 15 years, the real estate markets vary as to the exact point in the cycles of rental change that they are experiencing.

Table 6.1 Market performance indicators (2007, quarter 4)

	Office				Retail			Warehousing		
	Prime rent	% Rent change p.a.	Prime yield %	Vacancy rate %	Prime rent	% Rent change p.a.	Prime yield %	Prime rent	% Rent change p.a.	Prime yield %
Amsterdam	330	1.6	4.90	12.4	2,200	10.0	3.50	90	0	6.25
Barcelona	318	6.0	4.50	4.9	2,580	7.0	4.50	108	2.9	6.25
Berlin	252	2.4	4.90	9.4	2,460	7.9	4.75	54	0	6.75
Brussels	300	1.7	5.60	9.8	1,600	6.7	4.50	50	6.3	6.15
Budapest	264	18.9	5.75	10.3	1,800	25.0	5.50	72	0	6.25
Copenhagen*	1,900	5.6	5.00	4.3	19,000	0	4.00	600	0	6.00
Dublin	646	0	3.95	11.3	4,951	0	2.40	124	2.2	4.85
Edinburgh	307	2.0	5.25	4.9	1,128		4.50	75	7.2	5.75
Helsinki	305	4.5	4.80	7.0	1,154	5.7	4.75	130	0	6.00
Lisbon	276	12.2	6.00	9.0	1,020	0	6.50	90	0	7.25
London**	1,238	21.1	4.50	4.2	2,691	0	4.75	140	0	5.50
Madrid	480	15.9	4.25	3.6	2,652	7.8	4.50	90	7.1	6.00
Milan	500	0	4.25	7.2	2,200	0	4.00	58	1.8	5.90
Moscow	1,700	41.7	8.00	5.2	8,000	45.5	8.50	140	0	9.75
Oslo*	4,550	56.9	4.25	4.5	18,000	12.5	4.25	1,100	22.2	6.00
Paris	825	13.0	4.00	4.9	6,500	6.4	4.00	52	0	6.10
Prague	252	5.0	5.25	5.8	1,440	4.3	5.25	48	0	6.25
Stockholm*	4,300	10.3	4.50	11.7	13,500	8.0	4.50	900	5.9	6.30
The Hague	215	4.9	5.10	5.5	1,250	8.7	4.00	55	0	6.75
Warsaw	336	27.3	5.50	3.1	900	0	5.50	66	4.8	6.50

Notes: Rents in Euros per square metre per annum. * Rents in Danish, Norwegian or Swedish Kroner respectively, ** rents in Pounds Sterling.

Source: Adapted from Jones Lang LaSalle, Key Market Indicators, March 2008.

6.3 | Market institutions and characteristics

European countries vary in the legal arrangements governing the use of real estate assets. More recently many countries have adopted the Euro as their currency, and exchange rate risk for cross-border trade within the Eurozone has now disappeared. Markets also differ in the process of information formation, availability and exchange. Property rights may be non-standardised, and the degree of professionalisation varies across markets.

Figure 6.1 shows a 'property clock' for offices. It indicates phases of the rental cycle, beginning with rents falling in the north-east quadrant, moving clockwise to rents bottoming out, then accelerating rental growth, and finally slowing rental growth. At any one point in time different cities experience different rental change conditions. For example, in the 'clock' above, rental growth is accelerating in Edinburgh but slowing in Moscow, and many other cities lie somewhere in between these two. However the 'clock' does not indicate the amplitude of fluctuation as rent changes, simply the phases through which it can travel. Recent substantial annual rental increases in Moscow at 41.7 per cent (2006–7) and Oslo at 56.9 per cent (2006–7) suggest booming markets that are unlikely to persist. In fact, recent evidence suggests a slowing of rental growth in both cities, as indicated above. In contrast, office rental growth has been zero in both Dublin and Milan. The 'clock' above suggests acceleration in growth for Milan but not for Dublin. Hence similar experiences in the recent past do not imply similar experiences in the future. Underlying demand and supply conditions need consideration in order to arrive at a reasonable forecast for performance.

The European markets vary in their levels of maturity. The extent to which the characteristics of maturity exist varies, and this in turn has some impact on how the markets perform. Availability of market information varies significantly

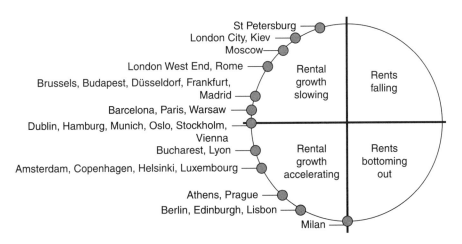

Figure 6.1 European office property clock (2007, quarter 4)

Source: Jones Lang LaSalle, European Office Property Clock, Quarter 4, 2007.

across Europe, as does the extent to which transactions take place through market professionals, research activity, the presence of professional bodies such as the RICS, the openness of markets, and the standardisation of market rules and processes. Jones Lang LaSalle have constructed an index of transparency that has global coverage. Their definition of transparency shares many of the elements of what would be considered to characterise a mature property market. They suggest that transparent markets are defined as '.. [an] open and clearly organised real estate market operating in a legal and regulatory framework that is characterised by the enforcement of rules and regulations and that respects private property rights. [There are] ethical and professional standards of private sector advisors, agents and brokers who are licensed to conduct business in each country' (Jones Lang LaSalle, 2006, Real Estate Transparency Index, p. 3).

Countries with immature real estate markets could be seen as less transparent markets where there is a lack of market information and historic data, no standardisation of rules or processes, no investment benchmarks, problems with title deeds and perhaps arbitrary expropriation of private property. Jones Lang LaSalle (JLL) show that real estate market transparency is broadly positively related to GDP per head, low levels of corruption and an attractive business environment. They also suggest that countries that have more mature or transparent real estate markets receive significantly more institutional real estate investment than less mature or transparent markets. For example, the UK, which has a high level of transparency, receives a disproportionately large amount of investment into direct real estate.

The transparency index they construct has five broad categories. The highest category contains markets where there is a history of market information (time series data) available, clear systems for accounting, standardisation in application of regulations, professionalisation and a robust legal framework defining and protecting private property rights and the ability to separate ownership and use rights, enabling the establishment of an investment market in real estate. These markets will be in transparency tier 1. Table 6.2 below ranks European countries using this approach.

The UK receives the highest transparency score within Europe and comes fifth in the world ranking. Within Europe, the Netherlands, Sweden and France are also amongst the highly transparent markets. This result indicates that market size itself is not an indicator of transparency, since the Netherlands and Sweden are much smaller markets than France and the UK.

Tier 2 contains 'transparent' markets. These markets typically have shorter time series information for market data and may in some cases lack published information available in English. In time more lengthy time series will become available, enabling further research to be more easily conducted in these markets. The difference between tiers 1 and 2, then, is not a difference in the views the societies have regarding real estate investment or, necessarily, regarding institutions and their role in real estate markets. It would be reasonable to expect that all countries listed above in tier 2 have standardisation in application of regulation, robust legal systems, and clear accounting systems.

Table 6.2 Transparency of real estate markets in European countries

	European rank	Transparency score	Transparency tier
United Kingdom	1	1.25	1
Netherlands	2	1.37	1
Sweden*	3	1.38	1
France	4	1.40	1
Finland	5	1.63	2
Germany	6	1.67	2
Denmark*	7	1.84	2
Austria*	8	1.85	2
Ireland	9	1.85	2
Belgium*	10	1.88	2
Spain*	11	1.91	2
Switzerland	12	1.94	2
Norway*	13	1.96	2
Italy*	14	2.14	2
Portugal*	15	2.44	2
Czech Republic*	16	2.69	3
Hungary*	17	2.76	3
Poland*	18	2.76	3
Slovakia	19	2.99	3
Greece*	20	3.13	3
Russia*	21	3.22	3

Note: *indicates an improvement in transparency over the past few years.

Tier 3 collects together 'semi-transparent' markets. This category contains former command economies whose accession to the EU occurred in 2004. Russia is also in this group of countries, together with Greece. These countries typically do not have investment performance data and generally have short time series information available. Institutional issues also exist, implying underdeveloped regulatory frameworks. This may not be surprising for former Communist states, where institutional frameworks would have been very different prior to moving back to a market system with its basic requirement for clear, legally defined private property rights. Somewhat more surprising, perhaps, is that Greece is also seen as a semi-transparent market. Greece joined the EU in 1981 and has operated as a market economy. However, there is no land registry and only poor data in terms of quantity and quality, and hence limited market and investment performance information is available.

The performance of the Greek real estate market is in sharp contrast to Poland, Hungary and the Czech Republic, countries that began the 1990s with no investment market in property but have since not only seen new investment but experienced strong economic growth and falling yields.

Prior to Spain's return to a market system, the 1980s saw institutional change that substantially impacted on opportunities for real estate investment. The Boyer decree of 1985 provided the key piece of institutional change that acted as the foundation for the development of real estate as an attractive asset class. Prior to this reform, tenants effectively had security of tenure and, although rents could be adjusted in line with the cost of living index, this was unusual. Furthermore, the landlord was unable to remove a low-value tenant and replace him with a higher-value use. Legal reforms in the Boyer decree effectively increased the attractiveness of real estate as an asset by weakening the rights of occupiers and strengthening the rights of landlords. The Boyer decree removed the tenant's automatic right to have the lease extended. Landlords could then remove tenants and redevelop or refurbish properties to attract high-value occupiers. Initially the legal changes affected only new leases; however, further reforms in the 1990s extended such changes to pre-Boyer leases. These 'institutional' changes have had a significant impact on the Spanish commercial real estate market.

Spain witnessed the development of an investment market in commercial real estate that has attracted substantial inward investment from overseas. Major real estate firms have now a presence in major urban centres (e.g., Madrid, Barcelona, Seville, and more recently Valencia). Companies such as CBRE, JLL, Cushman & Wakefield, and DTZ have offices in Spain and provide a wide range of services to clients. Their arrival in the market has also had an impact on the conduct and culture of business, for example, in relation to information availability. In addition, there is significantly more market information available than would have been the case 20 years ago. Market adjustment is also evident, with the development sector responding to increased demand via not only new supply but higher-quality supply, matching the requirements of international businesses.

The reforms in the Spanish real estate market coincided with relatively rapid growth in the Spanish economy. Membership of the EU and adoption of policies to enable Spain to meet the convergence criteria for monetary union and adoption of the Euro fuelled the macroeconomic boom. Spain's economy outperformed the EU average in terms of growth. Within the Eurozone it has outperformed the 'big three', France, Germany and Italy. Institutional reform and economic change have driven the real estate market. Demand for offices and retail have seen new development. Spain is a clear example of the impact that institutional and economic change can have on the real estate market. In a relatively short time period its real estate market has opened up to overseas investment and become more transparent, with more market information and research activity than many economies that were in a similar position 20 years ago. Keogh and D'Arcy (1994) had argued that, in comparison to London, Barcelona was at best an emergent market with respect to the characteristics of market maturity. It had limited user and investor opportunities, was less flexible and open than London and had poor information levels and little research available with an industry characterised by non-professional staff. Since then both markets have changed. Investor opportunities in both have increased. There is significantly more research available on the Barcelona market than there was previously (true of London too) and a wide range of professional services now available in the market. Compared with its position almost 15 years ago, Barcelona is relatively more mature, as is Madrid.

As highlighted in the transparency index above (and in the preceding discussion on Spain), institutional characteristics affect real estate transactions and can make markets more or less transparent. Countries that joined the EU in 2004 are all listed as having institutional factors adversely affecting real estate markets and investment. However, they have also seen the greatest changes in institutional behaviour, as these bodies themselves have been affected by legal change as the nations have moved to a market-oriented system. The Czech Republic, Hungary and Poland have witnessed significant inward investment in real estate.

Below, the links between the idea of market transparency (from JLL) and the concept of market maturity in Keogh and D'Arcy (1994) are explored.

In Keogh and D'Arcy (1994) six characteristics are identified for market maturity. The degree of diversification of user and investor opportunities refers to a market's 'ability to cater for a wide range of use and investment requirements...' (op. cit., p. 230). The more mature the market, the more flexibly it will be able to meet the diversity of motives and methods for property market participation. Flexibility will be aided by the availability of finance and financial products. While these may be available in a mature market, they may increase instability in property asset values. Hence maturity may exist alongside excessive volatility.

Professionalisation is often associated with market maturity. This relates to the education received and professional practice guided by professional bodies that effectively act to reduce the risks associated with unstandardised practices and hence facilitate investment in relatively inefficient real estate markets. This dimension of maturity also relates to the way in which business is done and the range of professions involved in real estate use, investment and development. As the role of real estate as an investment asset has increased, so there has developed a role for a wider knowledge base, which can be provided by accountants, economists and investment analysts in addition to the role played by chartered surveyors.

Associated with maturity is the presence of market research and greater information flows. Market research will be aided when longer time series of data are available and with a range of methods for investing in real estate. A culture of information-sharing is also evident in mature markets, which, together with

Table 6.3 A comparison of market maturity and transparency characteristics

Maturity characteristics	Transparency characteristics
The degree of diversification of user and investor opportunities	Investment performance
Flexibility of adjustment of property interests	Market data
Professionalisation	Disclosure and governance
The existence of information and research systems	Regulatory and legal framework
Market openness	Professional standards and transaction process
Standardisation of property rights and market practices	

Source: Adapted from Keogh and D'Arcy (1994) and Jones Lang LaSalle Real Estate Transparency Index (2006).

market research, increases transparency. However, it is still possible that information is inaccurate or that there is a bandwagon effect with all market participants (or at least enough of them) making inappropriate investment decisions based upon inaccurate, biased or misunderstood information.

Important for international real estate investment is market openness to the free inflow and outflow of foreign capital. Openness also relates to the functional divisions of the property market, namely use, investment and development. Overseas firms should be able to be active in all of these divisions. Finally, standardisation of property rights and market practice is also a feature of maturity.

These elements themselves may change and evolve through international transactions and the impact of international real estate service providers as they open branches in different countries.

The maturity characteristics are not unrelated to the characteristics related to transparency. Professional standards and the transactions process relate to the maturity characteristic of standardisation of property rights and market practice. Availability of market data and investment performance relate to research activity and the availability of appropriate market benchmarks. The regulatory and legal framework dimension of transparency can be related to the ability of the market to accommodate a full range of use and objectives plus flexible adjustment. For example, the legal framework should separate ownership and use rights, and lease laws could permit subletting. Disclosure and governance aspects can also be related to the legal dimension. As indicated by Keogh and D'Arcy (1999a), this has a number of dimensions. Legal institutions are one part of the institutional environment in a country. These relate to the property market, itself seen as an institution within which there are legal dimensions including property rights and covering land use and development. As the property market is affected by endogenous and exogenous influences, the legal dimension can change, and thus the behaviour of institutions can change along with the property market and the wider economic environment.

The characteristics listed above vary across real estate markets at any one time. Furthermore, over time changes in characteristics in different markets will occur. However, these do not necessarily have to be the same, although changes in Spain and more recently in some of the former Eastern Bloc countries do share some similarities, for example, establishment of an investment market in real estate through legal changes that themselves reflect deeper cultural change in attitudes to business.

The above characteristics vary across markets, and within markets over time. It could reasonably be argued that, since countries are attempting to increase economic welfare (whatever the exact means of measuring welfare), they adopt economic systems that seem the most successful at increasing GDP. Central and Eastern European nations have rejected centralised non-market-based economic planning in favour of market-oriented systems. In doing this they have, to varying degrees, begun to reform institutions that then provide the basis for trade in legally defined property rights. Progress on this is by no means uniform or rapid. However, in relation to the characteristics outlined in Table 6.3 above, countries have to varying degrees changed regulations in relation to disclosure and governance affecting real estate markets. Legal regulations also form the basis for diversification of user and investor opportunities. This has been evidenced in the Spanish market, but it is also evident at a more basic level where owner-occupiers are enabled to let out some space to tenants. The terms on which this letting occurs are also affected by legal regulations. In an extreme case it may not be legally permitted. Alternatively, and more commonly, the legal system may confer greater power on one party or the other. Changes in this balance of power have an impact on the extent to which an investment market in real estate appears.

Market maturity and transparency characteristics tend to be highly correlated with economies that have attracted relatively high levels of inward investment in relation to national GDP. These countries also exhibit significant outflows of investment funds. In the case of the UK, for example, many of the international real estate service providers have their head offices in the UK and have effectively exported a way of doing business that would be culturally related to business service provision in the London markets and other regional markets in Britain.

However, it is also important to consider the wider business environment across different countries. Investors often consider the Nordic countries as attractive for conducting business, and this covers countries in transparency tier two. New business formation in Sweden, particularly the Stockholm region, is above the EU average. The Danish capital, Copenhagen, is seen as a European leader in business innovation and technology, Finland, having experienced economic restructuring since the collapse of the former Soviet Union, is now a world leader in telecommunications, and Norway's economy is underpinned by the energy sector, leading to strong public finances and a balance of payments surplus. All of these countries share similar approaches to business and provide an attractive business environment. Interestingly, only one of these countries, Finland, has adopted the Euro, and another, Norway, is not a member of the EU. These have not in themselves been obstacles to real estate market development or investment, although their relatively small size has meant that domestic investors have often had to look further afield to find investment opportunities. This is currently the case with Norwegian pension funds, although their first port of call is Sweden and Denmark.

Spain, Portugal, Italy and Greece have lower levels of transparency than the Nordic countries, although, as mentioned above, Spain has made significant improvements in recent decades. Portugal has also seen developments in its real estate market, although legal reforms have been less successful than those in Spain. The presence of international real estate service providers, increased information and research activity are features of the market. There are notable developments in the retail sector, with shopping centres and retail parks being constructed. Greece remains relatively opaque, and this discourages international investment. However, there is some evidence of Greek investors playing a role in the Bulgarian market, which is still in its infancy.

The Italian real estate market is of interest because in many ways the Spanish market was more similar to Italy in the past than it is today. Keogh and D'Arcy (1994) suggested that the property markets in Barcelona and Milan were similar with respect to their relative maturity. While there is now more information available on both markets, it could be argued that Barcelona, and other markets in Spain, have improved more in relation to the characteristics of maturity than have markets in Italy. Rome, for example, is regarded as less transparent than Milan. The penetration of international real estate service providers has been less successful in Italy, which is dominated by many local real estate firms. There has therefore been less opportunity for overseas firms' business practices to permeate the domestic market. Thus, in terms of transparency and maturity characteristics, it may be less likely that the Italian market will approximate those in Northern Europe. Some evidence suggests that this may have had an impact on the quality of space being provided, with a particular lack of prime office space to meet international standards. In the retail sector, there is also evidence of a relatively low density of shopping centre floorspace per capita in comparison to the average for Western Europe. Italy now lags behind France, Ireland, Spain and the UK in terms of retail shopping centre floorspace density.

The UK, the Netherlands, Sweden and France are ranked first, second, third and fourth in Europe, respectively, for transparency of their property markets in Table 6.2. They score highly on the characteristics of maturity. The Paris office market is larger in size than the London market, is less expensive and is less dominated by financial services. The London office markets (like those in Paris), for example, provide a wide range of user and investor opportunities. The market is flexible in the short and long run. There is standardisation of property rights and market practice. The conduct, behaviour and professionalisation of the market are affected by the role of the Royal Institution of Chartered Surveyors (RICS), which sets standards for members. The Institution has successfully adapted to change in the real estate market and the broader range of skills that are now employed within it. Almost all transactions occur through professional agents (who will be members of the RICS), and there is a sophisticated property profession which has an increasingly wide knowledge base, as the real estate service firms provide a wider range of services to clients. The increasing importance given to the role of research within these firms is significant. With the major firms present in London, most now have research teams. These not only provide high value-added services to clients, but also publish market information that is widely available. This aids market transparency. In addition, financial and business service firms outside the real estate sector also undertake their own research into the property market. Financial firms such as Deutsche Bank and UBS undertake research and hold real estate portfolios for investment clients.

The London markets offer a high degree of openness, and large cross-border financial flows into and out of London are not uncommon. In recent years, when office occupier markets were relatively weak, overseas investors were still attracted into the city for buildings let to tenants on long leases. Interest rate and yield differentials played a role, as geared investors from the Eurozone still found it profitable to invest in London. A consequence of this investment behaviour was a disconnection with the weak user market, at least until the middle part of the first decade of the new millennium.

However, the London markets, while exhibiting high levels of transparency, are not necessarily stable. Volatility in returns and rents is a notable feature of the London markets, which tend to display higher volatility than regional markets in the UK. In addition, while information may be available, market sentiment may be biased by the views of the real estate industry. This may result in a band-wagon effect, where all agents make the same type of mistakes in the market at the same time; for example, they may all expect the market to continue to rise when in fact exogenous influences should suggest caution. A recent example can be taken from the performance of property yields. These had steadily fallen to very low levels, in part reflecting the level of investment into real estate assets. However, the industry played down the role of exogenous factors on yield expectations and, when liquidity problems arose in the finance sector and the macro-economic outlook became more unstable, yields in the property market began to increase (and quite rapidly). Thus, while information is available, misplaced emphasis on property-only variables or failure to account for exogenous factors may result in poor investment decisions being taken. It remains to be seen whether the increased research activity can overcome problems in information interpretation.

Furthermore, it has been argued that, in markets without professional bodies, firms will employ people from a wider range of backgrounds and that this might help to overcome problems of a bandwagon effect. However, given that firms in London employ a wide range of skill groups, this factor may be less significant. The culture of doing business within the industry itself may be a more important factor in formulating the weighting given to endogenous versus exogenous variables. In addition, given that information in property markets is not based upon homogeneous products, it may take time for the market to learn what any new events might imply, particularly when those events are external to the market itself. Market agents may set their expectations only adaptively rather than rationally. Thus, they may examine only historical information in making predictions about future performance. Instead, if they formed rational expectations, they would consider the impact of current and expected macroeconomic circumstances and policies in developing their expectations on the future performance of the property market. However, the extent to which agents are able to make rational expectations may be limited. Information within the property market remains relatively costly, given asset heterogeneity, and the added cost of examining the behaviour of exogenous factors may make agents place emphasis on past events to develop future forecasts.

The relative stability of other less mature markets and the relative volatility of markets like London could be used as a critique of flexibility, openness, cultures of information-sharing and professionalisation. However, both relative stability and relative volatility are measured over given time periods, and it is not necessarily the case that such relative differences in amplitude of fluctuations would persist into the future. Less transparent markets have less information upon which to base comparisons, and the information that is available may be more biased than in markets with fuller information. In addition, stability of capital values and rents may or may not imply high value-added by users of space. Stability at a low level of rents implies low value-added from occupiers.

Institutional change has also affected relatively mature markets, such as London. For example, the Landlord and Tenant Act 1954 permitted property investments to be valued at market value and rent to be set accordingly. It incentivised the leasing market and helped to underpin the investment market in commercial real estate. The Spanish Boyer Decree (mentioned above) 30 years later can be seen in a similar light. However, this does not necessarily imply that the Spanish markets will develop in exactly the same way towards 'maturity' as the London market. Local differences may continue. The pressures of globalisation, economic integration across countries, and national economic policy objectives to raise GDP may have had an impact on institutional change that sets the background against which markets can develop. Such changes may, together with the behaviour of real estate companies themselves, have made markets adopt similar practices.

Concepts of maturity and transparency are themselves relative concepts, subject to change. European markets regarded as mature today have not necessarily reached the end of a process of change that has led to their relative maturity. These markets seek to articulate user, investor and develop interests as efficiently as possible, and their characteristics as such enable this articulation to be achieved, *ceteris paribus*. Less flexibility, openness, standardisation of practice, information and research theoretically make this more difficult to achieve and thus turn investment away to other more mature destinations, *ceteris paribus*.

If this is the case, then why did firms still find more opaque markets attractive enough to risk investing? Modern Portfolio Theory, discussed earlier in Chapter 2, indicates that higher risk is associated with higher expected returns. High expected income growth rates in economies with relatively immature property markets would send a signal to investors that future expected returns would be high, and hence they would risk investment. However, Geurts and Jaffe (1996) regard this motive as naïve investment, citing other significant risks associated with foreign investment, many of those related to political behaviour patterns in the countries concerned. However, taking Spain as an example, such risks would have been minimised by the 1980s due to democratisation, entry into the EU and legal reforms creating an investment market in real estate assets. While risks were higher in the past, today, as the market has developed and investment volumes have risen, risk levels are comparable to those of other markets in Western Europe.

Another characteristic of more mature markets is the range of investment opportunities available. London, for example, while having a large direct (unsecuritised) property investment market, also has indirect (securitised) investment vehicles. Investors can purchase property company shares, buy units in property unit trusts or invest in tax transparent Real Estate Investment Trusts (REITs). Such methods of investment exist in other mature markets, such as France and

Germany. They are less prevalent in Southern Europe. Nevertheless, their existence points to a degree of market diversification and sophistication in the development of real estate investment opportunities. However, this financial innovation has recently been associated with problems with mortgage-backed securities, which has led to liquidity problems in financial markets. The real estate sector has been significantly exposed, and hence financial innovation has become another source of potential instability.

6.4　International real estate investment in Europe

The value of international real estate investment in Europe is substantial, reaching £95 billion (US$191 billion) in 2005. Most (67 per cent) international investment in European real estate involved non-European buyers or sellers, indicating both the global dimension to such investment and the openness of European economies to global financial flows. The main recipients of inward international investment were the UK, receiving 36 per cent of the total, Germany at 21 per cent, France at 14 per cent and Sweden at 8 per cent. Italy, the Netherlands and Spain received 3 per cent each. In comparison to the size of the economies, a disproportionately large amount of investment was received by the UK, the Netherlands and Sweden. However, these are ranked as the most transparent and most mature real estate markets, which may to some extent account for their attractiveness to overseas investors.

To a large extent foreign investors were not disadvantaged, since standard regulations are applied to foreign and domestic investors. However, local investors may have some knowledge advantage over foreign investors when it comes to the details of national tax systems and their ability to minimise their tax obligations. In addition, there is some evidence that local investors crowd out foreign investors, as they may have more market knowledge or access to greater information than overseas investors. Local investors in Ireland and Spain have dominated investment in their home real estate markets.

The last decade has seen an increase in the methods of investment into European real estate markets. The introduction of tax-transparent Real Estate Investment Trusts (REITs) in France (2003) and more recently in the UK and Germany has added to those already in existence in Belgium and the Netherlands. These vehicles might reasonably be expected to increase the amount of investment in indirect property vehicles. However, market conditions at the time of writing have not encouraged success of new REITs in the UK. Nevertheless, their presence increases the options for investors.

The increasing attractiveness of indirect investment options has also increased demand for market information and particularly the creation of accurate performance indices and benchmarks. These will be key to the development of a derivatives market. Again, at the time of writing, these markets have been weakened by the 'credit crunch' and the associated increases in market uncertainty and risk evidenced by the increasing cost of interbank funds.

Yield convergence has been a notable feature of European real estate investment over the past decade. There is still some premium for relatively less transparent markets in Eastern Europe, but these are smaller than they were. In fact, yields in the Czech Republic, Hungary and Poland are similar to those in Belgium. Issues still remain with the lack of land registry and uncertainty of ownership in Greece. These factors have deterred international investment.

6.5　Eastern European real estate markets

Most Central and Eastern European countries were part of the Soviet bloc until around 1989. They were not open to market forces, and instead had centrally planned economies. In this economic system, input–output analysis was used as the ordering principle in the absence of price signals. Private ownership of capital did not exist; nations owned capital collectively, together with firms and real estate assets. The use and development of real estate were also determined by the state. No investment market in real estate existed, just as no markets existed to allocate resources in other areas of economic activity.

Political change gathered pace rapidly after the collapse of the Berlin Wall in 1989. Across Eastern Europe, centrally planned economic systems that had failed to produce the living standards found in the West were replaced by market-oriented systems. The nature and model of the planned economy and the degree of liberalisation varied greatly between countries, as did the nature, processes and speed of subsequent change.

However, this change was somewhat uneasy, as countries often had outdated industrial structures that could not compete. The result was macroeconomic instability, exchange rate volatility, rising unemployment, inflation and balance of payments problems. Such structural problems in the macroeconomies of the former centrally planned systems mirrored structural problems in institutions that had been developed during the Communist era. For the real estate market in particular, there was a need to have legally defined private property rights that could form the basis of exchange in property markets. In addition, issues of restitution arose, as former owners of real estate had claims on assets that had been expropriated by the state when private ownership rights had been removed.

Successful transformation of these economies required reforms affecting both the economy and the institutional structure. The processes of transformation are summarised in Table 6.4.

The establishment of commercial real estate markets also required political, institutional and economic changes. Political stability is seen by investors as a prerequisite for establishing an asset market (see Geurts and Jaffe, 1996). Institutional changes are also required to establish a regulatory framework that encompasses the different interests in landed property. These are the necessary elements needed to establish a real estate market based upon the trade in legally defined private property rights (Parsa, 1995). Additionally, in former Communist economies a mechanism is required to address the issue of property restitution.

Table 6.4 Transformation processes

Object of transformation	Transformation process
Management of resource allocation	public → market
Ownership structure	state → private
Exchange measures	regulated → liberalised

Source: Sykora and Simonickova, 1994.

The setting up of institutions that permit the operation of a market economy is also necessary, since the real estate market responds to the wider economy; demand for real estate is a derived demand. These are necessary conditions that need to be in place for real estate transactions to occur and for markets to be created with investment, user and development sectors. They are not sufficient in themselves; further legal reforms and economic growth may be required before a real estate market can become more fully established.

Economic growth provides the basis for user demand. However, adjustment to a market mechanism was initially problematic for the former Communist states. Most experienced high inflation and, at the same time, structural economic changes leading to increasing unemployment, as their former industrial structures were uncompetitive. Even East Germany, which had been seen as having one of the strongest command economies, was faced with severe economic structural problems upon entering the market economy.[1]

The policy response has been to focus on controlling inflation and endure the discomfort of high unemployment. Liberalisation of prices, foreign trade and establishment of domestic capital markets have also been part of the adaptation to a market system. Despite the costs incurred by restructuring, setting a credible monetary policy has had benefits in attracting inward investment. Structural reform has included the privatisation of enterprise, restitution of private property rights, and institutional and legislative reform. From relative economic uncertainty and restructuring in the early 1990s, countries have experienced strong economic growth that has increased occupier demand for real estate. The establishment of the user market has also begun to encourage the investment market. This had a slow start, since there were relatively few investment grade developments and those that were constructed had not yet come back onto the market. However, this too is now changing.

Trade in the property market required that ownership rights be transferred from the state to the individual, since all land and buildings were state-controlled under the former Communist regimes. This raises the issue of restitution, whereby individuals who had owned property before the Communist era had that property returned to them or their heirs. This is not as simple a process as it might first appear. Identification of the appropriate heir may be difficult. Alternatively, no heir may exist. Also, properties owned before the Communist period may have multiple occupants or owners. Properties may also have been modified or refurbished by occupants, or land and property ownerships may differ. Proving previous ownership may also be problematic.

A variety of approaches to restitution emerged. In Russia there was no restitution policy. Instead, property was transferred from the state by transaction. In Hungary, reprivatisation of land has been permitted (and only where there is a five-year commitment to farm the land). A compensation scheme using tradeable vouchers has also been introduced. Restitution policies were also implemented in the Czech Republic and Poland. However, compensation introduces problems associated with valuing assets where there is no established market.

The development of a property market also required clarification of private property rights, as these are the basis for exchange in the market. The development of an institutional framework within which property market structures, including lease terms, transactions costs, professionals and land policy rules, can operate is also necessary.

This is important, as investors will not buy and sell assets if they cannot prove that they have legal rights of ownership. Hence the legislative system must define freehold and leasehold property rights. It must clarify the relationship between landlords and tenants. This is of particular importance for the development of an investment market in real estate.

For new markets coming from a system where prices were not used to signal resource allocation, attaching prices to property assets may not have borne any accurate relation to expected income streams or capital values (for investment purposes), or use values (for occupiers). Limited information and an absence of an established market framework thus implied that initial transactions prices were likely to provide only misleading indicators of price. This was exacerbated by the absence of registration systems. Subsequent transactions would be required to discover whether properties had been overvalued or undervalued at initial sale. Also, as official transactions recorded higher-value transactions in prime locations, this would introduce bias. This was compounded by the fact that such properties were sold to overseas investors. However, as the market develops, institutional frameworks are strengthened, and more transactions occur, such potential biases in pricing should be removed.

In addition to the development of user and investor markets in real estate is the establishment of a development sector to supply new product to the market and maintain and refurbish existing stock. The user and investor markets send price signals to the development sector. Rents, capital values and yields are the signals coming from use and investment divisions of the market to the development sector. As rents and capital values increase, development becomes more profitable and the development sector responds by increasing supply. As has been documented elsewhere and referred to in earlier chapters of this book, this is not an immediate response, due to supply lags in the development process. However, development is also affected by exogenous factors, particularly the planning system. In former Communist countries, land use was not directed by prices, and consequently relatively low-value uses could be found on what the market would have priced as high-value land. Institutional change was therefore required to ensure that high-value uses were in high-value locations. This has implications for the spatial development of property markets. For example, high-value offices tend to be centrally located within cities, with peripheral office parks being less costly. Industrial markets pay higher prices for good access, such as motorway junctions, which are important for distribution networks. Retail development may be located in central locations or in shopping centres/retail parks.

A new planning system should permit such development, as it has a role to play in enhancing economic welfare and GDP growth. Land law should clearly define development rights and consider, in the context of a market system, how development costs may be distributed, especially if externalities are present.

Removal of exchange controls is also important in attracting inward investment, as is removal of any restrictions on repatriation of profits by foreign investors. These types of reforms are consistent with economies in the EU. For Eastern European countries, reforms aided inflows of foreign direct investment, especially from neighbouring Germany and Austria. They have played a significant role in the development of the real estate market in countries such as Poland, Hungary and the Czech Republic.

From being rather opaque markets initially, with limited or no market information or exposure to the demands of international investors, these markets now have a degree of information previously not in existence. Market data are available and research is conducted. In addition, as the market has developed, there has been increasing professionalisation and standardisation of market practices. However, the markets in the countries above would not be regarded as mature or highly transparent. Nevertheless, they have formed the first group of Eastern European countries to open up their markets and experience the development of modern real estate use and development markets, and are increasingly an investment market.

Parsa (1995) suggests that there were three phases of market evolution in Eastern European markets. The first phase, from 1989 to 1992, saw liberalisation of prices and privatisation of real estate assets. This led to market rents being established and a rapid rise in property asset values. The second phase, from 1992 to 1994, saw foreign occupiers enter the market. This coincided with a severe shortage of supply and a consequent rapid rise in rents and capital values. This attracted foreign investors and stimulated development. The third phase, from 1995 to 1998, saw the establishment of domestic investors and developers. This phase also saw a downswing, as new supply reached the market when demand had fallen.

However, while the period immediately after the adoption of a market mechanism showed significant turbulence, foreign direct investment over the period 1989–96 was US$7.12 billion in the Czech Republic, US$13.26 billion in Hungary and US$5.39 billion in Poland (Adair *et al.*, 1999). Interestingly, as these economies grew and their property markets interacted with international users and investors, they still retained different planning systems, tax laws and legal systems. Changes in administrative and planning structures did not necessarily make the countries more similar, but investors and property developers did not consider the operating environment (currency controls, profit repatriation, etc.) to be restrictive. Regulations did not adversely affect international firms; however, local government planning and administration were generally thought to be confused, with difficulties in gaining planning permission (Prague) and local municipalities competing for investment and having inconsistent objectives (Warsaw).

McGreal *et al.* (2002) suggest that the property investment market within the cities (Budapest, Prague and Warsaw) was thin but starting to emerge, driven by German and Austrian investors. Financing, tax structures, information and land ownership were still seen as constraints on international investment. However, while the markets are still relatively non-transparent, there is evidence of improvement. In Poland, real estate markets in cities outside the capital have seen significant development. Yields have fallen and Warsaw offices now have yields lower than Prague, Budapest, Moscow and Brussels.

Retail has seen significant change and development. Building upon rapid economic growth, consumers' expenditure has risen and this has been met with a range of goods and services not previously available in the Communist era. Retail expansion has been a feature across the main Eastern European markets, with international retailers, such as Carrefour and Tesco, entering these markets.

Of the other countries in Eastern Europe, Bulgaria and Romania are still less transparent than Poland, for example. However, both countries are receiving increasing interest from overseas investors. Bucharest has shown falling yields over the past few years, office absorption and completions have both increased and retail expansion is expected to continue in the medium term. Obviously international macroeconomic cycles will have an impact; however, there are clear long-term trends of growth and development in commercial real estate. Investor confidence has also improved as GDP growth has been maintained against a background of falling inflation. The monetary authorities also aim for adoption of the Euro within the next decade, and this too generates an expectation of the type of policies they intend to adopt, providing some certainty to business.

Of the smaller Eastern European countries, there has been increased interest from the international investment community in the Baltic states of Estonia, Latvia and Lithuania. These countries are now EU members (as are the other countries discussed above) and this has helped to improve investor confidence.

One of the most risky markets is Russia. Outside the EU, overseas real estate investment interest has been limited and began only in 2001. By 2006, however, investors from over 10 countries were active in Russia, although it remains dominated by domestic investors. Economic growth is underpinning demand in the Moscow office market. This growth is expected to continue, especially in areas outside the CBD. Regional cities have also received inward investment. Quality stock is, however, limited, and this has reduced investment opportunities. However, foreign direct investment is likely to be around US$45 billion in 2008.

6.6 | Conclusions

European commercial real estate markets have experienced significant expansion of use, investment, and development activity over the past 20 years. Investment markets have been created where they previously did not exist and completely new markets have been established. Currently at the frontier of new interest from investors are Romania and Bulgaria. Yields remain high, due to the risks attached to investment, reflecting in part the institutional structure and capacity in these nations. In contrast to these are the established and highly transparent markets in the Nordic countries. Norway continues to export capital looking for good quality risk-adjusted returns. High productivity growth and a high value-added knowledge economy underpin the Danish capital, Copenhagen, as an attractive destination for investors, despite current cyclical fluctuations in European and world markets.

Table 6.2 above indicates the relative transparency of various European markets. Many of these have witnessed substantial improvements in levels of transparency and concurrent improvements in market efficiency. However, it is important to note that market development does not necessarily move at the same speed or indeed the same direction across countries. Institutions in individual countries will respond to change in varying ways. Further development may also be affected by competitive pressures from other parts of the world. Thus, for example, EU restrictions on national governments' support towards inward investment may discourage companies from opening Eastern European operations when they can benefit from significant local tax breaks available in particular states in the US. Increased global economic integration thus means that particular patterns of development that have been observed in the past may no longer be visible. New competitive pressures emerge, presenting challenges to existing institutional frameworks. However, it is clear that the institutional change that has occurred has enabled the development of a modern real estate investment sector, providing the appropriate type of real estate to meet changing economic circumstances.

Property Markets in Asia-Pacific

7.1 Introduction

The Asia-Pacific region as considered in this chapter includes countries bordering on the South China Sea and the western Pacific Ocean. With this description, the region includes Mainland China (China hereafter), Hong Kong Special Administrative Region (Hong Kong hereafter), Indonesia, Malaysia, the Philippines, Singapore and Vietnam around the South China Sea, and Japan and South Korea to the west of the Pacific Ocean. India has also been included in this chapter, having emerged as a major economy and property market in the last 10 years.

Economies in Asia-Pacific have responded to the forces of globalisation by reducing barriers to trade and foreign investment. The region has witnessed significant changes in economic and institutional structure over the last six decades. As a region, Asia-Pacific is culturally and institutionally highly diverse. Despite the formation of a regional trade bloc (ASEAN), economies in the region are far less integrated with each other than, say, regional trade blocs like NAFTA or the EU, and are dependent for trade on Europe or North America. The Asia-Pacific region has witnessed major political and economic changes, from the liberalisation of West Asian economies, leading to sustained periods of high economic growth, to the transformation in China from a command economy to market-based economic structures, to the handing over to China of Hong Kong by the UK and Macau by Portugal, to the opening up of the Indian economy for foreign investment and trade, etc. These transformations have had a significant impact on use and investment interest in the property market in these economies.

In this chapter we examine the economic and institutional context for property markets in Asia-Pacific. Section 7.2 discusses the pattern of economic development in Asia-Pacific. Trade-led economic growth began in Japan after the Second World War, and spilled over to other countries in the region. This section discusses the pattern and forces behind economic development in Korea, Hong Kong, Singapore, Taiwan, Malaysia, Indonesia, the Philippines, Vietnam, China and India. Section 7.3 presents the impact of globalisation on Asia-Pacific countries. Rapid growth has led to transformation of urban areas and institutions, which is discussed in Section 7.4. Section 7.5 looks at property market performance in Asia-Pacific. Property market institutions and maturity characteristics are discussed in Section 7.6. Asia-Pacific economies have witnessed significant growth in investment in property, and Section 7.7 discusses the motivation behind interest in property markets in this region by international investors. Section 7.8 concludes.

7.2 | Economic context

The Asia-Pacific region is growing at a much faster rate than the rest of the world (Figure 7.1). Despite economic downturns during the mid-1980s, the early 1990s and post-1997, Asia-Pacific has delivered above average economic growth. Unlike many other developing countries that have experienced boom–bust cycles since the 1960s, economies in Asia-Pacific witnessed a high degree of macroeconomic stability until 1997.

Macroeconomic policymakers in the region have, generally, focused on policies to create an environment for stable growth and trade. In Asia-Pacific countries, the fiscal and current account deficits since the 1960s have, in general, been less than half the average of other developing countries. Indonesia, Taiwan and Thailand used legislation to limit the size of public sector deficits. Political support for anti-inflationary policies acted as a constraint in Korea, Malaysia and Singapore. Hong Kong put in place the currency board arrangement, which disciplined fiscal policies and constrained monetary action. Monetary authorities have used monetary policy (via interest rate and reserve requirement increases) and administrative controls (such as sector-specific investment bans and restrictions on lending to excess capacity sectors) to control inflation. Disciplined macroeconomic policies provided a stable environment for private

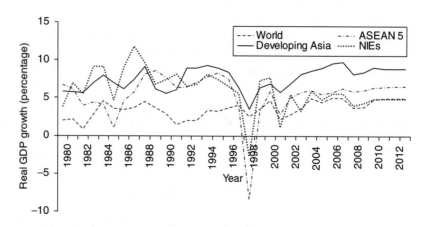

Figure 7.1 Real GDP growth in Asia

Table 7.1 Economic growth in Asia-Pacific (percentage)

Country	1960–70	1970–80	1980–90	1990–2000	2000–5
Japan	10.5	4.3	4.1	1.1	3.6
Korea	8.6	9.6	9.7	5.8	4.6
Hong Kong	10.0	9.2	7.1	4.1	4.3
Taiwan		9.7	7.8	6.4	3.7
Singapore	8.8	8.3	6.4	7.6	4.2
Malaysia	6.5	7.9	5.2	7.0	4.8
Indonesia	3.5	7.2	5.5	4.2	4.7
Thailand	8.2	7.1	7.6	4.2	5.4
Philippines	5.1	6.0	0.9	3.3	4.7
China	9.2		9.5	10.6	9.6

Source: World Bank Data Statistics; http://siteresources.worldbank.org/DATASTATISTICS/Resources/
table4_1.pdf; http://investintaiwan.nat.gov.tw/en/env/stats/gdp_growth.html

sector decision-making, high rates of savings, domestic and foreign investment and exports growth (IMF, 1999).

Growth in Asia-Pacific has followed a pattern which started with high growth in Japan during the post-Second World War period (Table 7.1). The newly industrialised economies (NIEs) of Hong Kong, South Korea, Singapore and Taiwan followed Japan. The ASEAN 5 countries (Indonesia, Thailand, Malaysia, the Philippines and Vietnam) were soon witnessing rapid growth.

The main features of the high-growing NIEs and ASEAN 5 economies included: high rates of investment, saving and human capital formation; exports having a leading role in the growth process; and stable macroeconomic conditions (IMF, 1999). Improving employment conditions have also supported income and consumption growth (IMF, 2006). The role of foreign investment differed widely across the region. NIEs (with the exception of South Korea) were less dependent on foreign investment than ASEAN countries. The composition of foreign investment has also differed from country to country. Malaysia and Singapore relied on portfolio and direct investment to finance domestic capital investment, while South Korea and Thailand depended largely on foreign borrowings. The regulations concerning foreign investment differed substantially. In South Korea, prior to the 1990s, restrictive limits on foreign ownership along with capital controls skewed the balance of foreign funds towards debt. Liberalisation of foreign ownership limits in the 1990s, however, led to a significant increase in foreign portfolio investment.

Financial systems in Asia-Pacific encouraged domestic savings and for the most part allocated financial resources to investments that yielded significant returns. Equity and bond markets were less important. The intervention of governments in the financial sector has been extensive, through regulations and state-owned financial institutions, and by guiding and rewarding financial market participants (IMF, 1999). The role of government in financial sector development has varied widely – from being limited to a prudential regulator in Hong Kong to actively directing allocation of credit in South Korea. In several Asia-Pacific economies, the public sector created, owned and managed financial institutions to encourage and intermediate savings. In South Korea, Malaysia, Singapore and China, postal savings systems were established to encourage small savers by offering secure ways to deposit their savings. Also in these countries, as well as in Indonesia, India and Thailand, development banks provided long-term credit to priority industries and social sectors. All commercial banks in South Korea were state-owned and managed until the early 1980s. The first private sector commercial bank was established in India in 1994. Most governments in Asia-Pacific, with the exception of Singapore, Hong Kong, and Indonesia, protected financial institutions from domestic and foreign competition by restricting entry and branch licensing (IMF, 1999).

The rapid expansion of financial intermediation in the economies of Asia-Pacific was not always matched by commensurate strengthening of regulatory and supervisory systems. All of these economies have suffered from financial distress to varying degrees. In several instances, such as in Hong Kong during the early 1980s, Indonesia during the early 1990s, Japan during the late 1990s, and Malaysia and Thailand towards the end of the 1980s, some financial institutions collapsed or were closed. Banking sector distress in these economies was caused by both external and domestic factors. External causes were related to world economic shocks such as increased cost of international borrowings, the fall in international demand for goods and worsening terms of trade. Domestic causes were mainly related to lax regulatory structure, speculative borrowing/lending and lending on non-commercial criteria, often to clients connected with bank management or government. From the mid-1980s onwards Asia-Pacific governments began to liberalise their financial sectors. Reforms included liberalisation of exchange and capital controls.

Though generally Asia-Pacific has offered stable macroeconomic performance, there have been periods of difficulties. Asian economies have faced bouts of overheating pressures, indicated by rising inflation in the asset market and sizeable current account deficits. During the period leading up to 1997, economies in Asia-Pacific witnessed sharp increases in private capital inflows, drawn primarily by high economic growth in the region. Goods price inflation remained moderate but asset prices rose sharply. Exchange rates appreciated in some countries, thereby eroding trade competitiveness. Current account balances deteriorated. With currencies in Asia-Pacific economies pegged to the US dollar, and with limited scope to undertake fiscal adjustment, the policy response to the capital inflows was limited. During the 1990s, leading up to 1997, the practicality of policy responses to sterilise monetary impact of capital inflows became questionable as the size of capital inflows grew large.

The recovery of Asia-Pacific was fairly quick, and most of the economies started turning around after 1999. In South Korea, where the recovery was fastest, GDP grew by 10.5 per cent in 1999. Malaysia and Thailand grew by 5.5 and 4.25 per cent respectively (IMF, 2000). The driving forces of recovery were strong export growth driven by strong US, European and, to a lesser extent, Japanese economies.

Public consumption and investment continued to support economic growth in all crisis-affected economies. Fiscal and monetary policies provided necessary support for the recovery in Asia-Pacific. One of the consequences of the Asia-Pacific financial crisis was the large-scale financial distress of the corporate sector, the counterpart to the non-performing loan problem. In response, these countries established out-of-court procedures to settle claims, and also introduced legal and institutional reform, where needed, to strengthen the bankruptcy system and improve financial transparency and corporate governance (IMF, 2000).

Asia-Pacific economies have once again emerged as the fastest-growing economies in the world. For the region as a whole, growth in 2007 was 7.4 per cent, with emerging economies in Asia recording growth of more than 9 per cent, led by China and India (IMF, 2008). Though trade is still an important contributor to GDP growth, domestic demand has become an important source of growth across most of Asia. Activity in emerging Asia, particularly China and India, has been investment-led in recent years.

Trade has played the most important role in the economic success of Asia-Pacific. These economies, except Hong Kong, went through an initial import substitution phase; they subsequently promoted exports, while, in most cases, continuing to protect domestic industries from import competition. Many governments' policies (in China, Taiwan and South Korea) assisted the export drive, and, despite a high rate of effective protection, exporters had access to imports at close to world price through a variety of channels such as free trade zones, export processing zones, special economic zones, bonded warehouses, duty drawbacks and tariff exemptions. In earlier years, Asia-Pacific economies provided incentives for foreign investment directed towards exports. One of the interesting features of the export drive in Asia-Pacific was that intraregional trade expanded substantially. A large part of this trade was in intermediate goods. The expansion was aided by the more advanced economies in the region, starting with Japan and followed by Korea, Singapore and Taiwan, investing directly and relocating firms to other Asia-Pacific economies like China, Indonesia, Malaysia, Thailand, the Philippines and Vietnam.

7.3   Globalisation and its impact on Asia-Pacific

The definition of 'globalisation' has a variety of conceptualisations, including history, internal dynamics and structural outcomes (Marcotullio and Lo, 2001). The broadest definition of the term is attributable to Held *et al.* (1999), who define globalisation as the widening and speeding up of worldwide interconnectedness in all aspects of contemporary social life, from cultural to criminal. Though globalisation has many dimensions, the one that is considered in this chapter is economic (international capital flows, trade and information). Thus the definition of globalisation, following Lo and Marcotullio (2001), is cross-border integration of economic activities and growing interdependency of countries and regional economic blocs. In analysis of the globalisation of Asia-Pacific economies, the approach that is subscribed to is a variant of 'one-world' analysis (Marcotullio and Lo, 2001). This approach focuses on analysis of international economic transactions among different countries rather than country-by-country analysis of social and economic change. Within this approach, property market development would be a product of the emergence of particular forms of international modes of production and their impact on the space market.

An interesting feature of the rapid rise of Asian economies has been the region's developing structural interdependence (Lo and Marcotullio, 2001). In defining and analysing structural interdependence, we would be limiting ourselves to the economic interdependence between nations. This perspective fits within the definition of globalisation that has been discussed above.

Flows in goods and services, capital, finance, people and information link nations through activities performed in major cities. Globalisation has led to economic adjustments in the nature and location of production and consumption. The structure of production in advanced economies has shifted from one based on industrial manufacturing growth and employment to service-oriented economies. There has been substantial growth in the share of the services sector in the GDP of G7 countries (Table 7.2). While the manufacturing base has not

Table 7.2 Share of services sector in GDP of G7 countries

Country	1960	1990	2000	2005	1990–2000 (annual growth rate)	2000–5 (annual growth rate)
USA	58	70	75	76	3.4	2.7
UK	53	63	71	75	3.4	3.1
France	52	70	74	77	2.2	1.6
Germany	41	61	68	70	2.9	1.0
Japan	42	58	66	69	1.9	1.7
Canada	60	66	65		3.0	3.0
Italy	46	64	69	71	1.7	0.9

Source: World Bank Data Statistics; http://ddp-ext.worldbank.org/ext/DDPQQ/

Table 7.3 Share of manufacturing in GDP of select Asia-Pacific countries

Country	1960	1990	2000	2005
South Korea	14	42	40	41
Taiwan	35	38	29	27
Singapore	12	35	36	33
Malaysia	9	42	51	50
Indonesia	8	39	46	47
Thailand	13	37	42	44
Philippines	20	34	32	32
China		42	46	48

Source: National Statistics, Republic of China (Taiwan).
World Bank Data Statistics; http://ddp-ext.worldbank.org/ext/DDPQQ/

completely disappeared from these countries, its share in the GDP of these economies has declined.

Another economic adjustment that has happened is the emergence of the manufacturing belt in East and South East Asia. Though advanced economies are still the major producers of manufacturing goods, the global manufacturing landscape has undergone substantial changes. Asia-Pacific has seen the emergence of a manufacturing belt over the last four decades. The share of manufacturing in the GDP of these economies has increased substantially (Table 7.3).

The four Asian NIEs, followed by ASEAN 5 (Indonesia, Malaysia, the Philippines, Thailand and Vietnam), were able to take advantage of the shifting location of industrial production. Asian NIEs have experienced spectacular manufacturing-driven growth during the last few decades. The expansion of industrial production has been responsible for the spectacular economic achievements of Asian NIEs. The per capita GDP of Taiwan increased from US$1,518 in 1962 to US$3,313 in 1972 and US$16,855 in 2007 (invest in Taiwan; http://investintaiwan.nat.gov.tw/en/env/stats/per_capita_gdp.html). Taiwan experienced 9.7 per cent annual growth during the 1970s and 7.8 per cent annual growth during the 1980s. South Korea attained average annual growth of 8.6 per cent in the 1960s, 10.3 per cent in the 1970s and 9.7 per cent in the 1980s.

With globalisation, spatial integration and interdependency among nations have increased. Indicators that present evidence of integration are extensive growth in trade and investment. World trade has grown significantly since the 1950s. During the last couple of decades, not only have growth rates been unprecedented, but they are also higher than the growth rates of global production. Since the 1950s, East and South East Asia have seen phenomenal growth in trade (Table 7.4). This region has followed a pattern, starting with Japan during 1950–60, followed by Asian NIEs in the 1960s and then phenomenal growth in trade in the ASEAN countries. Though the trade in most countries was growing, Asian economies saw much faster growth in trade. During the early 1980s, the global economy went into recession and primary commodity prices fell, but trade for countries in Asia continued to grow. There were exceptions – Indonesia and the Philippines. While the fall in demand for agricultural and fuel oil products depressed trade in Indonesia, political instability hurt economic growth and trade in the Philippines.

With the development of the global finance system, trade in capital also began to represent a separation of the real economy of production and trade in goods and services from the symbol economy of credit and financial transactions. The importance of the global finance system can be seen in the increases in volume of foreign currency trade. By the early 1980s, the volume of foreign currency trade amounted to 12 times the value of world trade in goods and services. By the end of the 1980s, the foreign currency trade had risen to 32 times the value of trade in goods and services (Drucker, 1986). While international capital flows contributed to the growth in Asia-Pacific during much of 1970–90, the currency and capital market crisis of 1997 and the global stock market fall that followed indicated the interconnected nature of the global financial system (Lo and Marcotullio, 2001).

Table 7.4 Country-wise annual average growth rates of trade in Asia-Pacific

Country	1950–60 %		1960–70 %		1970–80 %		1980–90 %		1990–2000 %		2000–5 %	
	Exports	Imports	Exports	Imports	Exports	Imports	Exports	Imports	Exports	Imports	Exports	Imports
Japan	15.87	12.27	17.47	14.36	21.6	21.96	8.32	5.06	11.12	4.59	7.32	7.23
Korea	0.82	17.21	39.81	21.28	37.20	29.12	15.04	11.86	10.10	7.12	12.9	12.07
Hong Kong	–0.31	3.41	14.53	10.68	22.35	22.06	16.79	15.01	8.25	8.81	8.47	8.06
Taiwan	6.83	6.62	23.05	19.05	28.88	28.11	11.68	12.37	3.88	8.54	1.59	8.32
Singapore	–0.11	0.80	3.32	5.40	18.39	24.65	3.93	8.03	18.84	7.83	1.69	9.30
Malaysia	0.56	3.27	4.26	3.45	–19.9	22.17	10.97	7.69	15.43	9.49	9.17	8.19
Indonesia	–1.12	–2.06	1.62	2.95	–6.65	26.44	17.99	2.57	26.79	3.55	16.45	11.93
Thailand	1.45	6.59	5.96	12.13	28.19	22.43	9.93	12.67	9.93	5.01	12.63	14.22
Philippines	5.01	4.70	5.39	6.41	14.79	21.76	–7.62	2.86	14.41	12.48	12.09	5.36
China	18.8	14.12	1.33	1.86	20.04	23.68	12.77	13.45	14.45	13.04	26.73	26.46

Source: UNCTAD Handbook of Statistics, 2008.

7.3.1 Foreign direct investment and growth of transnational corporations

Another important trend witnessed by the Asia-Pacific region has been the growth in foreign direct investment (FDI). Conduits of FDI are transnational corporations (TNCs). TNCs have driven the shift in economic activity globally. Prior to the 1960s, the extent of FDI was very small. However, since then FDI inflows have grown substantially. During the 1960s, FDI inflows grew at twice the rate of world gross national product and 40 per cent faster than world exports. During the 1980s FDI inflows to countries around the world grew at an annual rate of 24 per cent (Lo and Marcotullio, 2001). Recent years have seen phenomenal growth in FDI inflows, though compared with 2000 the inflow has declined slightly (UNCTAD, 2008; Development and Globalization: Facts and Figures). The destination of FDI has also seen changes over the last four decades. During the 1980s, most of the FDI transactions were limited to a 'triad' including the EU, North America, and East and South East Asia (with the focus on Japan). However, since the 1990s, developing countries in Asia have also received substantial volumes of FDI. The pattern was similar to the growth pattern in trade in Asia-Pacific. NIEs followed Japan and ASEAN 5 followed NIEs (Table 7.5) in attracting FDI.

Japanese trade and investments in the Asia-Pacific region have been the key to both the initial success of the region and the restructuring of many of the area's economies. Japanese trade in Asia grew with the importance of intrafirm trade among Japanese companies. The outward expansion strategy of Japanese TNCs has been to incorporate subsidiaries in economies in the region with which they

Table 7.5 FDI inflows by host regions and countries (US$ billion)

Host region/economy	1991	1996	2007
World	158.9	349.2	1,833.3
Developed countries	114.8	208.2	1,247.6
European Union	78.8	99.4	804.29
North America	25.5	91.3	341.4
Other	10.5	17.5	101.9
Developing countries	1.7	128.7	499.7
Latin America	15.4	38.6	126.26
South, East and South East Asia	21.2	81.2	247.8
Other	5.1	8.9	125.6
Central and Eastern Europe	2.4	12.3	85.9
South Korea	1.2	2.3	2.6
Singapore	4.9	9.4	24.1
Thailand	2.0	2.4	9.6
Indonesia	15	8.0	6.9
Malaysia	4.0	5.3	8.4
Philippines	0.5	1.4	2.9
China	4.4	42.3	83.5
Vietnam	0.2	2.2	6.7

Source: UNCTAD, FDI Statistics http://www.unctad.org/Templates/
Pageasp?intItemID=3198&lang=1

trade parts and services. Asian NIEs and ASEAN countries received 11.7 per cent of Japanese FDI in 1988. Japanese FDI and technologies have originally contributed to the region's growth (Tiwari *et al.*, 2003). The historical pattern of regional economic development within East and South East Asia is related to three waves of spatially concentrated investments (Lo and Marcotullio, 2001).

The first wave of relocation of Japanese manufacturing industries began in the 1960s and 1970s, when, faced with the rising cost of labour and material, Japanese firms moved their labour-intensive manufacturing to Asian NIEs. These countries provided not only cheap resources but also access to new markets for goods. The second wave occurred in the 1970s and 1980s, when NIEs started to lose production cost advantages due to the appreciation of exchange rates and rising labour cost. Japanese firms started locating in ASEAN countries, which offered labour, resource and access to market advantages. An interesting feature of FDI in these countries has been that the location pattern is not uniform. In Thailand and Malaysia it is heavily concentrated in specific regions, while in Indonesia it is fairly dispersed (Tiwari *et al.*, 2003).

Japan led the region in relocating light manufactured goods industries to NIEs in the 1970s. The Asian NIEs responded and shifted their exports to light manufacturing, and subsequently to durable consumer goods and machinery products. Almost simultaneously the ASEAN nations shifted from raw material exports to manufacturing exports and then to light manufacturing. The movement of industrial production followed the shift of investment from Japan to the NIEs and then to ASEAN (Lo and Marcotullio, 2001). Asian NIEs also followed Japan by relocating industries to cheaper neighbouring locations. Taiwan first, followed by South Korea, Singapore and Hong Kong, were extremely important sources of FDI in ASEAN countries. Hong Kong provided FDI to China, particularly to the immediate hinterland, the Pearl River delta. Singapore's direct investments also flowed to its neighbourhood. Two-thirds of the total investments from Singapore are located in Malaysia and another 24 per cent went to Indonesia (Lo and Marcotullio, 2001). The economic growth of ASEAN economies during the 1980s and early 1990s was the fastest in the world, and the industrialisation pattern that emerged attracted huge capital inflows, which, as has been argued in literature, caused the asset price bubble and later the Asian financial crisis of 1997.

Inflows of FDI also facilitated structural changes in trade orientation of recipient countries. ASEAN countries, which were commodity exporters in the 1960s, became manufacturing exporters in the 1980s. Export-oriented FDI in these countries stimulated the manufacturing sector (Lo and Marcotullio, 2001).

The third wave of foreign investment occurred after the mid-1980s and centred on China. In the early 1980s, China established four special economic zones (SEZs) in Guangdong and Fujian provinces, which offered incentives to attract foreign investment and export-oriented industries that located in these zones. In 1990, a new development area was designated in the Pudong area near Shanghai. During 1990 and 1995, Pudong New Area attracted FDI of US$8.52 billion, which helped transform Shanghai into an international metropolis (Lo and Marcotullio, 2001). An interesting consequence of China's general open policy has been that

FDI has converged on its coastal cities, making these cities generators of more than half of China's GDP.

The latest entrant to the global economy has been India. Economic reforms in India began in the early 1980s, but a comprehensive liberalisation and privatisation process started in July 1991, when India faced a balance of payments crisis. Since then, there have been attempts to integrate the Indian economy with the rest of the world, and a number of liberalisation attempts have been made through the removal of quantitative restrictions on trade, reducing tariffs and exchange rate flexibility (Sahoo, 2006). Indian policymakers were very cautious about the opening up of the economy to debt flows. The emphasis has, therefore, been on foreign investment – both FDI and portfolio investment. The limit for FDI in various sectors was raised in a phased manner, and by 2000 most sectors, except a few strategic sectors, had been permitted up to 100 per cent foreign direct investment (Shah and Patnaik, 2008). FDI flows in India have grown substantially from 0.14 per cent of GDP in 1992–3 to 2.34 per cent of GDP in 2006–7.

7.4   Globalisation and urban transformation of the Asia-Pacific region

Economic globalisation influences urban and regional planning. Planners attempt to enhance the competitiveness of their urban centres through developing urban and regional strategies that attract cross-border activities. Property market activity is an outcome of economic activity and urban planning. The influence of cross-border economic activity in the planning processes of cities in Asia-Pacific has been immense.

7.4.1   Urban transformation of Tokyo

As Japanese businesses started to relocate their manufacturing to NIEs and ASEAN countries during the 1980s, Tokyo started to reinvent itself by switching from a manufacturing to a service sector-based economy. Inner-city areas in Tokyo became sites of construction to house these activities. Demand for office floor space sky-rocketed during the late 1980s, and by the 1990s total office floor area in the core CBD of Tokyo exceeded available floor area in Manhattan, New York (Kidokoro *et al.*, 2001). As land prices soared, commercial use of space replaced all other types of uses in central Tokyo. In response to the globalisation of Japanese firms, the nature of employment in Tokyo changed from manufacturing-based to service sector-oriented (Kidokoro *et al.*, 2001). During the 1990s, Japan witnessed inflows of FDI, mostly in the non-manufacturing sectors, including finance and retail. Non-manufacturing FDI was concentrated in Tokyo, which became the hub of TNCs. However, the nature of the internationalisation of the city differed from other international cities such as London, New York, Singapore and Hong

Kong. Tokyo was servicing mainly Japanese TNCs, while other international cities also serviced foreign companies. An implication of this transformation was that manufacturing moved out of central Tokyo and started to concentrate in the western corridor of Tokyo Metropolitan Region. This led to the emergence of the Keihin industrial belt, where petrochemical and steel industries clustered. This transformation caused concerns among planners, and a set of policies aimed towards spatial decentralisation were enacted.

Planning in Japan is carried out at three levels – national, regional (for eight regions) and local. Japan has formulated strategic national plans in the form of national development plans, NDPs, since the 1960s. In addition, various regions also formulate regional development plans. Detailed land use and development plans are prepared at the local level as city plans. An important feature of the planning system in Japan has been strategic cooperation at various planning levels. Though balanced regional development has been the goal of plans right from the beginning, it became much more of an agenda as Tokyo became over-concentrated and high-density. The Fourth NDP specifically focused on decentralised multi-polar national development. Decentralisation was further reinforced in the Fifth NDP (Takafusa, 2004). National Capital Region Development Plans complemented the objectives of the National Development Plan.

At the local level there was huge support for national government policies concerning balanced regional development. During the 1960s and 1970s many communities lobbied with government to offer incentives and build large infrastructure to attract industries into their regions (Kidokoro *et al.*, 2001). The oil shocks of 1973–4 and 1978–9, and deteriorating environment due to rapid development of heavy industries, shifted the focus of national plans to high-tech industries such as microelectronics, automobile and consumer goods. Following up on the success of regional growth poles for heavy industrial development, in 1980 the Ministry of Trade and Industry promulgated the 'technopolis policy', which proposed the development of technopolis growth poles. The national development plan focused on complementary policies for regional development of a high-tech industry-based economy. Despite substantial funding, not all technopolis growth poles areas succeeded, and the technopolis programme did not succeed in producing R&D centres in high-tech industry (Kidokoro *et al.*, 2001). Successful R&D firms and high-tech industries continued to locate in Tokyo Metropolitan Region.

Japan's transition from heavy industry to high-tech industries allowed flexibility in outsourcing to other locations in Japan or abroad where factor costs were low. Another major push for industries to relocate overseas came after the Plaza Accord of 1985, following which Japan had to revalue its currency upwards against the dollar. To stay competitive, industries had to achieve lower production costs, and this was met by locating production sites to other countries in Asia, such as Indonesia and Malaysia. The headquarters of Japanese industries that were locating production abroad were still located in Japanese urban centres, particularly in Tokyo. Activities related to finance, insurance, and wholesale and business services became concentrated in Tokyo.

The decentralisation of Tokyo was one of the key objectives of NCRDPs. In order to implement the decentralisation of Tokyo, the government promoted other cities such as Yokohama/Kawasaki, Tsukuba Science City/Tsuchiura, Urawa/Omiya and Hachioji/Tachikawa. These cities are within a distance of 30 to 50 km and are well connected with Tokyo by rail/road. Prefectural governments implemented the plan with financial and other support from national governments. A huge amount of office space, residential and retail space has been developed. These policies have been successful in decentralising Tokyo to some extent. Many companies have moved their headquarters to locations like Yokohama and Chiba. The focus of urban policy in Japan has been on economic growth. National, regional and local plans have worked in harmony to achieve objectives set out for economic growth.

7.4.2   Urban transformation of Seoul

The economic development strategy of the South Korean government was led by the manufacturing sector. To attract foreign capital in manufacturing, in 1961 the government enacted the 'Foreign Capital Inducement Promotion Act', which offered tax benefits to foreigners and guaranteed repatriation of principal and earnings. Foreign capital inflows soared from US$147 million during 1962–5 to US$11 billion during 1973–8 to US$30 billion during 1986–92 (Hong, 1997). Much of the foreign capital inflow prior to the 1980s was in the form of public and commercial loans. FDI inflows increased substantially during the 1980s. With the appreciation of the Japanese yen during the1980s, Korea achieved a substantial current account surplus. Faced with increasing costs in their home market, Japanese firms started locating their labour-intensive production in Korea.

Investment was highly concentrated in Seoul, benefiting from the government's export-led industrialisation programme. Seoul emerged as a dominant city in Korea, with economic activities and jobs being concentrated there. This pattern of development led to a rise in regional inequality (Kwon, 2001). Planning responded by population decentralisation policies through various development control measures like a rigid zoning system, establishment of green belts, industrial relocation, and dispersal of government offices and universities out of Seoul. These policies did not succeed in population decentralisation (Cho, 2005). Increasing population in Seoul caused the city to expand. The CBD of Seoul, located north of the Han River, was formerly a residential zone. Commercial offices replaced older residential areas. Over time two more subcentres have emerged to the south of the Han River. Planning systems in Korea were highly concentrated at the national level. Central Government's containment policy has prevented Seoul from participating in its own urban development. Lack of local participation has caused tensions at local levels over the location of public facilities (such as garbage and solid waste disposal sites), allocation of new towns containing industrial and housing estates, and environment conservation.

Since the 1988 Olympic Games, Seoul has emerged as a key economic and political location in Asia-Pacific. FDI flows have also increased, mainly from Japan, the US and Europe. This helped Seoul establish economic links with other meg-acities in the region. Like Tokyo, Seoul also became the headquarters of Korean TNCs, which have had a significant impact on the spatial organisation of the city. Production of services for these headquarters is a growing part of the Seoul economy.

7.4.3   Urban transformation of Singapore

Singapore has a unique status, as it is a city state. In terms of population and land area it is smaller than most major capital cities in Asia-Pacific. In terms of natural resources, Singapore is severely constrained; half of its water supply is imported from Malaysia. Singapore's lack of natural resources has been compensated for by its unique geographical location within the region, which has helped in developing Singapore as a service economy. In economic terms, Singapore is the seventh largest in Asia. When Singapore started industrialising it faced challenges because of its small domestic market, which inhibited development of industries due to scale economies and lack of natural resources. Unlike other economies in the region, Singapore did not have advantages in terms of labour cost to enable FDI-led development of manufacturing. However, Singapore had a well developed infrastructure, commercial and financial expertise, which led the development of a service sector-based economy. Attracting TNCs to base themselves in Singapore and serve the region from there has been a strategy since the 1980s. Singapore has become a major transhipment hub and regional financial centre. International trade accounts for more than three times the gross national product. Until 1990, Singapore was the largest recipient of FDI in industries targeted for export markets in the region. Singapore is the third largest financial centre in Asia, after Tokyo and Hong Kong, and over the years it has developed as a risk management centre with active foreign currency trading, money market operations, and trading in capital market instruments (Chia, 2001).

Singapore is a highly planned and regulated economy. It has a single-tier government system that is responsible for planning at local and national levels. Being a city state, Singapore faces severe land constraints. Land use planning and management has aimed at controlling urban land demand through cross-border immigration restrictions and control of land supply through land acquisition (Chia, 2001). During the 1960s, the major objectives of urban planners were meeting the housing shortage, urban renewal to clear the slums, revitalising the city centre and improving the living environment. In 1971, Singapore prepared a concept plan to guide the city's physical growth over the next two decades. The plan provided for high-density housing, industries and urban centres in a ring formation around a central catchment area, linked together by an efficient public transportation system (Chia, 2001). Over time, central areas became congested, and the strategy of the next concept plan, introduced in 1991, became decentralisation. New centres in the east, north, north-east and west were planned, each serving up to 800,000 jobs with the objective of bringing jobs closer to homes. In the central location, a new downtown area incorporating hotels, shopping centres, offices and nightlife facilities was created to meet the needs of the expanding service sector.

7.4.4   Urban transformation of Chinese cities

The process of Chinese urban transformation began in 1949 with the establishment of the People's Republic of China. Modelled after the former Soviet Union, China followed a strong central command economy. Central government controlled fiscal power and instituted development policies. During the early phase of economic development, the Chinese government initiated policies of industrialisation focused on heavy industries. Cities became a focal point of industrialisation (Kamal-Chaoui *et al.*, 2009). The government policy during 1958–63 initiated industrial development in rural communities as well. Cities started urbanising at a rapid pace due to increasing demand for labour in urban areas. The government instituted a residency registration (urban and rural) system to control migration from rural to urban areas. The residency registration system, which is still in practice, controls access to employment in state-owned enterprises (SOEs) and urban services for households with rural registration. During the late 1960s, a slowing economy and growing Cold War tensions caused the government to shift its industrialisation programme from vulnerable cities and coastal areas to mountainous western regions (ibid.). In addition, to ease pressure on cities, the government embarked on a programme for relocating urban youth to rural areas by cancelling their urban residency registration. The bias towards rural areas led to the deterioration of urban economies and infrastructure.

In 1978, China embarked on an 'open door policy' and began far-reaching economic reforms. China established four special economic zones (SEZs) in 1980, and later increased their number by adding 15 more in 1984. These zones were open for foreign direct investment and spearheaded a Chinese era of rapid economic growth. By the late 1980s, the 'special economic zones' policy had led to the rapid development of the open coastal cities, triggering a first wave of urban construction and renewed urbanisation (ibid.).

In 1994, the Chinese central command economy started to decentralise. The process involved devolution of fiscal powers to local governments. Recognising that local governments would need new sources to raise revenue, central government allowed leasing of long-term land use rights of state-owned land. Much of this revenue could be retained by municipalities. This became the principal source of off-budget revenues for municipal governments, and led, in many cities, to massive redevelopment of inner-city neighbourhoods, and to new residential and industrial park development in outer urban and suburban areas. During the 1990s there was a huge inflow of foreign investment in manufacturing in many coastal cities, resulting in a real estate boom. The policies of the 1990s have largely driven China's economic growth for almost the last two decades.

As part of the Tenth Five Year Plan, during 2001–5, China squarely placed city and town-based urbanisation as the main policy thrust. An important policy reform was to allow agricultural land to be converted to town construction land.

The town-based industrialisation policy led to massive illegal conversion of agricultural land by some town governments into speculative industrial parks with low levels of service and hence low occupancy rates (Kamal-Chaoui *et al.*, 2009). After toying with various policies towards towns and cities, China has finally recognised the importance of large metropolitan regions for economic development in its Eleventh Five Year Plan (2006–10). Large cities such as Shanghai, Beijing and Chongqing are now implementing development strategies to foster growth of 'strategic' towns into satellite cities with strong connections to their respective metropolitan centres. To control unauthorised land conversions, China has set up an independent body called the Land Supervision Bureau (LSB), with powers to levy stiff punishments for conversion-related irregularities. In addition, municipalities are required to (i) record land leasing revenues and associated expenditures in their formal on-budgets, which are annually reviewed and approved by Municipal People's Congresses; (ii) retain land leasing revenues in a declining reserve for a period of three years; (iii) honour the revenue-sharing arrangement whereby 5–10 per cent of land leasing revenue is sent to the central government (a practice largely ignored for many years); (iv) allocate a portion of their land leasing revenues to land reclamation and protection; and (v) lease all land, including industrial land, through public auction or open tenders (ibid.).

China has evolved a unitary structure of governance, which is a five-tier hierarchical system. Functional responsibilities are delegated from the central to provincial governments (second tier); to a third tier of prefectures and prefecture-level cities; to a fourth tier of districts (only prefecture-level cities are permitted to have district governments), counties, and county-level cities; and to a fifth tier of towns, townships, and neighbourhood committees in cities. All organs of government are required to follow the directions of their higher-level counterparts.

Kamal-Chaoui *et al.* (2009) argue that urbanisation, structural changes under market reforms, and decentralisation over the past two decades are affecting the mandates, structure, and functional responsibilities of municipal governments. Prefecture-level cities are focusing on issues within their own municipal boundaries. Hard budget constraints (including credit limits), growing urbanisation pressures, the erosion of functional responsibilities under the 'city controlling county' system, and intense competition during the last 20 years for both domestic and foreign investment are leading them to define their roles much more narrowly. Their focus has become much more confined to the immediate boundaries of their urban municipality. Hierarchically subordinated cities are still required to obtain approvals from prefecture-level city governments for master plans and major infrastructure works, but these approvals have become routine, as prefecture-level cities do not co-finance these projects. Surrounding townships and towns (not part of urban areas), though not under the jurisdiction of the municipality for provisioning of major public urban services, are interacting more strongly with prefecture-level city urban areas and, in some cases, with county-level city urban areas. This interaction is leading to transition of suburban settlements into contiguous extensions of both prefecture-level city and county-level city urban areas. County-level cities and counties have become much more autonomous, and they are fully responsible for all social and infrastructure services. With the diminishing role of prefecture-level cities, these governments are increasingly dealing directly with provincial governments for policy direction, approvals and financing. Suburban districts are slow to integrate into municipal governments. Urban and infrastructure planning and investment by municipal governments generally focus on urban districts, leaving many suburban areas unserved by municipalities. Mechanisms for interjurisdictional coordination have not kept up with the new and expanding functional responsibilities and expenditure burdens that municipalities are facing. The core issue for local administrations is that the functional responsibilities of subprovincial levels of government have not been clearly allocated.

7.5   Current property market performance

Globalisation has had a significant impact on the urban form and demand for commercial property in Asia-Pacific. In value terms, the estimated size of commercial property markets in Asia-Pacific (covering nine countries; China, Hong Kong, Japan, Malaysia, Singapore, South Korea, Taiwan, Thailand and Australia – not included in this chapter) was around US$4 trillion in 2007, accounting for nearly 20 per cent of global investment. The growth in the size of the commercial property market has been fastest in Asia-Pacific. RREEF (2007a) estimated that by 2011 mature Asia would have grown by around 40 per cent compared with 2006. Within Asia-Pacific there are wide variations in property market development. On the one hand, countries like Japan, Singapore and Hong Kong have well defined and strictly governed property markets; on the other hand are fast-growing economies like China, India and Vietnam, which are closely studying regulatory frameworks in the rest of the region as a guide to establishing their own viable marketplace for international property investors. RREEF (2007a) estimated that by 2011 the size of the commercial property market in emerging Asia would grow by around 160 per cent.

Japan accounts for nearly half of the total commercial property stock in Asia-Pacific. The share of China is around 30 per cent. The size of commercial property stock in Hong Kong, Singapore, Malaysia and Thailand is small and accounts for only 6 per cent of total size. Of the total stock, the estimated invested stock is only US$1.4 trillion, and US$2.2 trillion is investible stock. Table 7.6 presents the estimated levels of investible stock in select Asia-Pacific countries (Chin and Dziewulska, 2006).

Asia-Pacific countries have a low level of invested stock, and a large proportion of commercial property stock is under owner-occupation (Figure 7.2).

China, South Korea, Taiwan, Malaysia and Thailand have a very high owner-occupation rate, above 80 per cent. Reasons for such high owner-occupation have been relatively poor institutional structure (Chin *et al.*, 2006), lack of a developed commercial lending sector, the low rate of participation of institutional investors, and relatively undeveloped indirect property markets (Chin and Dziewulska, 2006).

Table 7.6   Investible commercial property stock in select Asia-Pacific countries by end 2004

Country	Investible stock (US$ billion)	Investible stock as percentage of GDP	Investible stock as percentage of total stock
China	478.57	7%	19.8%
Hong Kong	75.98	39%	94.7%
Japan	1138.38	32%	75.0%
Malaysia	33.44	13%	40.5%
Singapore	48.23	39%	93.6%
South Korea	157.32	25%	51.3%
Taiwan	103.40	18%	45.0%
Thailand	35.00	11%	30.7%

Source: Adapted from Chin and Dziewulska (2006).

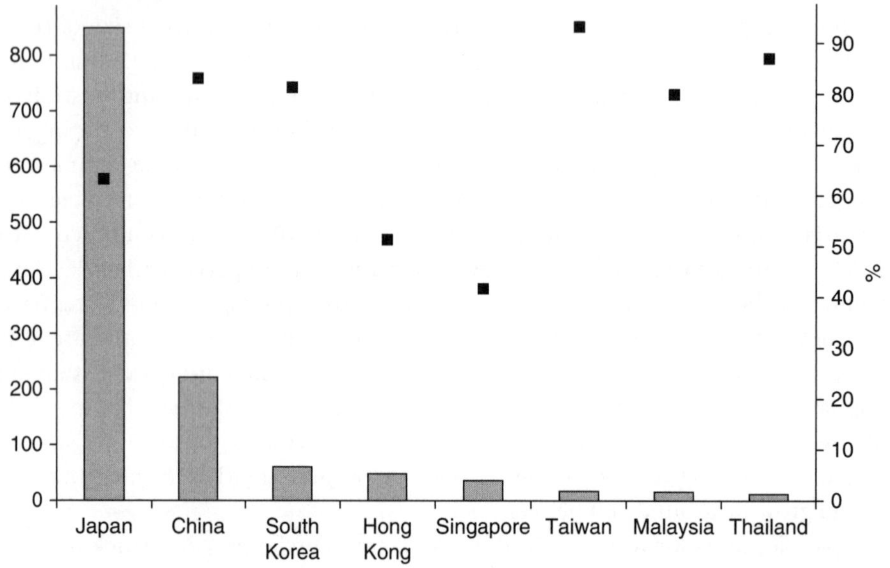

Figure 7.2   Invested stock and implied owner-occupation in select Asia-Pacific countries in 2004

LHS: Invested stock (US$ billion) as bars; RHS: Owner-occupation ratios as points
Source: Adapted from Chin and Dziewulska (2006)

Table 7.7 presents a snapshot of commercial property market indicators in major Asia-Pacific cities.

Asia-Pacific cities have far less property market information availability than European cities (see Table 6.1). The information base of retail and logistics property is far scantier. Hong Kong and Singapore, mature Asia-Pacific markets, have relatively better information than other cities. Japanese markets are outliers, and, for the world's second largest economy, market information, particularly for retail

Table 7.7 Market performance indicators (2008, quarter 1)

	Office				Retail			Logistics		
	Prime rent*	% Rent change p.a.	Prime yield %	Vacancy rate %	Prime rent**	% Rent change p.a.	Prime yield %	Prime rent	% Rent change p.a.	Prime yield %
Tokyo	1,796	13.4	3.2	3.0						
Seoul	595	5.6	5.5	0.0						
Beijing	430	21.2	7.5–9.5	16.5	986	–1.3	6.8–8.8			
Shanghai	456	13.6	7.3–8.9	2.0	2,265	11.6	11.1	113	10.9	9.6
Guangzhou	288	–0.7	7.8–9.4	27.1	948	14.0				
Chengdu	170	18.4	9.5–12	24.9	647	6.2	7.7			
Tianjin	241	11.5	9.7	26.0	635	22.5	8.9	46	4.6	9.5
Macau					1,857	11.7	6.0			
Taipei	300	7.3	4.8	8.4						
Hong Kong	1,796	38.7	4.9–7.4	1.1	1,960	13.5		118	4.3	6.5–7
Singapore	1,370	51.9	5.5–6.1	2.7	3,321	2.5	5.2			
Kuala Lumpur	160	2.4	7.15–7.35	9.3	970	14.7	7–10			
Manila					448	5.8	11–11.5			
Makati	207	18.2	10–10.5	3.5						
Bangkok	199	–2.6	6.6–8.2	14.3	569	2.5	11.4–12.4			
Jakarta	113	6.9	8–8.2	19.7	488	1.0	15–15.5			
Ho Chi Minh City	756	86.0		0.0						
Delhi	939	37.1	11.5	4.9	1,128	12.9	11.0			
Mumbai	898	17.6	11.3	3.8	967	9.1	10.9			
Bangalore	187	17.6	11.0	0.3	551	22.1	11.4			
Chennai	181	8.4	11.0	8.2	245	16.9	11.1			
Hyderabad	185	42.9	10.4	2.0	596	23.3	11.2			
Kolkata	366	42.3	11.2	1.4	934	5.5	11.1			

Notes: Rents in US dollars per square metre per annum.

* Office: refers to net rent except for Tokyo (gross rent), Singapore, Jakarta, Beijing, Chengdu, and Ho Chin Minh City (effective rent), Hong Kong (net effective rent on net floor area), Tianjin, Guangzhou and Shanghai (net rent on gross floor area), Taipei, Mumbai, Chennai, Hyderabad and Kolkata (gross rent on gross floor area).

** Retail: rents are net prime rent except for Beijing and Guangzhou (net effective rent on net lettable area), Chengdu and Tianjin (net rent on gross floor area), Delhi, Mumbai, Bangalore, Chennai, Hyderabad and Kolkata (gross rent).

Source: Adapted from *Jones Lang LaSalle, Asia-Pacific Property Digest*, First Quarter 2008.

and logistics markets, is not easily available. Another observation that could be made here (refer to the note to Table 7.7) is the difference in standards in reporting rent data. Different markets use different standards, which makes comparing data across different markets rather difficult.

Prime office rents display substantial variation across cities. Tokyo, Singapore and Hong Kong have far higher rents than other cities in Asia-Pacific. Indian cities, Delhi and Mumbai, also display high rents, though this does not indicate that market characteristics of Indian cities are similar to those of Hong Kong or Singapore. Hong Kong and Singapore are far more sophisticated and transparent markets. Tokyo, despite displaying the highest rent, is not as transparent as Hong Kong or Singapore. Rents in Indian cities are high due to shortage of space in the market and current economic growth, but again, in terms of market maturity, many of the characteristics of mature markets are absent.

As discussed in Chapter 6, the snapshot information does not suggest that relative rents will continue to be in the same order in the future, as this would depend on market fundamentals which determine demand and supply. The lack of information on retail indicates that investment activity in the retail sector is at a fairly early stage. For example, formal retail activity in India has grown during the last three to four years. Foreign direct investment in retail was permitted in 2005, which has led to the growth of a formal retail sector. Logistics as a sector has seen very little activity in Asia-Pacific, and this sector has started to emerge only recently.

7.6 | Market institutions and characteristics

Based on the market maturity criteria proposed by Keogh and D'Arcy (1994), reviewed earlier in Chapter 6, Asia-Pacific markets are at different stages of maturity. The level and diversity of property market activity depend not only on economic fundamentals but also on market maturity. In economic terms, Japan is the second largest economy in the world, but on the market maturity scale it ranks far lower. Singapore and Hong Kong are perceived as the most mature markets in Asia-Pacific. In a study of five cities (Bangkok, Hong Kong, Kuala Lumpur, Singapore and Taipei), Chin *et al.* (2006), based on a survey of researchers working with property consultancy firms, concluded that Singapore and Hong Kong are perceived as mature markets with a full range of use and investment opportunities, well developed property professional services, market flexibility, availability and standardisation of information, good quality of property products, and stability of development activity. Three other cities studied by them were classified as emergent markets. Bangkok, Kuala Lumpur and Taipei have well regulated and developed property markets, but in terms of market openness, availability and standardisation of market information these markets fall behind Singapore and Hong Kong. Market maturity is not a static feature, but keeps on evolving as institutions evolve. Few studies have studied market maturity according to the criteria suggested by Keogh and D'Arcy (1994), and this limits the discussion

Table 7.8 Movement across transparency index tiers

Country	2006 Tier	2004 Tier	2001 Tier
Hong Kong	1	2	2
Singapore	1	2	2
Malaysia	2	2	3
Japan	2	3	3
Taiwan	3	3	N/A
South Korea	3	3	3
Philippines	3	3	4
Thailand	3	3	3
India	3	4	5
China	4	4	4
Indonesia	4	4	5
Vietnam	5	5	5

Note: 1 – high transparency; 2 – transparent; 3 – semi-transparency; 4: low transparency; 5 – opaque.

Source: Adapted from JLL (2004; 2006).

on progress of markets over time. However, Jones Lang LaSalle has tracked the transparency index for various markets since 1999. There are close correlations between JLL's transparency index and the market maturity criteria of Keogh and D'Arcy (1994), as discussed in Chapter 6, which makes it possible to analyse market maturity over time. Since 2001, many of the Asia-Pacific markets have moved up on the transparency scale, as can be seen from Table 7.8, which reports Jones Lang LaSalle's transparency index.

Table 7.8 indicates that more than half of the Asia-Pacific countries have improved in terms of property market transparency. Many of these countries have adopted global accounting practices, and information is now far more readily available in English. Malaysia, which was a Tier 3 country, has now been classified as a Tier 2 country. Japan has also moved up on the transparency scale, from Tier 3 to Tier 2. India has moved from being classified as a Tier 5 country to Tier 3 during the last five-year period.

7.6.1 Property market institutions in Japan

Japanese property market institutions have been closely tied to the informal rules that exist in the country. In the property use market, there exist two kinds of lease systems (Kawaguchi, 2004). The more typically used is *Futsu-Shakuya*, and most leases are written according to this system. The other is *Teiki-Shakuya*, which was introduced in 2000. *Futsu-Shakuya* specifies a two years' renewable lease agreement and protects the tenant against eviction. However, tenants can break the lease agreement with six months' notice. The rent remains fixed during the lease term but may be reviewed at the time of renewal of contract. If a tenant quits, the landlord is required to pay for the cost of removal. In addition to rent, the tenant also pays a security deposit (*Shiki-kin*) or, in the case of pre-let properties, an advanced guarantee (*Hosho-kin*), which allows landlords of properties under construction to borrow part of the construction cost at 0 per cent interest. Rental incomes (other than for J-REITs) are taxed at normal corporate tax rate. The other type of lease system is *Teiki-Shakuya*, which is very similar to lease agreements in the UK/US. These are fixed duration lease agreements with no option for automatic renewal. Traditionally, most lease contracts were written according to *Futsu-Shakuya*. However, more and more leases are now being written according to *Teiki-Shakuya*.

Another problem for international investors with regard to the Japanese market has been an unclear institutional structure, and this was further complicated by lack of available information about market fundamentals. During periods of economic growth (which lasted until the 1990s), land prices in Japan continued to rise. During periods of high liquidity a huge flow of capital, often with high leverage, went into property. Accounting principles in Japan do not require businesses to mark their assets to market value. This practice made the latent value of assets non-taxable. In an environment where asset prices were always increasing, in order to realise non-taxable latent profits, firms invested in land for speculative purposes, which further fed into the growth in land values. This vicious circle led to an asset price boom in Japan. After the crash in the market during the 1990s, many firms were saddled with huge losses. Banks which had provided loans were left with huge non-performing loans.

Information on property transaction values is not available in Japan. By law, brokers and valuers are not permitted to disclose the actual market value at which a property was transacted. In the absence of this information, it has not been possible to construct a direct property price index. The only price information that is available is a land price index based on the appraised value of 31,000 monitored sites. These sites are assessed by the Ministry of Land every year in January. Local governments assess a further 28,120 monitored sites to interpolate the government official land prices. The official land price serves as a benchmark in general land dealings and also for valuers in their valuations (Kawaguchi, 2004). There are sampling and smoothing problems associated with such a benchmark, and these have distorted the market in Japan.

The improvement in Japan's position on the transparency scale has been due to changes in market practices and better availability of market information, which improved significantly after J-REITs were introduced following amendments to the Investment Trust and Investment Corporation Law in 2000. Following the development of J-REITs, there is now a higher level of international penetration in the market, which is putting pressure on the Japanese market to adopt international practices. This has also boosted the availability of information in English. The Association of Real Estate Securitisation, Japan (ARES), publishes various ARES-JREIT property indexes, which serve as new investment benchmarks.

7.6.2   Property market institutions in Taiwan and Hong Kong

Better disclosure and governance practices and better availability of market information have led to an improvement in transparency in Malaysia, Taiwan and

South Korea. Though there is market information available for indirect property, the direct property market information base is still very weak in these countries.

Until 2002, Taiwan did not allow foreigners to buy property for uses other than their own use. Transparency in Taiwan began to improve with the development of the indirect property market following the enactment of the Real Estate Securitization Act in 2003. The Act paved the way for issuing mortgage-backed securities and for raising REITs funds. Historically, Taiwan has had strained relations with Mainland China, which has consistently insisted that Taiwan is its sovereign part (Li *et al.*, 2000). This severely restricted economic relations with Mainland China. The political risk which existed due to soar relations with Mainland China is also beginning to reduce. With the Presidential Order of 29 October 2003, Taiwanese financial institutions are now permitted, with prior approval from the Ministry of Finance, to establish subsidiaries in Mainland China. Financial institutions from Mainland China would also be permitted to set up establishments in Taiwan. The economic interdependence of Taiwan and Mainland China has increased substantially, and Taiwan is now one of Mainland China's main trading partners. Taiwan suffers from poor transport connectivity with Mainland China and restrictions imposed on Mainland Chinese companies wishing to invest in Taiwan. This has limited the growth of property use markets in Taiwan. In March 2008, Ma Ying-jeou won the presidential election, and earlier Kuomintang (National Party) had won election to the legislative parliament. These political changes are expected to usher in regulatory and legislative reforms that are expected to bolster economic ties with Mainland China, which would certainly benefit property markets in Taiwan.

Another institutional risk faced by investors in Taiwan is the claim from Mainland China that Taiwan is one of its provinces. Some authors (e.g., Li *et al.* 2000) feel that Taiwan will eventually return to Mainland China. The difficulty that arises is in the land tenure system in Taiwan, which is different from that in Mainland China. Taiwan allows private ownership of land, but gains in land value due to 'natural causes and social progress' are taxed. The tax revenue is intended to be used for public works and social welfare projects. There are also constraints such as tenant protection and a form of rent control particularly for farm land, which limits the rent that can be charged to 37.5 per cent of crop harvest. Taiwan also imposed a ceiling of 0.1 ha on the undeveloped land, in an area zoned for planned development, which could be held by an individual in urban areas. Land tenure in Taiwan includes freehold and leasehold. In China the current land tenure system is a state-owned leasehold system which is modelled after the land tenure system in Hong Kong. Gains in value are attributable to those who have been assigned land use rights. These rights are freely tradeable in the market. Hong Kong's state-owned leasehold system is guaranteed to remain in place until 2047 under Basic Law. The land right system adopted by China is similar to that of Hong Kong, suggesting that land tenure in Hong Kong and China could converge. Taiwan has also introduced a land rights system of long leases similar to Hong Kong and Mainland China. This system is called Rights

Above Land (RALs) – different from the traditional leasehold system that existed in Taiwan. Under the leasehold system, leases longer than 20 years were not allowed by RALs. For leases longer than 20 years, flexibility in setting lease term was permitted. However, in the case of RALs, once the agreed term lapses, no renewal is foreseen by the government (Li *et al.*, 2000). The difference in the land tenure system compared with Mainland China or Hong Kong poses a potential risk for investors.

7.6.3 Property market institutions in South Korea

South Korean property market institutions have had a significant influence on the Japanese system. In fact, the cadastral system, land value taxation and land use planning were introduced by Japan when Korea was under Japanese occupation during the early twentieth century. South Korea witnessed substantial increases in land values during the late 1970s and late 1980s. A number of policies to curb speculative investment in land were introduced. These included: a progressive comprehensive landholding tax levied on cumulative value of all land registered nationally under the same owner; a ceiling on the holding of urban residential land per household; and a development charge and land value increment tax levied on undeveloped land owned by firms and excess residential land (Lee, 2000). The negative externality of the land value increment tax was that, to avoid paying this tax, firms and individuals undertook aesthetically blighting construction on the land, causing a shortage of building material and skilled labour (Lee, 2000). The tax was challenged in a court of law, and now the land value increment tax has become unviable in practice. South Korea follows an official land price assessment system which is similar to that in Japan. This price reporting system suffers from a selectivity bias and smoothing, which causes reported prices to be an inaccurate reflection of direct property prices. The Asia-Pacific financial crisis of 1997 affected South Korea severely. The bailout package from the International Monetary Fund required South Korea to undertake a series of structural and institutional reforms. The property market crash that followed the financial crisis led to an oversupply in the market caused by firms who had invested heavily, using debt, in land and property for speculative purposes wanting to offload these assets. Property market institutions in South Korea were too weak to effectively address the crisis. A number of changes to property market institutions were instituted. South Korea permitted foreigners (who had previously been excluded) to buy property, and various exemptions and reductions in transfer income tax were introduced (Lee, 2000). In addition, the urban residential land ceiling regulation and the land value increment tax have been lifted. Policy changes to develop indirect property markets have been undertaken. Mortgage-backed securities (MBSs) and asset-backed securities (ABSs) have been introduced. REITs were introduced in South Korea following the introduction of the Real Estate Investment Trust Act of 2001. With this move, the real estate and financial markets have slowly begun to be integrated. The development of an indirect market has led to better availability of property market information. Strengthening of the legal and regulatory framework has led to an improvement in transparency in South Korea.

7.6.4   Property market institutions in Mainland China

All land in Mainland China was either state-owned or under the collective ownership of village communities. The state retains the right to requisition rural land from rural collectives for public purposes, and it is permitted to transfer the ownership of rural land to the state (Qingshu *el al.*, 2002). Prior to 1980, the government allocated land use rights, mainly to state enterprises, on a no-fee basis. Further transfer of land use rights was not permitted. There was no mechanism for the determination of land values. The economic liberalisation policies that were introduced in China after 1978 required land market reforms, particularly related to land acquisition, property rights assignment from state to private entities, and transfer of land tenure in the market. Chinese property market institutions have been substantially transformed since the 1980s. Before 1980, there was no price mechanism by which property rights could be transferred. With the issuance of Provisional Policy on the Use of Land by Joint Venture Enterprises by the State Council on 26 July 1980, a land use fee system was established. All joint venture companies were required to pay a land use fee. In 1982, the city of Shenzhen, which was granted special status as a Special Economic Zone, became the first city to charge a land use fee based on location. The success of this system in revenue generation led other cities, like Fushun and Guangzhou, also to adopt a land use fee system in 1984. By 1988, a total of 100 cities in Mainland China had adopted a land use-based system (Feng and Yeung, 2004). Later that year, the State Council introduced an ordinance to levy urban land use tax throughout the country, which replaced the land use fee system. Tax rates were set according to the size of the city.

Another important institutional development in China took place in 1987, when a system, similar to that in Hong Kong, which permitted the user to transfer leases to other enterprises or individuals was introduced. Shenzhen Special Economic Zone was the first city to introduce this practice, but it was later adopted by several cities, such as Fuzhou, Haikou, Guangzhou, Shanghai and Tianjin (Feng and Yeung, 2004). In 1988, the Constitutional amendment provided the legal basis for the transfer of land use rights. Later in 1990, the State Council introduced the Provisional Ordinance on the Sale and Transfer of the Tenure of the Urban Land of the People's Republic of China, which prescribed sale, transfer, leasing, mortgage and termination of land use rights (Feng and Yeung, 2004). Shenzhen witnessed the interplay of developers, local government and state-owned enterprises, which formed a coalition in the development of the built environment (Han and Wang, 2003)

Land reforms were complemented by decentralisation policies, particularly to attract foreign direct investment. Cities around the Yangtze and Pearl River Deltas became a hub of economic activity. Han (2000) argues that the opening up of the Pudong area for foreign investment and associated capital flows, and local government initiatives of competition and growth, were important forces that have shaped the urban form of Shanghai and its property market.

The planning system in China, according to China's Urban Planning Act 1989, comprises three levels: master plans, which are usually made for 20 years and guide development of land use and location of major projects; detailed plans, which are made for five years and are for immediate implementation, setting out development codes such as plot size, building height density, etc., and zoning plans, which provide further details to the master plan so that there are enough guidelines to prepare detailed plans (Han and Wang, 2003). An example of these plans is Chongqing's development plan (Han and Wang, 2003), which has all three levels. An important feature of Chongqing's development plans is that these are flexible enough to take into account the interests (often commercial) of various parties.

Development activity in China is carried out by public and private sector companies. Developers are initiators of projects and work in close cooperation (usually partnership, to avoid red tape) with the government. The government is the supplier of land and regulates development process. At local level, city governments compete to attract investments by facilitating development of high-quality commercial buildings. A clean and modern built environment is considered as evidence of government achievement, which is so important for government officials to demonstrate progress to higher administrative levels. State-owned enterprises have land use rights. A large chunk of these use rights is located in central city locations. State-owned enterprises have also participated in the development process to boost their profits, which could subsidise their production costs and staff welfare (Han and Wang, 2003). The relationship with government has been very important, as government has the power to influence the project through various checks which could expedite or delay the project depending on the relationship between developer and government. This generated the potential for corruption and bribery. There have also been incentives not to let informational transparency emerge.

Prior to the 1980s, land was allocated without levying any rent. In land allocation, there was an absence of land value, no time frame was prescribed for land use and no further transaction was allowed (Qingshu *et al.*, 2002). While land users were not required to pay any fee to land owners (the state), land owners had to pay a 'land requisition fee' to rural collectives for requisition of land or a resettlement fee for the use of existing urban land. Acquisition of rural land and associated compensation has caused tensions between farmers and local government (Ding, 2005). Table 7.9 presents the nature of land markets, actors and basis for transaction price in China.

Mechanisms to determine prices for transfer of land use rights in China, particularly during the early stages of development, have been irregular. As documented by Han and Wang (2003) for Chongqing, the transfer of land use rights from government to developers used a negotiable price that was not made public. As the next stage of property market transactions has started to emerge, other price mechanisms based on open market auction or free market transactions have started to take place.

Table 7.9 Land market in China

Type of transaction	Nature of land market	Actors	Subject of transaction	Basis of transaction
Rural land acquisition for administrative allocation to work units	Land ownership by state	State (buyer) Rural collectives (sellers) Work units (users)	Land ownership	Requisition fee
Acquisition of rural land for leasing	Land ownership by state	State (buyer) Rural collectives (sellers)	Land ownership	Requisition fee
Conveyance of land use rights (LURs) by acquisition of rural land	LURs conveyance market	State (seller) Land users (buyer)	LURs	Land price
Conveyance of land use rights (LURs) by acquisition of urban land	LURs conveyance market	State (seller) Land users (buyer)	LURs	Land price
Conveyance of LURs of administratively allocated land on commercial basis	LURs conveyance market	State (seller) Existing land users (seller) New land user (buyer)	LURs	Payment to state and existing land user
Transfer of LURs on commercial basis	Market for transfer of LURs	Land user (seller) Land user (buyer)	Paid LURs	Land price

Source: Adapted from Qingshu *et al.* (2002).

China has strengthened its legal and regulatory framework considerably. The market-based pricing mechanism for land use rights has also evolved and matured over the last two decades. China has instituted effective legal measures for compulsory acquisition processes. With these measures in place and with much more information being available, Chinese property markets have been gaining maturity.

7.6.5 Property market institutions in India

The regulatory regime that governs urban land in India is regarded as restrictive for the growth and development of property markets (Ministry of Finance, 2002). Constitutionally, land is a state subject, and this has complicated the regulations within which land markets operate, as each state has its own set of regulations.

Various land regulations, such as the Urban Land (Ceiling and regulation) Act, Coastal Regulatory Zone (CRZ), Zoning laws – FAR norms and restrictions on development/redevelopment, have all created an environment which is anything but efficient. Pressure to reform land-related legislations has been immense since the process of economic liberalisation intensified in 1991. However, the progress has been slow and long drawn out. For example, the Urban Land (Ceiling and Regulation) Act was repealed by the Central Government in 1999. However, since land is a state subject, each state had to adopt the repeal Act. Even after seven years, some states, such as Maharashtra, Karnataka, MP, Rajasthan, Andhra Pradesh, Assam, Bihar, Orissa and West Bengal have not adopted the repeal Act (Ministry of Finance, 2002).

Besides formal rules (codified as Acts and Laws), traditions and customs play an important role in Indian property markets. During the last decade the informal rules that governed property markets for a long time have also undergone substantial changes. Traditionally the development industry was dominated by family-run and local players; however, in recent years a number of pan-Indian construction and development companies have grown (JLL, 2006). Increasing exposure to global capital markets is encouraging increasing transparency and professionalism in the developer community. A number of developers are seeking public listing, which is a strong divergence from the past, and will further improve transparency (ibid.).

Another tradition that is undergoing transformation is the mode of pricing for sale of properties. Commercial and residential premises in India are measured on three bases: carpet area (the total internal area of the premises measured from internal walls); built-up area (the total area of the premises measured from exterior perimeter wall surfaces, incorporating an allocation of common areas on the same floor, excluding lift core and fire stairs, usually 20–25 per cent larger than the carpet area); and super built-up area (incorporating the built-up area and a proportional allocation of common areas, including stairs, lift cores, ground floor lobby, caretaker's office, etc., usually 35–50 per cent over the carpet area). The convention is for all premises to be sold relative to their built-up area. However, capital values during the 1980s had risen so much that some developers were equating saleable/lettable area in super built-up terms to reduce the effective price per square foot. Variability in the ratio of the carpet area to the super built-up area was huge, making the actual carpet area opaque at the time of sale for properties under construction. The last few years have increased the transparency in property markets, and some developers have started quoting the prices on the basis of actual carpet area.

Property market transparency in India has also improved substantially over the last few years. Economic growth has attracted many international property consultants, which has significantly improved the availability of information. Regulatory developments such as permitting FDI in retail and other sectors, a regulatory framework for REITs (named real estate mutual funds) and mortgage-backed securities, and a legal framework for foreclosure of properties have helped in improving market maturity in India. Despite this progress, India lacks a direct property market index that could be used for benchmarking investment.

Vietnam has been at the lower end of the transparency scale, mainly due to weak property rights and a lack of availability of market information.

With the growth of REITs in Asia-Pacific, the transparency in various markets has improved. Japanese and South Korean property markets have benefited substantially from the introduction and growth of REITs. The information disclosure requirement associated with REITs has led to improvement in transparency in these countries. Japan has emerged as the largest REIT market in Asia-Pacific, with market capitalisation of US$31 billion in 2006. Singapore and Hong Kong have established strong legislation for REITs and are now hubs of local and cross-border REIT listings (So *et al.*, 2005).

7.7 International property investment in Asia-Pacific

Market maturity does not fully explain the flow of cross-border investment in the Asia-Pacific property market. There are other factors, such as economy and regulations, which attract cross-border investment. Property markets in the highly transparent markets of Asia-Pacific – Hong Kong and Singapore – are very small compared with other markets in the region, thereby limiting the scope for investment. The relatively less transparent markets of Japan and China together account for nearly 80 per cent of investible commercial property stock in value terms. Economic growth in China and increasing transparency have led to increased cross-border capital flows. In 2005, nearly 64 per cent of all investment grade properties in China were invested by foreign interests (JLL, 2006, Real Estate Transparency Index). Property market institutions in Japan, Malaysia, Thailand, South Korea and the Philippines have all become more transparent in recent years. Since the financial crisis of 1997, these markets have become far more open to international investors, and this has substantially improved transparency. The restructuring of the financial sector that happened in Japan after the crash of the bubble economy after the late 1990s required more transparency in property markets. Establishment of J-REITs has been a catalyst for improved transparency in Japanese markets. China, India and Indonesia are also moving towards greater openness and more transparency. Cross-border investment in direct and indirect property markets in Asia-Pacific, particularly in Japan and China, has increased substantially. In 2005, cross-border investment in Asia-Pacific was US$67.5 billion in direct property, and US$19.7 billion in indirect property. Half of the capital flow was destined for Japan and China. India, which has substantially improved in transparency, saw relatively small cross-border capital flows, due mainly to restrictions on foreign ownership of property, rather than to any lack of investor interest.

7.8 Conclusions

The analysis of the Asia-Pacific economic, institutional and property market presented in this chapter indicates that the region has significantly transformed, economically and institutionally. The region adopted an export-led economic growth strategy and has sustained high economic growth for almost six decades with few periods of difficulties. At national level, countries within Asia-Pacific have adopted a very different framework towards foreign investment. While Singapore and Malaysia preferred equity for domestic capital investment, South Korea and Thailand depended on foreign borrowings. Since the 1990s, these countries have liberalised regulation of foreign ownership, and this has led to huge inflows of foreign portfolio investment in this region. Despite institutional differences, there has been economic interdependence among nations in the region. The region has seen the emergence of a manufacturing belt over the last four decades, starting with Japan and followed by NIEs, the ASEAN 5 nations and China. With economic globalisation, cities in Asia-Pacific also started to internationalise, but the nature of internationalisation was substantially different in Tokyo, Singapore and Hong Kong. Tokyo became a hub of TNCs from Japan, but Singapore and Hong Kong became international gateways to investment in Asia-Pacific.

Economic development and internationalisation have had a profound impact on planning and other city administrative institutions. The region is witnessing significant changes as the market matures and becomes more institutional. These cities have become far more open to foreign investment in property markets. The size of institutional investment in commercial property is small, and a large proportion of properties are still under owner-occupation. Much of the institutional investment has been in Japan, where structures (such as J-REITs, etc.) for investment in stabilised commercial properties have evolved over the last 15–20 years. Hong Kong and Singapore have also developed structures for institutional investment in commercial properties. Other countries in the region have seen huge investment in the development sector, but are affected by relatively low market maturity. In countries like China and India, the pace of economic growth offers phenomenal opportunities for property investment by international investors. However, there is low liquidity and limited availability of market information, which limits the potential. With increasing liquidity, these markets are becoming more and more transparent, offering opportunities of investment.

The nature of economic growth in Asia-Pacific is also changing from 'export and investment-led' to 'consumer-driven', and this will have implications for property markets. The region has the potential for larger internationalisation of property markets, but problems related to information and liquidity of the market remain.

Real Estate Markets in North America

8.1   Introduction

The United States of America has the largest real estate market in the world. It accounted for just over half the value of total world transactions in 2007. While the Canadian market is significantly smaller, it had the eighth highest transactions value. These markets are also regarded as highly transparent mature real estate markets. They comprise many individual city markets spread over a substantial geographic area. These cities display a wide variety of rental levels, vacancy rates, and mix of occupiers. They also vary in terms of both absolute and relative size of the different sectors that comprise the commercial real estate market.

In comparison to other real estate markets across the world, the US has more data available than any other market and for a much longer time period. More research has been undertaken to examine the US real estate market than in any other country, enabled by the availability of data and market information. Major academic journals provide coverage of residential and commercial real estate occupation, investment and development sectors. Market analysis is advanced and provided by real estate service providers, among others, for all major centres across the US and Canada.

In this chapter we examine the US and Canadian real estate markets. As the legal and institutional framework already clearly establishes private property rights and creates the basis for an investment market by defining occupation and use rights and permitting flexible leases, we do not consider the North American markets in the same way as we examined transitional or emergent markets. In 2006, JLL, listing countries by level of transparency, placed the US and Canada in the highest tier, having the joint first (with Australia) and fourth most transparent property markets in the world, respectively.

The US also has a wide variety of mechanisms permitting investment into real estate assets. These aspects add to its maturity and flexibility. However, as in other markets, this does not imply an absence of market volatility. The relative ease of access to capital and financing has to some extent encouraged development. In addition, land supply is high in comparison to many other locations (in Europe for example), and planning less restrictive. These factors further encourage development, and there can be significant booms followed by 'busts' with high excess supply of real estate.

In this chapter we examine investment into the real estate market in North America. We consider the evolution of real estate investment vehicles. Also, we provide an overview of the commercial property markets across the continent, commenting on key differences in rental values, vacancy rates and occupier base, and consider whether or not global economic integration has implications for portfolio diversification across the US and other countries.

8.2 Investors and investment mechanisms in North American real estate

Fifty years ago, the US commercial real estate market was essentially local in nature. Local demand for space drove the development sector. Developers responded by forming partnerships with investors who provided equity for the projects, and local banks were the providers of debt finance. The value added by local occupiers essentially determined the rents that could be obtained from the properties. Types of occupiers varied across location, as did their value added. Hence there arose the development of the mix of commercial real estate and the spatial variation in rents.

The real estate market was not at this stage strongly linked to the financial markets, and means of investing in real estate were limited. As more sources of finance have been found, the nature of the market itself has changed, being more closely linked into exogenous national and international factors.

Eppli and Tu (2004) suggest that '[the] real estate capital markets in the US are most often described using a "four quadrants" approach: private debt, private equity, public debt, and public equity. The primary difference between public and private sources of real estate capital is whether the capital source is publicly traded' (p. 220). Private debt sources include life assurance companies and banks (if the mortgage debt is not publicly traded). Private equity sources include pension funds and limited partnerships. Public debt and equity sources are raised in public auctions; for instance, stock and bond markets in New York play a significant role. One of the more recent developments is the CMBS products. These provide fixed incomes and are pooled mortgage products. These pooled loans diversify property and market-specific risks. The pooled product is divided into 'tranches', each having a credit rating. Of the total institutional investment in US real estate, just over 60 per cent is combined private and public debt.

The range of methods available to permit investment in real estate resulted in capital chasing the best risk-adjusted return in the years immediately after the millennium. This could be interpreted as 'too much money chasing too few goods', and hence should indicate potential asset price inflation above fundamentals.

US pension funds began to take an interest in property in the 1970s, when stock was falling and government debt provided a negative real return. Real estate proved to be a hedge against inflation, which was significant during this period. The National Council of Real Estate Investment Fiduciaries (NCREIF) was established, and its real estate index came to be seen as the investment performance benchmark.

Pension funds and savings and loans (S&Ls) companies acted as major sources of development finance. Excess supply resulted, and the 'bust' phase of the early 1990s (similar to those experienced elsewhere) saw many financial intermediaries declare bankruptcy. Thus it could be argued that there were institutional aspects to what might have been regarded as 'over-investment' in real estate. For the companies lending to real estate, though, the bust of the early 1990s would have been the first they would have experienced in this market.

The failed S&Ls were taken over by a government body called the Resolution Trust Corporation (RTC). It liquidated the assets of the S&Ls; however, this took time. It was new opportunity funds that made the difference. These firms had to be able to price indirect investment assets. '[The] Wall Street houses were well suited to [this]. Structuring their investment vehicles as highly leveraged closed-end limited partnerships, the opportunity funds had a simple investment strategy: buy as much as they could, leverage it ..., and wait for the markets to recover' (Winograd, 2004, p. 205).

Two other sources for investment funds in real estate are also important in the US context: debt finance via Commercial Mortgage-Backed Securities (CMBS), and equity via Real Estate Investment Trusts (REITs). REITs first appeared in the US in 1960, and mortgage REITs were established in the 1970s. However, poor performance left them with a small share of the market by the early 1990s.

Umbrella Partnership REITs (UPREITs) saw changes to the attractiveness of REITs. UPREITs admitted 'a REIT into existing real estate partnerships as a partner and then [sold] REIT shares to the public to raise capital to recapitalise the partnership' (op. cit., p. 207). The consequence of this structure was a rise in the capitalisation of REITs from US$6 billion in 1990 to US$128 billion in 1997 (EPRA, 2004).

CMBSs also saw substantial growth from the mid 1990s. CMBSs overcame problems associated with 'the complexities of servicing a mortgage, the lack of a secondary market, the problems of measuring risk of default without employing a sophisticated and large real estate organisation, and the uncertainties of cash flows that resulted from ... these problems' (ibid., p. 209).

During the 1990s, transparency improved with the availability of new information, as REITs made public disclosures and rating agencies analysed their creditworthiness. Information on default rates also affected investment decision-making. Liquidity problems in 1998 brought some form of market discipline in the removal of more high-risk loans.

The growth of REITs has made real estate investment more similar to investing through the general stock market, while the growth of CMBS increased the exposure to debt. The new sources of finance enabled lending to the industry but highlighted the importance of exogenous factors. Problems in the capital market outside the real estate sector could now more greatly affect the industry in the absence of any imbalance in property markets themselves. Real estate was now more closely integrated into general (and increasingly global) financial markets. Recent difficulties show how significant this integration can be. However, the changes to sources of finance for real estate and the requirements of the investment market have resulted in greater market transparency. More market information is now available, market reports proliferate, and consequently there should be greater awareness and appreciation of market risk, although recent events in risk pricing following on from the sub-prime mortgage default crisis might lead independent observers to conclude otherwise.

8.3   Real estate investment trusts (REITs) and mutual fund trusts (MFTs)

In the US, Congress created REITs in 1960. Its objective was to make investments in high unit value, income-producing real estate feasible for smaller investors. The method of investment would be via the purchase of shares, as with other standard investments. 'The way shareholders benefit by owning stocks of other corporations, the stockholders of a REIT earn in the same way a pro rata share of the economic benefits that are derived from the production of income through commercial real estate ownership' (EPRA, 2004, p. 45). REITs overcame the problem of limited diversification when owning one property. They provided the investor with the ability to avoid the high unit cost of real estate, while the purchase of lower unit cost shares permitted the investor to diversify his or her portfolio across a wider range of assets than would have been possible previously.

There are legal requirements with which US REITs must comply. The key requirements are:

1. They must pay at least 90 per cent of their taxable income to shareholders;
2. Most of their assets must be real estate-related (including investments in mortgage loans);
3. They must derive most of their income from real estate held for the long term; and
4. They must be widely held.

If these requirements are met, the REIT benefits 'from a dividends paid deduction so that most, if not all, of a REIT's income is taxed only at the shareholder level. On the other hand, REITs are limited in the earnings they may retain to meet their business needs. As a result, much of the capital for growth and property maintenance and betterment must come from new money raised in the investment marketplace from investors who have confidence in the REIT's future prospects and business plan (op. cit., p. 45).

In Canada, REITs did not come into existence until 1994 and the term 'REIT' does not exist. Canadian REITs qualify as 'mutual fund trusts' ('MFTs') under the Canadian Income Tax Act (ITA), which has comprehensive and detailed rules. 'An MFT provides for a flow through of income and capital gains and, in addition, has many tax benefits necessary for a publicly traded vehicle which are not available to trusts that do not qualify as MFTs. A MFT must qualify as a "unit trust" under the ITA. A unit trust is an *inter vivos* trust (being a trust other than a testamentary trust) in which the interests of each beneficiary is described by units and either (i) 95 per cent of the units are redeemable at the demand of the holder (an "open-end trust") or (ii) the trust complies with numerous conditions regarding its investments and income (a "closed-end trust"), as noted below' (ibid., p. 45).

Although REITs could exist as MFTs before 1994, they had to exist as open-ended trusts, and this was unattractive to investors due to a shortage of liquidity needed to pay for redemptions when there was a high value of redemptions at any one time. Legislative changes in 1994 relating to closed-end trusts made REITs much more attractive as investment vehicles. The MFT has subsequently become the most attractive public investment vehicle for real estate investment in Canada.

In the US, REITs must have at least 100 shareholders. In relation to the spread of share ownership, no more than 50 per cent of shares can be held by five or fewer investors. In Canada, an MFT must have at least 150 unit holders. There is a minimum requirement to hold one 'block of units' valued at no less than CA$500. Units are also required to be listed on the appropriate stock exchange. Mandatory listing is not required in the US. Various restrictions are also placed on the activities of REITs.

In the US, REITs must hold at least 75 per cent of their assets in real estate, government securities and cash. They must earn at least 75 per cent of their gross income from rents on real estate assets or from interest payments from real estate mortgages. At least 95 per cent of gross income must be earned from these sources plus mortgage interest and dividends (see EPRA, 2004, p. 47). It must distribute at least 90 per cent of its taxable income. In Canada, the trust must invest its funds in property. It can own, manage, and lease property and it pays out all income in each tax year to the unit holders, although this is not required by the ITA.

In the US, REITs (public equity) accounted for US$173 billion of investment in real estate, private debt accounted for US$1.3 trillion, public debt US$534 billion, and private equity US$735 billion in 2002.

8.3.1   Evolution of investment sources for US real estate

Borrowers in the US have a wide range of sources of capital to draw upon. Above we have briefly mentioned the sources of public and private debt finance available for real estate. Over time their relative contribution to funds has varied. Public debt played only a minor role in the 1980s, with significant inflows of funds from private debt. Between 1984 and 1988, over US$80 billion per annum of private debt flowed into the real estate market (and in 1987 alone US$100 billion), resulting in new development and general excess supply. Over-building was characteristic of most US cities. By the early 1990s, however, private debt showed an outflow of over US$150 billion, reversing the picture from the previous period. Inflows of private debt resumed by the mid-1990s as the economy improved and space absorption increased. The impact and significance of public debt sources can be seen in the 1990s, particularly from the mid-1990s. Of these, the most important, as mentioned above, has been the CMBS. Since the late 1990s, the value of CMBS to real estate has averaged US$47 billion per annum.

Private equity markets display patterns of real estate investment somewhat similar to the private debt markets. They were active in the 1980s, although not on the same scale, and came out of real estate during the recession of the early 1990s. Their role after the mid-1990s is significantly less than the private debt market. Public equity (like public debt) has become more significant since the early 1990s recession. This is due to the behaviour of REITs, 91 per cent of whose investments are in commercial real estate equity.

In contrast to the volatility in investment volumes into real estate, yields have remained relatively stable. Data are available on US capitalisation rates (initial yields) from 1965, and the long-run average value lies between 9 and 11 per cent. The boom/bust of the late 1980s and early 1990s does cause cyclical variation in yields, and more recently they moved below their lower long-term average value as capital chased the best risk-adjusted return. This part may have caused risk spreads on CMBS to fall relative to corporate debt spreads, and is consistent with the weight-of-money argument used by market agents to explain yield convergence in recent years. Falling default rates were also seen as part of this explanation. However, recent problems with a shortage of liquidity have seen yields increase and defaults rise.

Table 8.1 above shows the breakdown of REIT values across property sectors and also across different categories of REITS. Equity REITs are clearly the most significant, having approximately 20 times the value of mortgage REITs. Also evident from the table is the total return performance in the year following August 2007. Hybrid REITs have performed extremely poorly, followed by significantly negative total return performances of both home and commercial mortgage REITs.

Total return volatility is indicated in Figure 8.1 below. All of the commercial real estate sectors exhibit similar degrees of unconditional volatility, with industrial somewhat less than offices and retail. Changes in retail returns also seem to lag behind the other sectors between 1999 and 2002. All sectors show a distinct fall to zero or negative total returns in 2007. The relatively high transparency in the US real estate market has, therefore, been able to reduce volatility in return performance, although whether returns would have been even more volatile without the current level of market information is unclear, so the impact of market transparency remains an unanswered question.

Table 8.1 REIT values by sector and subsector

| Property sector/subsector | Investment performance by property sector and subsector[*] (Percent change, except where noted. All data as of August 31, 2008) | | | | | | |
| | Total return | | | Dividend yield[**] | Number of REITs | Equity market capitalization[***] | Implied market capitalization[3] |
	2007	August	Year to date				
FTSE NAREIT Equity REIT Index	−15.69	2.21	1.96	5.04	108	288,206,770	312,929,234
Industrial/Office	−14.86	−0.04	−4.66	5.04	25	66,969,557	73,069,711
Industrial	0.38	−9.26	−25.05	5.46	6	19,562,481	20,414,367
Office	−18.96	4.76	6.40	4.43	14	38,869,816	42,541,148
Mixed	−33.09	2.95	14.03	6.87	5	8,537,261	10,114,196
Retail	−15.77	4.07	−2.82	5.19	26	76,832,022	87,980,019
Shopping Centers	−17.68	5.06	0.37	5.09	14	31,989,137	33,073,692
Regional Malls	−15.85	3.13	−5.54	5.17	7	37,926,504	47,971,808
Free Standing	−0.43	4.88	−0.48	5.87	5	6,916,381	6,934,519
Residential	−25.21	−1.22	14.57	4.82	18	42,324,003	45,534,525
Apartments	−25.43	−1.53	14.96	4.83	14	40,494,660	43,350,864
Manufactured Homes	−19.34	6.35	5.99	4.44	4	1,829,343	2,183,661
Diversified	−22.29	5.40	15.07	4.34	8	20,647,342	22,882,459
Lodging/Resorts	−22.37	8.48	−21.73	8.75	10	14,430,907	14,913,494
Health Care	2.13	0.91	10.03	5.34	11	29,898,139	30,418,496
Self Storage	−24.82	7.04	20.51	3.26	4	17,921,297	18,085,699
Specialty	14.56	1.87	9.30	3.80	6	19,183,505	20,044,830
FTSE NAREIT Hybrid REIT Index	−34.77	−13.09	−59.09	32.88	4	2,089,599	2,089,599
FTSE NAREIT Mortgage REIT Index	−42.35	−1.89	−28.77	15.86	22	14,915,118	14,915,118
Home Financing	−38.23	−0.36	−26.46	14.63	10	11,886,881	11,886,881
Commercial Financing	−48.79	−7.77	−36.46	20.96	12	3,028,237	3,028,237

Notes: [*]Data represent the constituents of the FTSE NAREIT Composite REIT Index.
[**]Dividend yield quoted in percent and for month end.
[***]Equity market capitalization and implied market capitalization in thousands of dollars.
Source: FTSE® Group and National Association of Real Estate Investments Trusts®.

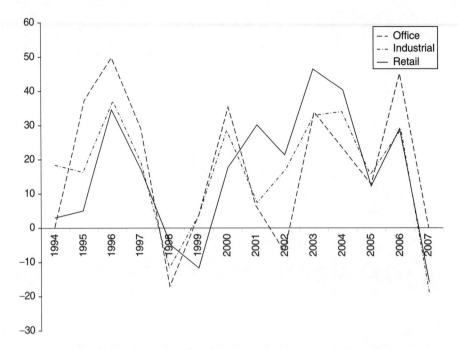

Figure 8.1 Annual nominal percentage change in total returns on US real estate
Source: National Association of Real Estate Investment Trusts.

8.4   Trends in North American real estate markets

In this section we examine some recent trends in US and Canadian markets. These markets have been particularly exposed to the recent liquidity problems and the sub-prime mortgage crisis originating in the US. Although this by itself does not necessarily mean that the real estate sector will perform worse in the US than elsewhere, exposure to debt financing has been more significant than in other parts of the world.

The most recent available data for 2008 suggests that markets in Canada are performing better than most markets in the US. Compared with US cities, the main Canadian office markets display higher rents and lower vacancy rates. However, since Canada depends upon US demand for most of its exports, expectations for future trends in Canadian real estate will have to take into consideration the expected performance of the US economy.

Canada, the US, and Mexico form the North American Free Trade Area (NAFTA); however, Mexico is listed by JLL in transparency tier 3. In some senses, NAFTA is a combination of Mexico on the one hand, and the US and Canada on the other. Mexico has benefited, as manufacturing has moved to the country, leaving higher-cost areas. Canada and the US are heavily service sector-oriented. More recently Canada has experienced significant growth in natural resource-based industries, particularly oil exploration.

At the time of writing, the US economy faces a turning point. Economic growth has slowed, and the shortage of liquidity has led to the failure of large financial institutions, most notably Lehman Brothers. Insurers are also under scrutiny, and the US government has been forced to underwrite both Fannie Mae and Freddie Mac, which had exposure to over US$5 trillion of US mortgage debt. There is slower consumer expenditure, and this has been affecting the retail sector.

8.4.1   North American office markets

The years since 2000 have witnessed a cyclical pattern in space absorption and vacancy rates. In 2000, vacancy rates were below 5 per cent, and for many markets were below their long-run average values. However, by 2001, they had risen sharply to approximately 15 per cent nationally, peaking at around 17.5 per cent in 2003. As the market improved, vacancy rates fell to 13 per cent in 2007, but by the first quarter of 2008 they showed signs of an increase as the market weakened following on from the shortage of liquidity, a weaker user and investment market, and a slowing down of the growth in absorption.

The events of 9/11 and the dot.com bubble contributed to a reduction in space absorption in the period from 2001 to 2002, with a small rise in absorption in 2003. 2004 to the first quarter of 2008 saw increased absorption from office occupiers, but this now seems to have halted. New job creation has decreased significantly, which implies lower demand for space.

The market in the US, and elsewhere, can be seen to be at a turning point in the economic cycle between 2007 and 2008. The initial restriction in credit has only begun to have an impact on growth. Financial markets remain highly volatile, being affected by uncertainty regarding the future direction of the economy and the impact that bad debt will have. Commodity price fluctuations have been substantial, as investors have moved funds from the financial sector into other areas that would seem to provide a better risk-adjusted return. Between 2007 and 2008 oil prices rose by over 60 per cent, and more recently have fallen by around 50 per cent. Thus it is extremely difficult to predict what the pattern will be over the next 12 months, since prices seem to have diverged from fundamentals.

This type of uncertainty, and the associated rising food and energy costs, is having an adverse impact on consumer sentiment and expenditure, which in turn is adversely affecting demand for services, feeding through into weaker demand for office space. This is in sharp contrast to the first half of 2007, which saw rental increases of over 20 per cent in New York, San Francisco and Seattle on the coasts, plus Austin and Houston in Texas. New York midtown remained the most expensive office location; New York downtown was the third most expensive, just behind Calgary. Of other Canadian cities, Toronto and Vancouver were also within the top ten most expensive office locations, along with San Francisco, Washington DC, Boston, and New York midtown south.

Of the mid-western markets, Chicago is the most expensive, although it still has higher rental values than Los Angeles or San Diego on the West coast. However,

Los Angeles has the second most expensive suburban markets after San Mateo, south of San Francisco.

Vacancy rates have also reached a turning point in many markets. At any one time the variability of vacancy rates is significant. While recent statistics show that the most expensive office market is just over six times dearer than the least expensive market,[1] the highest office vacancy rate is almost 20 times that of the market with the lowest vacancy rate.[2]

In the fourth quarter of 2007, the lowest central business district vacancy rates were found in the Canadian cities of Calgary (1.5 per cent), Vancouver (2.7 per cent) and Edmonton (4.1 per cent). In the US, the lowest office vacancy rate was also found in the most expensive market, New York (4.5 per cent). Toronto has the fifth lowest vacancy rate, at 4.6 per cent. It also has the fifth highest rent. The mix of occupiers varies significantly across these cities, as does their value added and rent levels achieved. It may also be difficult to judge long-term trends in vacancy rates from such snapshot statistics. This becomes more problematic since the macroeconomy is at a turning point in the economic cycle during this time period. Changes in prices for natural resources, particularly oil, will affect cities such as Calgary and Edmonton. This will be less relevant to Toronto, while New York faces physical supply constraints and still remains a key world financial hub location.

The rent and vacancy rate data reflect the underlying demand and supply conditions within each market. The locations with higher added value have the lowest vacancy rates and highest rents (such as New York), while those with lower rents and higher vacancy rates have lower added value and may suffer from problems relating to declining industrial structures (such as Detroit). In contrast to some European countries, policies to regenerate declining areas or regions are either absent or work differently (they may not have a specific property focus). Hence, while places such as Detroit and other mid-western locations are less expensive, they still find it difficult to attract new industries, which have tended to cluster on the coasts, where employees may prefer to live and where they may have a (real or perceived) improvement to their quality of life. Thus, for example, Microsoft has its headquarters in Seattle, a more expensive location with a lower vacancy rate than Detroit.

The most recent statistics for Canadian office markets in the first quarter of 2008 suggest a weakening of suburban markets as the economy slows. Office absorption has shown a decline from 2007, although Calgary showed an increase. Ottawa and Halifax have shown negative absorption through the first quarter of 2008. Thus again there is experience of markets reaching a turning point in Canada. Since the overwhelming majority of Canadian exports go to the US, changes in the behaviour of the US economy will be expected to have a significant impact on Canadian economic performance and office markets.

8.4.2 North American industrial markets

Industrial markets in the US displayed cyclical variation in absorption between 2000 and 2008. 2001 saw negative absorption and 2002 saw only small increases in absorbed space. Absorption rose significantly between 2003 and 2005. Whilst it has fallen from its 2005 peak of close to 175 million square feet, it was still over 100 million square feet by early 2008. Vacancy rates have remained just below 8 per cent for most of this time period, suggesting that the development sector is responding well to market signals and meeting occupier needs. Key seaports and distribution hubs have seen a significant proportion of new development activity. These include locations from Los Angeles to Dallas/Fort Worth, Houston, Atlanta, Chicago, and the east of Pennsylvania. Rents in warehousing/distribution ranged from over US$11 per square foot in Orange County, California, to under US$3 per square foot in Columbus, Ohio. In Canada, Calgary, Edmonton, and Vancouver had higher than average rents, around $6.50 to $7 per square foot.

As a significant proportion of industrial units are for warehousing, one of the key demand drivers for space in the market will relate to consumer expenditure. This key variable will be under pressure as real disposable incomes are reduced due to rising commodity prices and a more insecure jobs market. As exogenous drivers of the market weaken, absorption may be expected to fall. Negative absorption therefore remains a distinct possibility.

8.4.3   North American retail markets

Growth in retail consumers' expenditure slowed from over 8 per cent per annum in 2006 to almost zero growth per annum by the end of 2007. The retail market has seen declining leasing activity, and those retail sectors most closely related to housing, such as furniture and household electrical goods, have experienced more difficult trading conditions. Some commentators have taken comfort from the recent reductions in interest rates and the fact that most of the rest of the world economy is still growing and that corporate debt levels are low, suggesting fewer redundancies. This is expected to cushion the market and obviate a crash. However, the US economy, which has tended to import from the rest of the world, runs a significant balance of payments deficit. This suggests that the US slowdown may lead to slower growth elsewhere, reducing world demand for US exports. Falls in asset wealth in the US and elsewhere may also reduce consumers' expenditure due to negative wealth effects. At the time of writing, it remains to be seen how the balance of opposing forces resolves.

As with office and industrial rents, there is significant variation across the US and Canada. Retail rents are highest in New York, followed by San Francisco. Toronto is also among the top five highest retail rent locations. Retail also displays very high rents in prime streets. In New York, for example, the highest retail rents of US$1,250 per square foot occur on 5th Avenue between 48th and 59th streets. Rodeo Drive in Los Angeles, the second most expensive street, has rents of US$600 per square foot.

In Canada, Alberta has the highest retail spend per head of population. Significant increases in retail expenditure have been experienced in recent years due to the growth of the state's resource-based economy. While eastern Canada and Ontario, in particular, may enter recession, Alberta's economy remains strong with low unemployment, below the Canadian average. High oil prices continue to make oil extraction profitable. This further underlines the importance of considering the exogenous drivers of local real estate markets.

8.5 | Real estate markets and the macroeconomy

One of the interesting features that arise from comparing US and Canadian real estate markets is that Canadian markets tend to have relatively low vacancy rates in comparison to markets in the US. Where vacancy rates are similar, the US locations seem to produce higher added value. This difference could be due to a number of reasons. Planning policy may place a larger restriction on supply in Canadian cities. Hence absorption of space is high relative to new supply. Further investigation of the institutional differences between the two countries will be necessary to shed further light on this apparent anomaly.

The macroeconomy continues to strongly affect the behaviour of the real estate market across the different sectors and across both nations. However, local economic factors are still important. The strength of the natural resource market is having a clear positive impact on Edmonton and Calgary, and also, perhaps to a lesser extent, Vancouver. This has enabled real estate markets in these locations to be somewhat insulated from turbulence in financial markets, which has more strongly affected economies less reliant on oil and other natural resources.

However it is also clear that office, retail, and industrial markets are coming to, or have reached, a turning point just as the macroeconomy has reached the same point. While this is not unusual, there is increased uncertainty about the future direction of both the US and the Canadian economies. Both inflationary and recessionary pressures are being felt concurrently. In addition there is the impact of the liquidity shortage, originally linked to the sub-prime residential mortgage debt that is leading to market uncertainty and increased costs for borrowers, making this period similar in some ways to the late 1920s, which preceded the prolonged depression of the 1930s.

Given the degree of integration of international financial systems, many countries have become exposed to problems created by the liquidity shortage. However, market integration and the forces of globalisation may reduce the opportunities for portfolio diversification across countries. Global economic convergence may not have occurred, but it is possible that cities with similar economic structures in different parts of the world have more synchronous cycles than other locations. For example, New York and London may behave similarly, since they are both world leading centres for international finance. Jackson *et al.* (2008) suggest that there are linkages between total returns in the two markets but not between rental series. They argue that this could be because 'links may be originating in the capital market through investor behaviour and, in particular, due to the fact that New York and London are two of the largest and most liquid international markets' (op. cit., pp. 90–1). They also suggest that more general economic forces could also contribute to similarities between the cities. Thus New York may be more different from Chicago and San Francisco than it is from London. This further implies that within-country diversification opportunities may be greater than those between countries, at least for certain types of real estate investment. The scale of the real estate industry in the US, and the varied economic structures affecting local markets across the country, also enable within-country diversification to take place.

8.6 Conclusions

Both the US and Canada are highly transparent real estate markets. They are mature in the sense that they provide a wide range of user and investor opportunities, have significant market information and are open to investors globally. They thus score highly on the market maturity characteristics as outlined by Keogh and D'Arcy (1994) and the characteristics of transparency as listed by JLL. Some authors have suggested that the increased market information and strengthened links with the capital market might make real estate markets less volatile. The allocative efficiency of the market should thus be improved.

However, there is no clear indication that this might be the case. Thus far the volatility of the late 1980s and early 1990s has been avoided, since exogenous factors affecting real estate have themselves been less volatile. But the market is at a turning point in 2008, and it remains to be seen whether a full recession can be avoided. Recession would place significant downward pressure on rents, capital values, and returns. Internally, variables endogenous to the real estate market may be less imbalanced than in the recession of the early 1990s, and this may contribute a cushioning effect to future falls in demand, since there would be less of a supply overhang caused by new development.

From the text above it is clear that there are a wide variety of ways of investing in commercial real estate in North America. For the earlier part of this decade, capital was chasing the highest risk-adjusted return, even in the face of relatively weak user markets. This was also true of London. This experience is rather like the simple description of inflation as 'too much money chasing too few goods'. Either there have been structural changes that can support these investment volumes, or real estate asset prices are being inflated above fundamentals, and therefore a correction can be expected. More recent events might point to the latter being a more accurate interpretation of these events.

Property Markets in Latin America

9.1   Introduction

Latin America as a region refers to those countries in the Americas where the Spanish or Portuguese languages are spoken. The region includes Mexico, most of Central and South America, Cuba, the Dominican Republic, and Puerto Rico in the Caribbean, as well as the smaller numbers of French and Papiamentu speakers who reside in the region. Though this chapter describes property markets and institutions in a general sense, the reliance is on the markets for which data and description are accessible in the literature. This would mean that some countries, such as Cuba, Bolivia, Guatemala, Jamaica, Honduras etc., or smaller countries, though geographically part of the region, are not covered by the property market discussion later in this chapter.

Historically Latin American countries have witnessed periods of substantial macroeconomic volatility. The region has been prone to hyperinflation, exchange rate devaluations, failed currency reforms, banking sector collapses and debt default (Singh, 2006). Hyperinflation has been a recurrent phenomenon in all major countries in the region. During the 1970s, inflation started to soar high, and reached four-digit levels in countries like Argentina, Brazil and Peru during the 1980s and early 1990s. Alongside hyperinflation, the region also witnessed financial and exchange rate turbulence. As shown in Figure 9.1, Latin American countries have witnessed a number of financial and banking crises (Singh, 2006). One of the consequences of such developments has been high financial dollarisation in many countries (Figure 9.2). Countries like Argentina, Peru and Paraguay had more than 60 per cent of total deposits in US dollars. The region has also witnessed many episodes of restructuring or defaults on debt, higher than any other region in the world. A consequence of macroeconomic instability in the region has been that the periods of growth have been quite short. Singh (2006) reports that during the post-World War period in Latin America less than half of the growth spells continued beyond seven years, while growth spells in over 85 per cent of the developed world, and

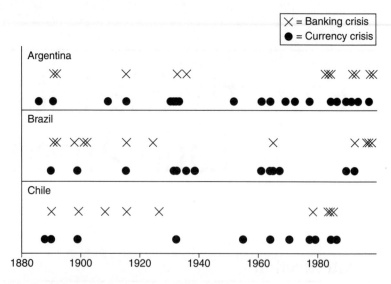

Figure 9.1 Banking and currency crises 1880–1997
Source: Bordo, Eichengreen, Klingebiel, and Martinez-Peria (2000).

Figure 9.2 Dollarisation in 2001 (as percentage of total deposits)
Source: Adapted from Singh (2006).

100 per cent for Asian economies, lasted more than seven years. The business cycle volatility in Latin American countries has been generally higher than in the developed world, and the cyclical instability rose sharply to double the average in developed countries. Despite the fact that Latin American countries have limited regional trade or integration of capital markets, there is evidence of substantial cyclical co-movement. Singh (2006) attributes this to the vulnerability of these economies to external shocks, particularly to world commodity prices and terms of trade. Besides external shocks, the domestic political and macroeconomic environment has also been responsible for volatility in output in Latin American countries. A number of countries in Latin America have exhibited higher levels of political instability compared with many other countries and regions. Political instability weakens macroeconomic policy discipline. Monetary policy in the region has also acted pro-cyclically – loosening during growth phases and tightening during downswings, amplifying the cycle. Monetary authorities have been forced to provide easy access to central bank credit in the past, causing inflation and leaving growth phases highly vulnerable to macroeconomic and financial shocks.

The region followed a fixed exchange rate regime, which further exacerbated any negative effect of terms of trade shocks on output. The inability of the domestic price and labour market to adjust in response to external conditions only worsened conditions during downswings. Due to volatility and underdeveloped capital markets, Latin American countries tended to borrow in foreign currencies and in short maturities that were 'inherently inconsistent with sustaining exchange rate pegs and macroeconomic stability' (Singh, 2006). As and when the region faced adverse shocks, risk premiums, contagion and borrowing costs increased sharply. High levels of debt limited the ability of monetary policy to respond counter-cyclically.

Since 2002, Latin American economies (except Argentina, Uruguay and Venezuela, where the period of growth started in 2003) have seen positive sustained growth (Table 9.1). The region has depended on exports for a long time and has emerged as an important supplier of oil and non-oil commodities to the world. Venezuela is a key crude oil supplier to the US and has benefited from higher oil prices in recent years. The liquidity in the capital market and low interest rates also helped in channelling huge amounts of capital into investment-grade countries like Mexico, and countries recovering from crises during the 1990s, such as Brazil. Most countries in the region have benefited from a growth spurt that also reflects cyclical recoveries (Singh, 2006).

Many countries in the region have made progress in advancing market-based reforms and have also instituted sound macroeconomic policy frameworks. There is more willingness for fiscal prudence and to tackle inflationary pressures. There is more political commitment to controlling inflation. A range of reforms to improve central bank autonomy, inflation targeting, and flexibility in setting up exchange rates have been undertaken. Brazil, Chile, Colombia, Mexico and Peru adopted inflation-targeting frameworks in the late 1990s and early 2000s (Singh, 2006). These policies have paid dividends in terms of sustained growth

Table 9.1   GDP growth 2002–8

	2002	2003	2004	2005	2006	2007	2008
Argentina	−10.9	8.8	9	9.2	8.5	8.4	6.1
Brazil	2.7	1.2	5.7	3.1	3.7	5.1	4.4
Chile	2.2	4	6	5.7	4	5.3	4.4
Colombia	1.9	3.9	4.9	4.7	6.8	6.8	5
Costa Rica	2.9	6.4	4.3	5.9	8.8	6.4	4.6
Cuba	1.5	2.9	4.4	9	12	6.5	6.1
Dom. Republic	4.3	0.5	1.2	9.5	10.7	7.9	4.9
Ecuador	4.2	3.6	8	6	3.9	2.1	2.6
El Salvador	2.3	2.3	1.8	2.8	4.2	4.2	2.9
Mexico	0.8	1.4	4.2	2.8	4.8	3.2	2.6
Panama	2.2	4.2	7.5	7.2	8.7	9.2	7.8
Paraguay	0	3.8	4.1	2.9	4.3	5.4	4.1
Peru	5.2	3.9	5.2	6.5	8	8.5	6.6
Uruguay	−11.0	2.2	11.8	6.6	7	6.5	4.3
Venezuela	−8.9	−7.8	18.3	10.3	10.3	8.6	5.6
Total	0.5	1.9	6	4.4	5.4	5.3	4.1

Source: Economic Intelligence Unit, *The Economist*.

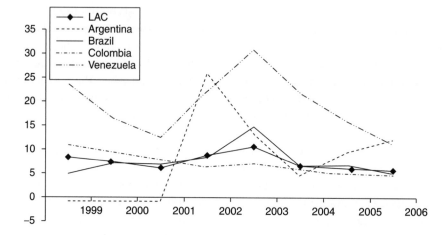

Figure 9.3   Annual inflation rates (%)

Source: Adapted from Singh (2006).

and relatively stable inflation rates (Figure 9.3), with an average of 7.5 per cent since 2000 for the region. The overall macroeconomic environment has resulted in a balanced pattern of growth and has avoided the over-appreciation of currencies and widening external current account balance that arrested recoveries in the past. Since 2002, the growth in exports has been geographically diversified and has led to the region's current account surpluses and reduced dependence on external capital inflows.

Latin American countries have also strengthened their banking systems by improving bank supervision and financial sector regulation. Financial regulators have been accorded greater power and independence. These efforts have made the banking and financial sector resilient.

Latin American countries have also tried to achieve consistency between monetary and fiscal policies and frameworks. A number of disciplinary fiscal rules have been instituted in many countries. Brazil has framed a number of fiscal norms and regulations, including fiscal responsibility law and debt restructuring agreements with subnational governments, and rules that limit public wage expenditures. Chile's fiscal rule targets structural surpluses equivalent to 1 per cent of GDP in the account of central government. Columbia and Peru have also instituted fiscal responsibility and transparency laws (Singh, 2006).

Debt levels in Latin American countries have also declined since 2000. Better management of debt and reduction in foreign currency denominated debt have provided macroeconomic stability. Countries such as Brazil, Chile, Colombia, Mexico and Peru have increased their reliance on debt issuance in domestic currency. Brazil, Colombia and Uruguay have issued debt in domestic currency even in international markets. These efforts have achieved economic stability for the region.

Latin American countries, which are among the world's largest producers and exporters, particularly for bulk and soft commodities, have benefited significantly from the surge in global commodity prices. Rising commodity export revenues have turned out to be a real catalyst for the development of these economies, with many other sectors, such as infrastructure, real estate and financial markets, benefiting. And, although prices (mainly metal) are currently trending lower due to global economic slowdown, the uptrend has the potential to go further once the global economy recovers. In this context, Brazil, Argentina, Chile and Mexico are the main beneficiaries of the commodity boom (Merath, 2008). However, there are also countries like Venezuela, which have large commodity revenues, but benefit only to a limited extent due to political and economic problems.

9.2 Institutional development in Latin America

Political parties and the military have historically influenced the political climate and institutions in Latin American countries. Both these groups have tried to manoeuvre control of resources, which in turn has meant the creation of institutions and appointments made to bureaucratic posts based on favouritism. The role of the military in the political process arose as political actors chose, in many instances, not to abide by the rules of the political game but rather to call the military to their aid. The consequence of such a system was that nine constitutional Latin American regimes fell to military insurgencies.

Latin American economies followed an import substitution policy that resulted in solid economic growth and led to a rise in per capita income. Argentina saw its per capita GDP more than double. The economic growth ensured the survival of the political system based on populism until the 1980s, although tensions between left-wing labour movements and capital were often present and marked the basis for much of the continent's political instability. However, social democratic leaders with political platforms based on redistribution and land reforms, such as Venezuela's Gallegos or Chile's Frei, were unable to hold together the delicate coalitions necessary to keep them in power for long; giving way either to right-wing dictatorships or to radical leftist experiments.

Political agents, worried about their long-term survival, engaged in populist politics and adopted short-run economic policies funded by debt and causing huge fiscal deficits. The consequences were repeated cycles of growing budget deficits, high or hyperinflation, balance of payments crises and temporary but highly contractionary stabilisations. Such a system lacked the institutional capacity to react to the negative external shocks that were to hit the region during the early 1980s. By the late 1980s, most Latin American economies were in disarray, heavily weighed down by accumulated external debt, delayed adjustment to negative external shocks and a desperate need for reserves.

The collapse of the USSR weakened left-wing movements during the 1990s. Developing countries which had adopted market-friendly strategies had enjoyed much better economic performance. These factors led to a shift towards market liberalisation in Latin American countries as well. The 1980s and 1990s were characterised by a wave of economic liberalisation and democratisation.

A stable and efficient federal/national governance structure ensures the stability of macroeconomic and regulatory policies, which are important for investors (institutional – local or foreign) in understanding and pricing country-level risks associated with their investments. In addition, city-level administration also plays a very important role. Location is an important feature of property. The policies of local governments and administrative efficiency influences the activities of property market players – users, investors, developers, service providers, etc. Mature markets have efficiently functioning local government with transparent regulatory regimes. Inefficient local government and unclear regulatory regimes lead to rent-seeking behaviour by local government officials, which hinders the efficient functioning of property markets, thereby deterring investors, particularly those who are not local or do not have local connections.

Since 1990, with democratisation at the national level, local governance has also undergone changes in Latin America. There has been greater decentralisation and devolution of powers from national to local governments. Following austerity measures adopted by national governments, they have been more willing to embrace decentralisation and administrative reorganisation (Ward, 1996). Urban authorities in Latin America have had to confront cuts in public expenditure and often pressure to privatise public utilities. This has meant a greater fiscal responsibility being vested in local governments, and they are expected to raise more of their own revenues (ibid.). Many countries have been introducing greater transparency in city budgeting, and increasing the efficiency with which urban services are delivered.

Though the political and fiscal powers are increasingly being devolved to local levels, all major cities in Latin America suffer from a multiplicity of political–administrative units, often with overlapping jurisdictions. Although there may be a municipality that is dominant, a multiplicity of municipalities in an urban area leaves very little incentive to cooperate. This is particularly evident in cities like Sao Paulo, with 39 municipalities, or Santiago, with 34 separate communes. In some cities, urban areas are administered by two levels of governments – federal and local. Rio de Janeiro has 13 municipalities, Buenos Aires has 20 local government units and Mexico City falls under the jurisdiction of 16 delegated areas of Federal District and 27 municipalities. Administratively, complications arise as many of these municipalities are themselves managed by higher-level administrative units (Ward, 1996). Differing political allegiance of different tiers of governments has also posed problems with city administration and allocation of responsibilities. Another feature associated with city governance in Latin American city is weak legislature relative to executive, because executive officers are not appointed by legislators. Unlike some of the Mayors, who hold cabinet office, elected councils are weak and have only nominal powers, mostly consultative in nature or as public 'watchdogs' (Ward, 1996). Political allegiance is far more important than individual qualities in appointments to the Mayoral office.

Since 1990, however, most Latin American cities have been undertaking fiscal and governance reforms. One of the trends towards fiscal reform has been to cut down expenditure and improve efficiency through privatisation of public utilities. Now there is far more transparency and accountability in local governments. These changes are leading to improvements in the way regulations (such as planning restrictions, zoning, building regulations, etc.) are applied, which clearly has positive implications for property markets.

9.3   Current property market performance

Table 9.2 presents a snapshot of market performance indicators for various Latin American cities by asset class. The first observation that could be made on looking at Table 9.2 is that there are many blank cells. Availability of property market information in Latin America is poor. Many of the Latin American cities are in the early stages of development of their real estate investment market. One of the reasons is the lack of availability of investment-grade real estate. For example, out of a total of 32 million square metres useable office space in 10 Latin American countries (Brazil, Mexico, Chile, Colombia, Argentina, Venezuela, Peru, Ecuador, Costa Rica and Uruguay), only 10.3 million square metres are in class A buildings (Cushman and Wakefield, 2008). Nearly 28.5 per cent of this space is located in Mexico (Mexico City) and 28 per cent in Brazil (Sao Paulo and Rio de Janeiro). With economic growth, demand for office space has surged in the region. The new supply in 2007 of 'class A' office space was 400,000 square metres for an absorption rate of 624,000 square metres. The small size of the investment market makes it less attractive to large investors.

Table 9.2 Market performance indicators (2006)

	Office				Retail			Warehousing		
	Prime rent US$	% Rent change p.a.	Prime yield %	Vacancy rate %	Prime rent US$	Prime yield %	Vacancy rate %	Prime rent US$	Prime yield %	Vacancy rate %
Rio de Janeiro, Brazil	28.0	20.0%		5.5%	70.0		2%	4.7–6.5	13.0%	
Buenos Aires, Argentina	28.0	20.0%		3.0%	70–80		2–4%	4.0–5.0	19.0%	3%
Montevideo, Uruguay	30.0	20.0%	7.2%	5.0%	40.0					
Santiago, Chile	21.0	25.0%	11.4%	4.1%						
Lima, Peru	13.3	8.0%	12.2%	10%				3.50	15.0%	
Quito, Ecuador	12.0	9.0%	15.6%	6%	15.0	8.5%	3%	2.30	15.3%	40%
Bogota, Colombia	17.8	36.0%		1.8%	20.0	12.8%		4.90	29.4%	
Caracas, Venezuela	36.0	25.0%	13.5%	2.5%	60.0	12.0%	8%	9.0	12.0%	12%
San Jose, Costa Rica	16.0		9.6%	5.0%				3.5–6.0	10.5%	5%
Mexico City, Mexico	19.0	−14.0%		8.15%	20–50					

Note: Rents in US$ per square metre per month. Prime yields are authors' est mates.

Source: Adapted from Cushman and Wakefield, Marketbeat Latin America 2007.

Another point to note from Table 9.2 is the wide variation in level of rent across various cities. In 2006, Caracas had the highest rents for office space. Rio de Janeiro and Buenos Aires had the same level of rents. High rent does not necessarily mean high market maturity. On the JLL transparency scale for 2008, Venezuela is an opaque market. Among Latin American countries, Brazil is the most transparent and is expected to move further up the transparency scale as institutional strengthening and regulatory reforms take place.

Retail rents also display significant variations across cities. Rio de Janeiro and Buenos Aires have the highest retail rent. Brazil and Mexico are the two largest economies in Latin America. Brazil is projected to grow to become the eighth largest economy in the world by 2020 and the fifth largest economy by 2050. Demographic trends in Latin America are favourable, as more and more of the young population is entering the labour market. Economic growth, the rise in disposable income, stable inflation rate and increasing access to credit are some of the factors that will drive retail demand in the future.

Industrial space rents for larger markets in Brazil, Argentina and Colombia are very similar. Rents are highest in Venezuela, an oil economy. Another feature to note is the high levels of yields and vacancy rates for industrial property compared with other types of real estate. A reason for the high vacancy rate is the poor quality of industrial space, and in countries like Brazil the industrial real estate sector is going through the modernisation process.

Figure 9.4 presents the Latin American office clock. Not only do different markets have different rental levels, but they are also on a different phase of the property cycle. Most markets (except San Juan) are in the rental growth phase. Santo Domingo and Sao Paulo have reached the peak of the rental cycle, and rents are

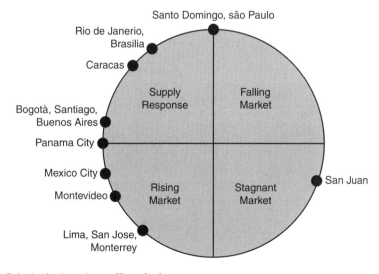

Figure 9.4 Latin American office clock

Source: Adapted from Jones Lang LaSalle, Latin American city profile: Buenos Aires, Argentina, 3Q2008.

expected to fall in the future. Economic growth in Latin America has meant that office rentals in cities such as Buenos Aires, Bogota, Santiago, Caracas and Rio de Janeiro have been growing significantly since 2004. Increasing rentals and favourable credit conditions have also led to supply responses, which are likely to slow down the growth in the future. Markets such as Mexico City, Montevideo, Lima and San Jose are observing high demand for space, reflected in rental growth. The only market that is struggling is San Juan (Puerto Rico).

9.4   Market maturity

The paucity of market-based institutions in the past has meant that Latin American economies have lacked the flexibility to cope with shocks. These economies have lacked institutions relevant for the business climate, such as legal and regulatory systems. Figure 9.5 indicates that the number of procedures required to start a business in Latin America is among the highest in the world. Procedural complexity to enforce contracts in this region is also quite high (Figure 9.6).

In general, Latin American countries have smaller real estate markets, lack institutional-quality real estate and are thinly traded. This in turn means that most of the investment is in new development, market information is weak and there are fewer opportunities for economies of scale in investment in real estate.

The degree of market maturity of the real estate sector varies substantially across Latin American countries (Table 9.3). According to the JLL transparency index for 2008 (a measure of market maturity; see Chapter 5 for more details), some countries, such as Brazil, Mexico and Argentina, are far more transparent than other markets in the region, such as Colombia, Peru and Venezuela. Macroeconomic stability, market size and business sophistication are correlated

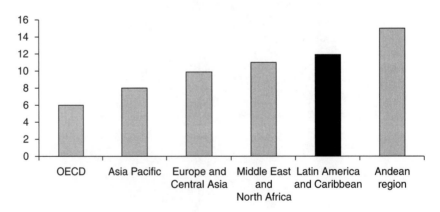

Figure 9.5 Number of procedures in starting a business

Note: OECD denotes the member countries of the Organization for Economic Cooperation and Development.

Source: World Bank, doing business database.

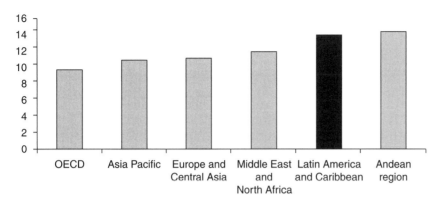

Figure 9.6 Contract enforcement procedural complexity index (%)

Note: OECD denotes the member countries of the Organization for Economic Cooperation and Developmen.

Source: World Bank, doing business databaset.

Table 9.3 JLL transparency index – Latin America, 2006–8

Country	Latin American Rank	2008 transparency score	2006 transparency score	Transparency level
Brazil	1	3.06	3.31	Semi-transparent
Chile	2	3.11	3.11	Semi-transparent
Mexico	3	3.15	3.20	Semi-transparent
Argentina	4	3.56	3.56	Semi-transparent
Costa Rica	5	3.8	3.83	Low transparency
Panama	6	3.85	4.18	Low transparency
Colombia	7	4.0	4.10	Low transparency
Peru	8	4.05	4.08	Low transparency
Uruguay	9	4.10	4.13	Low transparency
Venezuela	10	4.2	4.08	Low transparency
Dominican Republic	11	4.30	N/A	N/A

Source: Adapted from JLL, Real Estate Transparency in Latin America, 2008.

with real estate market transparency (JLL, 2008). As discussed earlier, the region has lacked a stable macroeconomic environment, with inflation running high, shorter economic growth spells, huge government deficits and weak financial institutions. These conditions have deterred foreign investors from considering Latin America as a long-term investment destination.

Brazil, Mexico and Colombia have instituted a number of regulatory reforms and have undertaken measures to protect property rights. These developments have led to increased investment and economic growth in these countries. The region also varies in terms of the quality of business networks, quality of firms' operation and strategies, and technological innovations. Brazil, Mexico and Chile have far better business environments than other countries in the region. On the JLL transparency scale, Brazil, Mexico and Colombia have shown substantial improvements during 2006–8. The trend, however, is not uniform across the region. Argentina and Venezuela have fallen back on the JLL transparency scale during the same period, as governments continue to interfere with the economy, which has affected private investment in these countries.

For real estate investors, availability and duration of public and private investment indices, as well as real estate valuation frequency and credibility, are important. Latin American countries have been lacking on these counts. Data related to market fundamentals like rent, yield, demand, supply, etc. are available for most major markets. Brazil and Mexico are far more transparent in availability of information related to market fundamentals (JLL, 2008: Real Estate Transparency in Latin America).

For real estate investors it is important that the market offers a wide range of products, including those that are traded on public markets. The lack of credible performance indices delayed the development of a public market for real estate for a long time. Latin America has made progress with regard to the development of public markets for real estate. Brazil, Colombia, Costa Rica, Peru and Panama have put together financial disclosure and corporate governance systems that have contributed to the development of public markets for real estate in these countries. Many of these countries have seen real estate company initial public offerings (IPOs) and the introduction of REITs.

Fairness and consistency in application of real estate legal and regulatory regimes to different investors are necessary for transparent markets. The legal and regulatory regime should cover such issues as taxation, zoning, building codes and contracts. Latin American countries (except Venezuela) have liberalised their regulatory regime by minimising restrictions and improving property rights. Venezuela has reversed some of the free market policies (JLL, 2008: Real Estate Transparency in Latin America).

The availability of real estate market information and professional standards of agents and service providers involved in real estate transaction play a very important role in the real estate transaction process. Real estate agents and service providers are also market-makers, as they play a crucial role in the provision of market information. In countries like Mexico, the presence of institutional investors and international occupiers has helped in the professionalisation of real estate service providers.

9.5 | Property investment

When compared with regions such as the emerging markets in Asia, the level of international investment in real estate in Latin America is low. The data on international investment flows in commercial real estate in individual countries is not easily available. Most of the investment that flows is in the big four countries – Mexico, Brazil, Argentina and Chile. One of the reasons for the low investment levels is that the size of the Latin American commercial real estate market in value terms is quite small, 3.6 per cent of the global real estate market. The presence of institutional investors in Latin American commercial real estate markets is limited to specific types of assets in specific markets. Industrial property in Mexico has seen a huge presence of institutional and international investors. Investments by foreigners have created sophisticated industrial property markets in the three largest cities – Mexico City, Monterrey and Guadalajara. Retail real estate is also undergoing transformation in Mexico. With rising income and changing shopping preferences, traditional retail formats are giving way to hypermarket-anchored formats. According to an estimate by Prudential Financial, there were 295 retail centres with an area of more than 100,000 square metres that were planned or were under construction in Mexico during 2005–8. The sector is also witnessing a huge amount of investment activity by institutional investors. Office property is largely owner-occupied, with little presence of institutional investors. Institutional investment in Brazil is in the fairly early stages for retail and industrial properties. Retail has taken off in a big way on the back of economic growth. According to Prudential Financial, there are 262 shopping malls in Brazil. Industrial property in Brazil is largely owner-occupied. However, some investment activity is beginning to emerge, led largely by local investment managers. The owner-occupied nature of real estate assets indicates that, as the market matures, the potential for investment by institutional and foreign investors will grow.

9.6   Conclusions

Latin America as a region has moved towards economic and political stability during the last decade. However, there are differences across different countries in the region with regard to the progress made. On the macroeconomic front, these economies have introduced policies for fiscal prudence, open trade and debt management. These policies have borne fruit and the region as a whole is growing rapidly. Demographic trends for the region are also favourable, as the age of the population is young. Economic growth, low unemployment levels and rising household incomes are positive factors for use and investment in property. The region, however, suffers from a lack of investment-grade property. The size of the individual investment market is small, and a large proportion of commercial property is owner-occupied.

Many of the countries in the region have suffered from political uncertainty and weak city-level institutions for a long time. Since the 1990s progress has been made towards stabilising political structure at the national level and moving towards decentralisation and devolution of fiscal and administrative powers to local levels. Regulatory systems at the urban levels, involving property rights, zoning, building regulation, planning systems, etc., are being strengthened and the transparency of administration at the local level is improving. These trends are contributing to market maturity. However, the trend is not uniform across countries. Argentina and Venezuela still suffer from institutional opacity.

Information availability related to property market fundamentals is weak. However, with the development of public markets for real estate (with attempts such as the introduction of REITs or property company IPOs), information availability would improve.

Towards an Internationalised Real Estate Market

10.1 Introduction

In this concluding chapter we summarise the main elements within this book and consider the extent to which an internationalised real estate market can be said to exist.

We introduced this book by stating that the concept of an international real estate market is a relatively new phenomenon. It is true that some (large) real estate companies have an international presence and that they have changed the way in which real estate is viewed in many countries. Today it is more common to regard real estate as an income-producing asset than it was a generation ago. This in itself is in part a consequence of global economic change, greater pressures for economic integration and a change in preferences that have been more strongly supportive of more liberal economic policies.

It may be going too far to suggest that there is just one international real estate market. Perhaps a better conceptualisation is that there are international markets in real estate that have low barriers to entry, and within which new entrants are more certain of the rules of the game and these are more consistent across countries. There is a sense in which market knowledge about how to do business and the framework within which it will be most profitable is more widely accepted and understood. This is turn has implications for the institutional framework within which the market and market actors operate. However, the quality of information (even when relatively plentiful) remains an issue.

This book has discussed various theoretical bases for understanding real estate markets. These markets are at best weak-form efficient and have heterogeneous assets and limited information. Direct (unsecuritised) real estate is a high unit-value asset and can be relatively illiquid. The characteristics of the market mean that it cannot provide instant adjustment to exogenous changes in demand; rather, adjustment is slow and the market exhibits notable cyclical volatility. The inefficiency of the market's operation has led to the formation of market institutions that aid (or in some countries hinder) exchange. Both the property rights strand and the transactions cost theories within institutional economics are relevant to help explain processes and institutional structures in real estate markets.

The past 30 years have seen substantial change in real estate industries. This covers the major international expansion period against a background of deregulation and the removal of barriers to international financial flows. An increasingly interconnected, globalised and integrated world economy has emerged. This is a process that does not seem to be ending, even in the face of the liquidity shortage and recessionary forces across the globe.

This process has seen production move to less costly countries, with a consequent expansion in their industrial bases and a requirement for commercial property development. Global regions have been identified, including Europe, North America, and Japan and South East Asia. It is these world regions that have witnessed the greatest change in commercial real estate markets and the internationalisation of the real estate service companies themselves. Some continents have seen less rapid economic growth and expansion. South America has not received the same interest from RESPs, and it remains a continent with institutional structures that have remained more intact and faced less intrusion from alternative business and corporate cultures emanating from the US, the UK and Northern Europe. Africa has also not experienced the same economic growth rates as many other locations. Its markets remain underdeveloped and opaque. Markets in the Middle East also remain highly opaque, with limited or no information on market prices, rents or yields available. However, even within the key global regions, some countries have been less exposed to change than others. For example, in South East Asia, Vietnam has only recently begun to be more exposed to global economic forces. Laos is still regarded as relatively closed and has not attracted foreign investment. Political problems in Myanmar have also significantly deterred investors. Within NAFTA, Mexico remains significantly more opaque than the US or Canada.

Internationalisation of real estate companies and world economic growth over the past few decades have also been accompanied by changes in the behaviour and structure of real estate markets. Jones Lang LaSalle, as we have discussed earlier, rank countries by their level of property market transparency. Many countries have seen improved levels of transparency, although there remain significant differences. However, countries which were not listed in earlier transparency league tables are now being recorded. This suggests that, even if they are seen as being highly opaque, their markets have begun to open up to some level of analysis.

From a European perspective, it is interesting to witness the significant changes in Eastern and Southern Europe. Countries such as Poland have created a private commercial real estate investment market since the early 1990s. This contrasts sharply with the non-market centrally planned system it experienced for most of the post-war period. Similar changes have been seen in Hungary and the Czech Republic. In Southern Europe, institutional change has underpinned the growth and development of the commercial real estate market in Spain. In many senses it can be seen to have overtaken Italy in the availability of market information and the openness of its real estate industry to overseas firms. Portugal has also experienced new development and investment in commercial real estate, albeit without effective legislative changes. But, across Southern Europe, Greece remains one of the most opaque markets.

Market volatility, in rents and total returns, can be seen in markets with different levels of transparency or maturity. For example, markets in Spain, China, the UK, and the US have experienced volatility and cover a wide spectrum of levels of relative market maturity. Thus, if market efficiency is positively correlated with transparency, more efficient markets are not necessarily more stable. Property markets still remain relatively inefficient in comparison to other markets. However, some recent evidence suggests that market adjustment is faster in more mature or transparent markets than in less transparent or transitional markets (Ke and White, 2009).

10.2   From national to international real estate markets

Internationalisation of MNCs in the post-war period has played an important role in the internationalisation of real estate service providers. MNCs directly affected economic development in different countries and essentially increased global economic integration. The role for real estate provision increased substantially. This has been particularly noticeable in South East Asia during and after the 1980s. Since the Asian financial crisis in 1997, China has seen dramatic developments in its real estate service industry, in which many US and UK firms are present and playing an active role.

Alongside this internationalisation have been changes in the nature and range of services provided by real estate companies. In an earlier chapter we have argued that they have become professional business services providers. Their service base has widened from more traditional valuation services to, for example, investment and research services that can provide bespoke services to high-value clients. Their relationships with clients tend to be ongoing, and there is a value to maintaining high services standards across international markets where their clients have or seek to have a presence.

Coinciding with this internationalisation process has been the view of real estate as an asset class. The ability of investors to enter different real estate markets has been facilitated by an increasingly varied range of real estate financial products in addition to unsecuritised investment opportunities, which themselves have increased. REITs have become more widely available in different countries and have increased in scale in countries in which they were already established. Interestingly, only recently, the UK passed legislation to permit the creation of these tax-efficient investment vehicles. With their introduction coinciding with a recessionary phase in the property market, they have yet to prove attractive.

Thus the last 30 years have seen the global economy becoming increasingly integrated. Real estate investment markets have developed, real estate investment products have also developed, real estate companies have changed their size, coverage, and range of services, and there has been significant institutional change across different markets. Such institutional change has occurred in part because of macroeconomic pressures. It also reflects changes in societal preferences and a desire to remove barriers, real or perceived, to the realisation of higher living standards. In many societies institutional change has been adopted to permit economic development and integration with the global economy. Few, if any, economies remain completely isolated, and, where they do, they tend to have experienced low economic growth rates and little or no investment, either domestic or international, that would encourage growth in value added. Such economies also tend to have experienced political risks of the kind described by Geurts and Jaffe (1996). The substantial changes in the world economy and real estate markets have passed them by. Nevertheless, it is possible for them to benefit from economic integration in the future. Living standards have improved in countries that have become part of the global economic system, and there is no obvious barrier to keep those countries that have thus far not been part of this system from joining.

The internationalisation processes at work and the interlinkages across world economies raise the possibility of increasing synchronisation of macroeconomic cycles in different countries, and consequently it could be expected that real estate cycles would also become more synchronised. Increasing demand for space in one country would reflect positive economic growth, and through interlinkages across economies in different countries it is reasonable to expect increasing demand in other nations also. The amplitude of fluctuation in rents and capital values may vary, but the timing of peaks and troughs of a cycle may therefore become closer.

Alternatively, cycles may vary in timing depending upon specific national or local factors. Thus, newly industrialising economies with a larger proportion of their workforces employed in manufacturing may not experience office market cycles at the same time as more developed economies with large service sectors. Further, the geographical concentration of particular industries means that local real estate market cycles may differ from national cycles in relation to both timing and amplitude of cycles. If the process of internationalisation continues, and economies become more similar in relation to the mix of industries, then it might be reasonable to assume that the cycles in economies and real estate markets may then become more synchronised. Specific local factors will remain and cause some differences to persist. The amplitude of fluctuation may remain different due to different institutional characteristics, which may persist. Specific government policies impacting on the real estate market can also affect the amplitude of fluctuation. For example, policies reducing land prices may encourage a relatively high supply of new space in response to growth in rents and capital values, and such a supply would reduce the rate of rental inflation. However, given the cyclical nature of the industry, new supply may only be completed when absorption has ceased, leading to relatively high vacancy rates and large reductions in rents and capital values. Such a fluctuation has been seen in Shanghai, where significant new floorspace has been added to the market.

Variations in supply are perhaps more directly affected by public policy than other variables. Cheshire and Hilber (2005) examine the impact of regulatory restraint imposed by public policy (mainly planning systems) across different cities and discuss the impact this has on office markets. They argue that constraints imposed by the planning system in Britain significantly raise the costs of supplying commercial real estate. They make a comparison between offices in Manhattan and Birmingham, England. Manhattan is geographically constrained, whereas Birmingham does not face the same geographical limitations. They state that 'the cost of constructing a m² of office space in Birmingham, England, in 2004 was approximately half that in Manhattan. ... In the same year, the total occupation costs per m² were 44 percent higher in Birmingham than they were in Manhattan (King Sturge, 2004)' (p. 1). They argue that this difference is due to planning restrictiveness in Britain.

Such institutional characteristics may vary substantially across countries, and thus land and development costs can be significantly different. Translating these into higher costs of occupation will in the long run affect the profitability of industry using the space, and may affect long-term economic competitiveness as high costs cause business to move elsewhere. Cheshire and Hilber also suggest that office markets in Britain face higher levels of regulatory restraint than those in Europe, and that European office markets are more constrained than those in the US. They suggest that this is related to the concept of urban constraint that is embodied in the British planning system. However, since its impact may be felt more clearly in the long run, it may take more time for the fuller negative impact on national competitiveness to be felt. This matters because other nations do not seem to suffer from the same degree of restrictiveness, and therefore the UK is at a competitive disadvantage in the long run.

Interestingly, though, the same restrictiveness has not been applied in the City of London or London Docklands. The City of London Corporation has a more proactive approach and is focused on maintaining London's role as a major world financial centre. The development of high-rise offices both in the City and at Canary Wharf has enabled London to remain an attractive location for international finance. However, even with the benefit of less restrictive policies and the added value from the agglomeration economies the industry has in London, excessive restraint on development could cost London its position as a key global centre.

This picture of restraint is in sharp contrast to the urban transformation seen in countries in Asia as rapid economic growth has led to substantial changes not only in urban form but in the size of cities and urban areas. The success of East Asian industrialisation and the extent to which Asian countries have become integrated into the global economic system have been among the key features of economic development over the last 30 years. Many of these markets are still in the early stages of maturity and provide significant investment opportunities for those willing to take on higher risk.

Cultural attitudes remain important. The American and Northern European business 'model' finds support in some South East Asian countries. The high level of interest in business and finance in East Asia complements the business models exported from the US and Europe, and, while many cultural differences may remain and persist, differences in business culture seem less apparent. There do not seem to have been any ideological differences of significance, and countries such as Singapore, South Korea and Hong Kong have been major recipients of inward investment for many decades. This, and the economic dominance of Japan in the region, may also have encouraged other countries to adopt similar policies that encouraged business development.

10.3 Implications of internationalisation for occupiers, investors and developers

The internationalised real estate market is partly a consequence of changes in the shape of business. Large firms dominate world trade in manufactured commodities, and the majority of US international trade is produced by MNCs. The perfectly competitive model is no longer appropriate in a world economy dominated by oligopolistically structured industries. International RESPs may also be seen to be highly oligopolistic in structure, although they meet varied national and local real estate structures in other countries. International occupiers receive an international standard of service that can affect the quality of development in markets across the globe. Investors may themselves be international firms having a presence in different markets. They also receive an international standard of professional business service advice from real estate firms. This advice, however, will also remain bespoke to their specific requirements.

The nature of such advice has become relatively complex, requiring a significant amount of knowledge on the part of both service provider and client. For example, many firms now use econometric analysis of property markets as a basis for providing their investment advice to their clients. Such approaches have been adopted not only by real estate companies but also by financial corporations that have real estate portfolios.

The real estate sector has also generated significant international investment flows. It is more strongly interconnected with the financial sector, and, as large flows of funds can freely cross borders, volatility of values is potentially increased. Minor differences in expected returns can also generate sizeable investment flows. Thus both direct and indirect real estate assets will be affected by a more laissez-faire attitude to international financial movements.

The development sector also has been affected by internationalisation and economic forces of global integration. Prime property is the highest-quality asset class within real estate, and internationalisation has helped to raise awareness of the meaning of prime real estate across the globe. This is not a static concept, being subject to change as business requirements have changed. However, the internationalisation of MNCs and RESPs has given global significance to prime real estate.

Interestingly, development companies remain largely national or even local. In this sense their industrial structure differs from that of many occupiers or, indeed, investors. This may be due to persistent local differences or the nature of the industry precluding any competitive advantage being generated by international mergers or alliances. Also, the largely bespoke nature of many buildings may mean that there are no economies of scale at an international level. Techniques of building may be more similar, but as yet there are no dominant international players in this field.

10.4 Future directions

At the point of writing, the real estate markets have passed a cyclical peak and are heading towards a period of significant negative growth. This type of event has occurred previously in the UK and almost concurrently in many other countries. London is currently experiencing its 'fourth major market cycle of the post-war period. The current cycle, like that of the late 1980s/early 1990s, has been a global phenomenon, and across Europe a synchronized cycle of office take up, vacancy, rental growth and building has affected most markets with varying degrees of severity' (Barras, 2005). But this cycle has features that distinguish it from its most recent predecessor, namely the constraint on liquidity. This could make the trough of the recession deeper and longer than other recessions in the post-war period. In response to these threats, governments in different countries have adopted expansionary monetary policies. Whether these will be thwarted by forthcoming fiscal restraint required to control ballooning budget deficits remains to be seen.

After a relatively long period of world economic growth, increased global economic integration, and a more rapid pace of international real estate market development, the recession will affect more countries more visibly than before. Increased interconnectedness has meant not only the spreading of investment and development to new countries and the development of new real estate markets, but also the spread of recessionary forces. In a globally integrated economy, such economic shocks may be transmitted more quickly across different markets, increasing the synchronisation of economic cycles.

Local differences will remain because of differences in the composition of each region's economic base. Locationally specific production processes imply that some regions will be less or more exposed to international economic cyclical forces than others. This provides a diversification opportunity to real estate investors holding an international property portfolio. However, while the real estate market has been highly cyclical and remains so, longer-term trends may also be discerned from recent developments.

The expectations for future trends are dependent upon the world economy and continuing processes that increase global economic integration. Economic growth has increased wealth over the past two centuries. These processes have momentum and it seems reasonable to expect them to continue in the long run. The structure of the world economy has changed and continues to do so. It has changed in both the quantity of commodities and the quality of provision. As wealth has increased, markets have developed in different countries, and in addition there has been evidence of what might be termed market deepening in the sense that there is increasing (and probably income elastic) demand for higher value-added bespoke services to individuals and corporate clients. These may be expected to bring significant growth in revenue as the world economy grows.

The real estate industry is relatively well placed to provide similar types of services within its area of expertise. It would, therefore, seem reasonable to expect that such high-value services will become an increasingly important source of revenue generation. However, business models may also need to consider potential changes in the institutional environment. This is particularly apposite in the era of the liquidity shortage. There is now an incentive to re-evaluate the effectiveness of regulatory regimes. As real estate has been highly exposed to debt financing, this may in turn have implications for the industry in the short term. Not only may the scale of the industry be adversely affected, but also there may be structural changes in the medium term. It may not be unrealistic to expect a new round of mergers and acquisitions to occur as a response to the need for at least some restructuring of the industry. There may be further implications for the exportability of the Anglo-Saxon model of corporate culture as well as the 'relaxed' regulation viewed by others as the modern day beggar-my-neighbour policy that has led to excessive risk-taking in the financial sector and the consequent macroeconomic problems affecting the world economy.

However, the real estate sector has displayed flexibility and adaptiveness to economic change both within countries and internationally. It has increased its interlinkages with other related areas, for example, in finance, and its corporate culture has changed to accommodate a wider range of (unbadged) professionals. This has happened in order to develop its ability to reach a wider range of high-value clients.

There still remain many areas of the world less connected to the global economy and less exposed to, or open to, the international real estate sector. It remains difficult to predict how these world regions (for example, in Africa) will develop. Unpredictability of political and institutional processes remains a major factor discouraging investment. Financial instability in South America remains problematic, as is a lack of market information. However, there is already evidence that RESPs have begun to open branches here too, although this expansion remains in its infancy.

However, many markets across the globe have shown increasing transparency, and it could be argued that they have begun travelling along a road (although there is not necessarily only one road) to increased maturity. This will also be correlated with national economic growth and industrialisation processes.

Transparency itself brings challenges, since it may weaken the role of particular skill groups that might previously have benefited from keeping market information to themselves. On a macroeconomic scale, more (and better-quality) information will lead to greater efficiency of resource allocation and hence make a positive contribution to national income. However, there are also distributional consequences for groups that lose out. Institutional structures may help to maintain the status quo and information imbalance, or alternatively they may encourage information-sharing because of the expected uplift in national income. The evidence also suggests that there is a positive correlation between more transparent markets and markets with higher income per head of population.

Changes in real estate markets and their own processes of internationalisation may be seen as both cause and effect of wider economic growth and international economic integration. They play a key market mediation role in developed and developing economies. As a transactions cost-minimising institutional structure, they obviate the inefficiencies inherent in property markets to improve resource allocation. Related institutional changes that raise the attractiveness of real estate as an asset also widen investment markets and can not only permit quantitative changes in the form of investment flows but also raise the quality of real estate product to international standards, creating international (financial) institutional-grade investment assets in unsecuritised property. This in turn is often the foundation for the development of securitised real estate vehicles. These too have increased in importance internationally.

Informal institutional structures within real estate markets continue to vary across countries. Cultures relating to information-sharing vary widely. This may relate to the depth of the market in particular locations. Where there are more exchanges and transactions with a small number of agents, information-sharing may become prevalent. As a key component of transparency, information levels have increased in many countries. Most rapid changes can be seen in Eastern Europe, where a real estate investment market has emerged since the mid-1990s. Thus there has been a rapid movement from centrally planned economic systems not simply to market-oriented systems but to market systems that have become rapidly integrated into Western Europe and, for many of those countries, the EU. They have seen commercial property development occur at the same time as many RESPs were internationalising and when removal of foreign exchange controls permitted large inflows of financial capital and FDI.

Cyclicality remains a feature of international real estate markets and may remain so in the long term. Even if information sources improve, the asset remains highly illiquid and the development sector may be slow to adjust to short-run changes in demand. Policy intervention may also add to volatility, in the case of restrictive planning in the UK or weak restrictions on new development such as have been experienced recently in the Shanghai market.

While institutions will continue to change, and their structures evolve, it could be argued that such change will accommodate further internationalisation of the real estate industry. In this context it would also seem reasonable to expect further growth and consolidation within the real estate sector. Long-term trends, then, seem to imply greater economic integration and the Northern European – North American business model, if that is not too heroic an assumption. But change may not be gradual; specific events and market shocks can cause more rapid structural changes within markets, and regime changes affect the context within which markets operate.

The recent events surrounding the liquidity shortage may be the catalyst for regime change that has a significant impact on market relationships as the world economy moves forward. Hence, not only is the property market experiencing one of many cyclical fluctuations, but there is a real possibility that the trajectory of future growth may take a different path from the one it would have followed in the absence of the liquidity shortage. Interestingly, problems with market information lie close to the core of recent market turbulence.

Other potentially interesting outcomes may also emerge from recent economic events. These relate to geopolitical factors outside the scope of this book. But increasingly indebted nations in Europe and the US will have weaker global bargaining positions than large creditor nations. This could lead to institutional change in directions not previously anticipated. However, the basis for such conjecture is still limited.

It is, however, noticeable that there are no international organisations that directly regulate or define institutional structures within real estate markets. Within the EU, harmonisation policies have often focused on fiscal and monetary policies, and the outworking of the latter may be most clearly seen in the establishment of the Euro, the single currency. On issues related to planning, there are no EU policies on harmonisation, although many authors have argued that such regulations may impact on economic competitiveness. Also, there are no international regulations making market exchange in real estate identical in different countries, although in practice there may be many similarities. Further, there are no supranational bodies overseeing or encouraging regulation or setting a clear international framework within which real estate transaction would take place. This may be because the cost of establishing such a body and making it effective, given the wide range of specific processes in operation, would be costly. Recent developments in the real estate markets, too, may suggest that such overarching regulation would be unnecessary.

However, internationalisation of the real estate industry may cause individual firms to become large relative to the size of the market. In this case the real estate industry becomes like other industries producing differentiated products; it becomes oligopolistic. In this situation regulation may be necessary to prevent oligopolies from price-fixing and earning 'excess' profits. National regulatory bodies now exist to oversee conduct and performance of other oligopolies that have arisen as economies or economic policies have changed. Would such an approach be needed in the real estate sector?

Identifying the exact shape of future development in the real estate market will always be difficult. However, the text above and in the earlier chapters highlights the key variables that should be taken into consideration when analysing real estate markets in different cities, regions and nations. Processes for change may go through periods when change itself is gradual or more rapid. Nevertheless, the mixed-market system has increased in importance in the last 30 years. It has proved relatively successful at delivering economic growth over the long term, despite short-term cyclical fluctuations.

In the first chapter we set real estate within an economic context and used this as a basis for understanding market processes and internationalisation strategies, and for analysing institutional forces impinging on the market. An understanding of these processes remains central to extrapolating future market trends. As more countries have opened up to letting prices allocate resources, more countries have then interacted with the global economic system. Even for those countries where this is a recent phenomenon, there is evidence that the knowledge already learned by agents involved in earlier internationalisation of business has been quickly brought to, and applied in, new markets. In a sense, the 'pattern' for an internationalisation strategy is now embedded by key economic agents, and thus it seems reasonable to expect that once an economy opens to global economic forces it will, with appropriate institutional change if necessary, be of interest to real estate service companies as they follow (or lead) clients into new markets.

As some continents or global regions remain opaque, there still remain significant opportunities, not only for future developments in the real estate sector but also for other economies to become more integrated into global economic systems.

Real estate investment will continue to carry risk, and over time this will vary relative to other asset classes. However, as the market grows internationally, there will be opportunities to develop investment strategies within specific property sectors (e.g., retail, office, industrial, residential, leisure) across a wide range of countries that can benefit from expected growth in these markets. The potential range of investment services that could be provided and the range of investment products that could be created may only be in its infancy.

While market risks remain and institutional features may change, it seems that, as more economies develop, real estate markets, real estate companies and the range of services they offer will continue to grow and adapt to changing circumstances.

Notes

2   Theorising international real estate I

1. A TNC is an enterprise that controls assets of other entities in economies other than its home economy, usually by owning a certain equity capital stake (usually at least 10 per cent of ordinary shares). A foreign affiliate or direct investment enterprise is an enterprise in which a foreign direct investor, resident in another economy, owns a stake that permits a lasting interest in the management of that enterprise.
2. FDI is an investment involving a long-term relationship and lasting interest in, and control by, a resident entity in one economy in an enterprise resident in another economy. In FDI, the investor exerts significant influence on the management of the enterprise resident in the other economy. The ownership level required for a direct investment to exist is 10% of the voting shares (UNCTAD, 2008).

4   Property market activity

1. "Total" stock refers to the overall stock of commercial real estate. "Investible" stock means investment grade properties. This stock might currently be institutionally owned or owner-occupied but, in time, it should all become "institutional". This is smaller than the total stock as much commercial real estate is of too poor a quality to become institutional, or will always remain owner occupied. "Invested" stock, or the current stock refers to those properties which are currently owned by professional real estate investors for investment purposes (Adapted from RREEF, 2007).

6   European real estate markets

1. This may have been exacerbated by the exchange rate chosen after German reunification between the former currencies of East and West Germany.

8   Real estate markets in North America

1. See Grubb and Ellis (2007) National overview.
2. See Grubb and Ellis (2007) Office Market Trends: North America.

References

Adair, A.S., Berry, J.N., McGreal, W.S., Sykora, L., Ghanbari Parsa, A. and Redding, B. (1999) Globalization of Real Estate Markets in Central Europe, *European Planning Studies*, 7(3), 295–305.

Adams, D., Dunse, N. and White, M. (2005) Conceptualising State-Market Relations in Land and Property: The Mainstream Contribution of Neo-Classical and Welfare Economics, in D. Adams, C. Watkins and M. White (eds) *Planning, Public Policy and Property Markets*, Oxford: Blackwell.

Addae-Dapaah, K. and Kion, B. (1996) International diversification of property stock: a Singaporean investor's viewpoint, *The Real Estate Finance Journal*, 13(3), 54–66.

Addae-Dapaah, K. and Yong, G. (1998) Currency risk and office investment in Asia Pacific, *Real Estate Finance*, 5(1), 67–85.

Aharoni, Y. (1993) Globalization of Professional Business Services, in Y. Aharoni, (ed.) Coalitions and Competition, the Globalization of Professional Business Services, London: Routledge, pp. 1–19.

Asabere, P., Kleiman, R. and McGowan, C. (1991) The risk–return attributes of international real estate equities, *Journal of Real Estate Research*, 6(2), 143–52.

Ball, M. (1998) Institutions in British property research, *Urban Studies*, 35, 1501–17.

Ball, M. (2002) Cultural explanation of regional property markets: a critique, *Urban Studies*, 39, 1453–69.

Ball, M., Lizieri, C. and MacGregor, B.D. (1998) *The Economics of Commercial Property Markets*, London: Routledge.

Bardhan, A., Edelstein, R. and Tsang, D. (2008) Global financial integration and real estate security returns, *Real Estate Economics*, 36(2), 285–311.

Barras, R. (1994) Property and the economic cycle, *Journal of Property Research*, 11(3), 183–97.

Barras, R. (2005) A Building Cycle Model for an Imperfect World, *Journal of Property Research*, 22(2/3), 63–96.

Barry, C., Rodriguez, M. and Lipscomb, J. (1996) Diversification potential from real estate companies in emerging capital markets, *Journal of Real Estate Portfolio Management*, 2(2), 107–18.

Baum, A. (2002) *European private property vehicles: the emerging property market*, paper presented at the 5th Annual European Property Company Conference.

Bigman, T. (2002) Investing in international listed property companies, *PREA Quarterly*, Winter, 53–61.

Bond, S.A., Karolyi, G.A. and Sanders, A.B. (2003) International real estate returns: A multifactor, multicountry approach. *Real Estate Economics*, 31(3), 481–500.

Bordo, M., Eichengreen, B., Klingebiel, D. and Martinez-Peria, M.S. (2001) Is the Crisis Problem Growing More Severe?, *Economic Policy*, 32 (April), 51–82.

Case, B., Goetzmann, W. and Rouwenhorst, K.G. (1999) *Global real estate markets, cycles and fundamentals*, Working Paper No. 99–03, Yale International Center for Finance.

Casson, M.C. (1991) *The Economics of Business Culture: Game Theory, Transaction Costs and Economic Performance*, Oxford: Clarendon Press.

CBRE (2008) *Global market rents May 2008: office rents and occupancy costs worldwide*, US: CB Richard Ellis.

CBRE (2008) *Global REIT market trends and outlook*, presentation by W. S. Carroll, 16 September 2008, CB Richard Ellis.

CBRE (2006) *Who is buying the world?* US: CB Richard Ellis.

Cheng, P., Ziobrowski, A., Caines, R. and Ziobrowski, B. (1999) Uncertainty and foreign real estate, *Journal of Real Estate Research*, 18(3), 463–80.

Cheshire, P. and Shepherd, S. (2005) The Introduction of Price Signals into Land Use Planning Decision-making: A Proposal, *Urban Studies*, 42(4), 647–63.

Chia, S.Y. (2001) Singapore: global city and service hub, in F-C. Lo (ed.) *Globalization and Sustainability of Cities in the Asia Pacific Region*, Tokyo: United Nations University Press.

Chin, W. and Dziewulska, K. (2006) *Money into property: keeping on track in Asia Pacific real estate capital markets*, paper presented at Pacific Rim Real Estate Society Conference, Auckland, New Zealand, January 2006, http://www.prres.net/Papers/Chin_Money_into_Property.pdf

Cho, J. (2005) Urban planning and urban sprawl in Korea, *Urban Policy and Research*, 23(2), 203–18.

Chua, A. (1999) The role of international real estate in global mixed-asset investment portfolios, *Journal of Real Estate Portfolio Management*, 5(2), 129–37.

Coase, R.H. (1937) The Nature of the Firm, Economica, 4, 386–405.

Coase, R.H. (1960) The Problem of Social Cost, Journal of Law and Economics, 3, 1–44.

Colwell, P. (2002) Tweaking the DiPasquale and Wheaton Model, *Journal of Housing Economics*, 11, 24–39.

Conner, P. and Liang, Y. (2003), The expanding frontier of institutional real estate, May, *Pramerica Real Estate Investor*, Pramerica Financial.

Conover, C., Friday, H. and Sirmans, G. (2002) Diversification benefits from foreign real estate investments, *The Journal of Real Estate Portfolio Management*, 8(1), 17–25.

Conover, M., Friday, H. and Howton, S. (1998) The relationship between size and return for foreign real estate investments, *Journal of Real Estate Portfolio Management*, 4(2), 107–12.

Cushman and Wakefield (2007), Marketbeat Latin America 2007.

Cushman and Wakefield (2008), Marketbeat Latin America Office 2008, Sao Paulo.

D'Arcy, E. and Lee, S. (1998) A real estate portfolio strategy for Europe: a review of the options, *Journal of Real Estate Portfolio Management*, 4(2), 113–23.

D'Arcy, E., Keogh, G. and Roulac, S. (2000) Business culture and the development of real estate service provision in the UK and the US, Aberdeen Papers in Land Economy 2000–03.

Davies, H. and Ellis, P. (2000) Porter's competitive advantage of nations: time for final judgement?, *Journal of Management Studies*, 37(8), 1189–213.

Dehesh, A. and Pugh, C. (2000) Property Cycles in a Global Economy, *Urban Studies*, 37(13), 2581–602.

de Magalhaes, C. (2001) International property consultants and the transformation of local markets, *Journal of Property Research*, 18(1), 99–121.

Di Maggio, P. (1994) Culture and Economy, in N.J. Smelser and R. Swedberg (eds) *The Handbook of Economic Sociology*, Chichester: Princeton University Press.

Ding, C. (2005) *Land acquisition in China: reform and assessment*, Working Paper WP05CD1, Cambridge, MA: Lincoln Institute of Land Policy.

DiPasquale, D. and Wheaton, W. (1996) *Urban Economics and Real Estate Markets*, New Jersey: Prentice Hall.

Drucker, P. (1986) The changed world economy, *Foreign Affairs*, 64, 768–91.

DTZ (2006/07) *Money into property: global*, June, London: DTZ Research.

Dunning, H.H. and Bansal, S. (1997) The cultural sensitivity of the eclectic paradigm, *Multinational Business*, 5, 1–16.

Dunning, J.H. (1977) Trade location of economic activity and the multinational enterprise: a search for an eclectic paradigm, in B. Ohlin, P.O. Hesselborn and P.J. Wiskman (eds) *The International Allocation of Economic Activity*, London: MacMillan.

Dunning, J.H. (1993) Internationalizing Porter's 'diamond', *Management International Review*, 2, 7–15.

Dunning, J.H. (2000) The eclectic paradigm as an envelope for economic and business theories of MNE activity, *International Business Review*, 9, 163–90.

Economic Intelligence Unit, *The Economist*.

Eichholtz, P. (1996) The stability of the covariance of international property share returns, *Journal of Real Estate Research*, 11(2), 149–58.

Eichholtz, P. (1997) Real estate securities and common stocks: a first international look, *Real Estate Finance*, 14(1), 70–4.

Eichholtz, P. and Huisman, R. (1999) The cross section of global property share returns, in S.J. Brown and C.H. Liu (eds) *A Global Perspective on Real Estate Cycles*, Boston: Kluwer Academic Publishers.

Eichholtz, P., Mahieu, R. and Schotman, P. (1993) *Real estate diversification: by country or by continent?* Working paper, Limburg University, Maastricht.

Eichholtz, P., Hoesli, M., MacGregor, B. and Nanthakumaran, N. (1995) Real estate portfolio diversification by property type and region, *Journal of Property Finance*, 6(3), 39–59.

Eichholtz, P., Koedijk, K. and Schweitzer, M. (1997) *Testing international real estate investment strategies*, paper presented to the *Real Estate Research Institute Annual Seminar*, Chicago.

Eichholtz, P., Huisman, R., Koedijk, K. and Schuin, L. (1998) Continental factors in international real estate returns, *Real Estate Economics*, 26, 493–509.

EIU (2007) *Asset management in the Middle East*, London: Economic Intelligence Unit.

EIU (2008) *Latin American data*, Economic Intelligence Unit online, *The Economist*.

Eppli, M.J. and Tu, C.C. (2004) Real Estate Markets in the United States, in W. Seabrooke, P. Kent and H.H.H. How (eds) *International Real Estate: An Institutional Approach*, Oxford: Blackwell.

European Public Real Estate Association (EPRA) (2004) *EPRA Global REIT Survey: A Comparison of Major REIT Regimes in the World*, Shipol: EPRA.

Feng, C.C. and Yeung, S.C.W. (2004) Real estate markets in mainland China, in W. Seabrooke, P. Kent and H.H.H. How (eds) *International Real Estate: An Institutional Approach*, Oxford: Blackwell.

Geurts, T. and Jaffe, A. (1996) Risk and Real Estate Investment: An International Perspective, *Journal of Real Estate Research*, 11(2), 117–30.

Giliberto, S. (1989) *Real estate vs. financial assets: an updated comparison of returns in the United States and the United Kingdom*, New York: Salomon Brothers, Inc.

Giliberto, S. (1990) *Global real estate securities: index performance and diversified portfolios*, New York: Salomon Brothers, Inc.

Glascock, J.L. and Kelly, L.J. (2007) The Relative Effect of Property Type and Country Factors in Reduction of Risk of Internationally Diversified Real Estate Portfolios, *Journal of Real Estate Finance and Economics*, 34, 369–84.

Goetzmann, W. and Wachter, S. (1995) The global real estate crash: evidence from an international database, in *Proceedings of the International Congress on Real Estate, Vol. 3* (unpaginated), Singapore: AREUEA.

Gordon, J. (1991) The diversification potential of international property investments, *Real Estate Finance Journal*, 7(2), 42–8.

Gordon, J. and Canter, T. (1999) International real estate securities: a test of capital markets integration, *Journal of Real Estate Portfolio Management*, 5(2), 161–70.

Gordon, J., Canter, T. and Webb, J. (1998) The effects of international real estate securities on portfolio diversification, *Journal of Real Estate Portfolio Management*, 4(2), 83–92.

Hamelink, F. and Hoesli, M. (2004) What factors determine international real estate security returns?, *Real Estate Economics*, 32, 437–62.

Hamilton, W.H. (1932) Institutions, in E.R.A. Seligman and A. Johnson (eds) *Encyclopaedia of Social Sciences*, 8, 84–9.

Han, S.S. (2000) Shanghai : between state and market in urban transformation, *Urban Studies*, 37(11), 2091–112.

Han, S.S. and Wang, Y. (2003) The institutional structure of a property market in inland China: Chongqing, *Urban Studies*, 40(1), 91–112.

Hargreaves-Heap, S.P. and Varoufakis, Y. (1995) *Game Theory: A Critical Introduction*, London: Routledge.

Healey, P. (1991) Models of the development process: a review, *Journal of Property Research*, 8, 33–44.

Held, D., McGrew, A., Goldblatt, D. and Perraton, J. (1999) *Global Transformations: Politics, Economics and Culture*, Stanford: Stanford University Press.

Hendershott, P. and White, M. (2000) Taxing and Subsidising Housing Investment: The Rise and Fall of Housings Favoured Status, *Journal of Housing Research*, 11(2), 257–76.

Hendershott, P., MacGregor, B. and Tse, R. (2002a), Estimation of the Rental Adjustment Process, *Real Estate Economics*, 30(2), 165–83.

Hendershott, P., MacGregor, B. and White, M. (2002b), Explaining Commercial Rents Using an Error Correction Model with Panel Data, *Journal of Real Estate Finance and Economics*, 24(1), 59–87.

HENDERSON INVESTORS/AMP (2000) *The case for global property investment*, London: Henderson Investors Ltd.

Hodgson, G.M. (1989) Institutional economic theory: the old versus the new, *Review of Political Economy*, 1, 249–69.

Hodgson, G.M. (1999) *Economics and Utopia*, London: Routledge.

Hoesli, M. and MacGregor, B. (2000) *Property Investment. Principles and Practice of Portfolio Management*, Harlow: Pearson Education Ltd.

Hoesli, M., Lekander, J. and Witkiewitz, W. (2002) *International evidence on real estate as a portfolio diversifier*, working paper.

Hofstede, G. (1991) *Cultures and Organisations*, London: MacGraw-Hill.

Hong, S.W. (1997) Building a power house: Korea experiences of regional development and infrastructure, Seoul: KRIHS Press.

IMF (1999) *World Economic Outlook*, Washington, DC: International Monetary Fund.

IMF (2000) *World Economic Outlook*, Washington, DC: International Monetary Fund.

IMF (2006) *Regional Economic Outlook: Asia and Pacific*, Washington, DC: International Monetary Fund.

IMF (2008) *World Economic Outlook*, Washington, DC: International Monetary Fund.

ING Real Estate (2008) *Global Vision 2008*, www.ingrealestate.com

ING Real Estate (2008) *Global retail markets: Is the retail real estate sector defensive in this downturn*, September, www.ingrealestate.com

Jackson, C., Stevenson, S. and Watkins, C. (2008) NY-LON Does a Single Cross-Continental Office Market Exist? *Journal of Real Estate Portfolio Management*, 12 (2), 156–74.

JLL (2004) *Real Estate Transparency Index*, London: Jones Lang LaSalle.

JLL (2006) *Real Estate Transparency Index*, London: Jones Lang LaSalle.

JLL (2006) *India A real estate investment future*, Jones Lang LaSalle.

JLL (2007) *European Office Property Clock*, Quarter 4, London: Jones Lang LaSalle.

JLL (2008) *Americas road to transparency*, London: Jones Lang LaSalle.

JLL (2008) *Asia Pacific property digest, First Quarter*.

JLL (2008) *Key market indicators*, March, London: Jones Lang LaSalle.

JLL (2008) *Latin American city profile: Buenos Aires, Argentina, 3Q 2008*.

JLL (2008) *Real Estate Transparency Index*, London: Jones Lang LaSalle.

JLL (2008) *Real Estate Transparency in Latin America, 2008*, London: Jones Lang LaSalle.

JLL (2008) *The Big Five: Shopping centre investment in core Western Europe*, London: Jones Lang LaSalle.

Kamal-Chaoui, L., Leman, E. and Rufei, Z. (2009) *Urban Trends and Policy in China*, OECD Regional Development Working Papers, 2009/1, Paris: OECD.

Kawaguchi, Y. (2004) Real estate markets in Japan, in W. Seabrooke, P. Kent and H.H.H. How (eds) *International Real Estate: An Institutional Approach*, Oxford: Blackwell.

Ke, Q. and White, M. (2009) An econometric analysis of Shanghai office rents, *Journal of Property Investment and Finance*, 27(2), 120–39.

Keogh, G. and D'Arcy, E. (1994) Market maturity and property market behaviour: a European comparison of mature and emerging markets , *Journal of Property Research*, 11(3), 215–35.

Keogh, G. and D'Arcy, E. (1999a) Property market efficiency: an institutional economics perspective, *Urban Studies*, 36, 2401–14.

Keogh, G. and D'Arcy, E. (1999b) The property market and urban competitiveness: a review, *Urban Studies*, 36, 917–28.

Keogh, G., D'Arcy, E. and Roulac, S. (2000) Business Culture and the Development of Real Estate Service Provision in the United Kingdom and the United States, *Aberdeen Papers in Land Economy*, 2000–03, 1–34.

Kelly, J. (2002) *Commercial real estate development and the 'city offer'*, presentation at Gemaca II Seminar on Economic Performance of the major European metro regions improving their competitiveness, 8 February 2002.

Key, T. and Law, V. (2005) *The size of the UK market*, IPF Seminar May, City University.

Kidokoro, T., Onishi, T. and Marcotullio, P. (2001) The impacts of globalization and issues of metropolitan planning in Tokyo, in F-C. Lo (ed.) *Globalization and Sustainability of Cities in the Asia Pacific Region*, Tokyo: United Nations University Press.

Krugman, P.R. and Obstfield, M. (2000), *International Economics*, 5th edn, Addition Wesley Longman.

Krugman, P.R. and Obstfield, M. (2004), *International Economics: Theory and Policy*, 6th edn. Harper and Collins, New York.

Kwon, W-Y. (2001) Globalization and the sustainability of cities in the Asia Pacific region: The case of Seoul, in F-C. Lo (ed.) *Globalization and Sustainability of Cities in the Asia Pacific Region*, Tokyo: United Nations University Press.

Lau, L. (1994) The competitive advantage of Taiwan, *Journal of Far Eastern Business*, 1(1), 90–112.

Lee, S. (2000) *The risks of investing in the real estate markets of the Asian region*, mimeo, University of Reading, UK.

Li, L.H., McKinnell, K.G. and Walker, A. (2000) Convergence of the land tenure systems of China, Hong Kong and Taiwan?, *Journal of Property Research*, 17(4), 339–52.

Lin, X. and Song, H. (1997) China and the multinationals – a winning combination, *Long Range Planning*, 30(1), 74–83.

Ling, D.C. and Naranjo, A. (2002) Commercial real estate return performance: a cross country analysis, *The Journal of Real Estate Finance and Economics*, 24, 119–42.

Liu, C.H. and Mei, J. (1998) The predictability of international real estate markets, exchange rate risks and diversification consequences, *Real Estate Economics*, 26, 3–39.

Lo, F-C. and Marcotullio, P.J. (2001) Globalization and urban transformations in the Asia Pacific region, in F-C. Lo (ed.) *Globalization and Sustainability of Cities in the Asia Pacific Region*, Tokyo: United Nations University Press.

Løwendahl, B.R. (2000) The Globalisation of Professional Business Service Firms: Fad or Genuine Source of Competitive Advantage? in Y. Aharoni and L. Nachum (eds) *Globalisation of Services: Some Implications for Theory and Practice*, London: Routledge.

McGreal, W.S., Parsa, A. and Keivani, R. (2002) Evolution of property investment markets in Central Europe: opportunities and constraints, *Journal of Property Research*, 19(3), 213–30.

Maclennan, D. and Whitehead, C. (1996) Housing economics – an evolving agenda, *Housing Studies*, 11, 341–44.

Marcotullio, P.J. and Lo, F-C. (2001) Introduction, in F-C. Lo (ed.) *Globalization and Sustainability of Cities in the Asia Pacific Region*, Tokyo: United Nations University Press.

Markowitz, H.M. (1952) Portfolio Selection, *Journal of Finance*, 7(1), 77–91.

Markowitz, H.M. (1959) *Portfolio Selection: efficient diversification of investments*, New York: John Wiley & Sons.

Marks, E. (1986) Real rates of return among foreign investors in US real estate, *Real Estate Finance Journal*, 1(3), 56–61.

Merath, T., Rohner, P., Schubert, S. and Simioni, B. (2008), *Latin America more attractive investment market*, Credit Suisse, published 25 August 2008.

Miles, M. and McCue, T. (1982) Historic returns and institutional real estate portfolios, *AREUEA Journal*, 10, 184–99.

Miles, M. and McCue, T. (1984) Commercial real estate returns, *AREUEA Journal*, 12, 355–77.

Ministry of Finance (2002) *The tenth five year plan (2002–07)*, New Delhi.

Montet, C. and Serra, D. (2003) *Game Theory and Economics*, Basingstoke: Palgrave Macmillan.

Mouzakis, F. and Richards, D. (2007) Panel Data Modelling of Prime Office Rents: A Study of 12 Major European Markets, *Journal of Property Research*, 24(1), 31–53.

Mull, S. and Soenen, L. (1997) U.S. REITs as an asset class in international investment portfolios, *Financial Analysts Journal*, 53(2), 55–61.

Mundell, R. (1957) International Trade and Factor Mobility, *American Economic Review*, 47(2), 321–35.

Needham, B. (1994) Comment, *Journal of Property Research*, 10, 65–7.

Newell, G. and Webb, J. (1996) Real estate performance benchmarks in New Zealand and South Africa, *Journal of Real Estate Literature*, 6(2), 137–43.

Parsa, A.R. (1995) Property Investment and Development in Central Europe 1989–1995, *Proceedings of The Cutting Edge 1995 Conference*, RICS, London, 2, 277–90.

Pierzak, E. (2001) *Exploring international property securities for US investors*, Henderson Global Investors Property Economics & Research.

Porter, M.E. (1986) Competition in Global Industries: a Conceptual Framework, in M.E. Porter (ed.) *Competition in Global Industries*, Cambridge: Harvard Business School Press.

Porter, M.E. (1990) The competitive advantage of nations, London: MacMillan.

PREI (2003) *A bird eye of real estate markets*, March, US: Pramerica Real Estate Investors.

Qingshu, X., Parsa, A.R.G. and Redding, B. (2002) The emergence of the urban land market in China: evolution, structure, constraints and perspectives, *Urban Studies*, 39(8), 1375–98.

Ravenhill, J. (2005) *Global Political Economy*, Oxford: Oxford University Press.

Reid, I. (1989) Creating a global real estate investment strategy, *Money Management Forum*, 101–4.

Ricardo, D. (1817) *On the Principles of Political Economy and Taxation*, London: John Murray.

RREEF (2006a) *Asia Pacific property cycle monitor Nov 2006*, London: RREEF Limited.

RREEF (2006b) *European property cycle monitor December*, London: RREEF Limited.

RREEF (2007a) *The future size of the global real estate market*, London: RREEF Limited.

RREEF (2007b) *RREEF global real estate insights, October*, London: RREEF Limited.

RREEF (2008) *Global real estate investment and performance 2007 and 2008*, London: RREEF Limited.

Rutherford, M. (1994) *Institutions in Economics: The Old and the New Institutionalism*, Cambridge: Cambridge University Press.

Sahoo, P. (2006) *Foreign direct investment in south Asia: policy, trends, impact and determinants*, ADBI Discussion Paper 56, ADB Institute, Tokyo.

Samuels, W. (1995) The present state of institutional economics, *Cambridge Journal of Economics*, 19, 569–90.

Samuelson, P. A. (1948) International trade and equalization of factor prices, *Economic Journal*, June.

Schott, J.J. (1991). Trading blocs and the world trading system, *World Economy* 14(1), 1–17.

Shah, A. and Patnaik, I. (2008) *Managing capital flows*, ADBI Discussion Paper 98, ADB Institute, Tokyo.

Sharpe, W.F. (1964) Capital asset prices: a theory of market equilibrium under conditions of risk, *Journal of Finance*, 19(3), 425–42.

Singh, A. (2006) *Macroeconomic volatility: the policy lessons from Latin America*, working Paper WP/06/166, International Monetary Fund.

Sirmans, C.F. and Worzala, E. (2003) International Direct Real Estate Investment: A Review of the Literature, *Urban Studies*, 40(5–6), 1081–114.

Smith, A. (1776/1976) *An Inquiry into the Nature and Causes of the Wealth of Nations*, Oxford: Oxford University Press.

So, K.K., Chan, G. and Chan, R. (2005) *Eye on Asia*, US: PricewaterhouseCoopers.

Stevenson, S. (1998) *The role of commercial real estate in international multi-asset portfolios*, working Paper BF No. 98–2, University College, Dublin.

Stevenson, S. (1999) Real estate's role in an international multi asset portfolio: empirical evidence using Irish data, *Journal of Property Research*, 16(3), 219–42.

Stevenson, S. (2000) International real estate diversification: empirical tests using hedged indices, *Journal of Real Estate Research*, 19(1/2), 105–31.

Sweeney, F. (1989) Investment strategy: a property market without frontiers, *Estates Gazette*, 89(35), 20–30.

Sykora, L. and Simonickova, I. (1994) From totalitarian urban managerialism to a liberalised real estate market: Prague's transformation in the early 1990s, in M. Barlow, P. Dostal and M. Hampl (eds) *Development and Administration of Prague*, Amsterdam: Institut voor sociale Geografie.

Takafusa, S. (2004) *The role of development planning in Japan*, paper presented at International Conference on China's Planning System Reform, 24–25 March 2004, http://www.adb.org/Documents/Events/2004/PRC_Planning_System_Reform/takafusa7.pdf

Tiwari, P., Swamwil, I.B. and Doi, M. (2003) Spatial pattern of Japanese manufacturing industry in four ASEAN countries, *Papers in Regional Science*, 82(3), 403–15.

Tripathy, M. (2008) *Managing a global real estate portfolio*, Deloitte Development LLC.

Trompenaars, F. and Hampden-Turner, C. (1997) *Riding the Waves of Culture: Understanding Cultural Diversity in Business*, London: Nicholas Brealey.

ULI and PwC (2007) *Emerging Trends in Real Estate*, US: PricewaterhouseCoopers.

UNCTAD (2007) *World Investment Report, Transnational Corporations, Extractive Industries and development*, United Nations.

UNCTAD Handbook of Statistics 2008.

UNCTAD (2008) *World Investment Report, Transnational Corporations, and the Infrastructure Challenge*, United Nations.

UNCTAD, FDI Statistics http://www.unctad.org/Templates/Page.asp?intItemID=3198&lang=1

Van der Krabben, E. and Lambooy, J.G. (1993) A theoretical framework for the functioning of the Dutch property market, *Urban Studies*, 30, 1381–897.

Walker, A. and Flanagan, R. (eds) (1991) *Property and Construction in Asia Pacific: Hong Kong, Japan, Singapore*, Oxford: BSP Professional Books.

Ward, P. (1996) Contemporary issues in the government and administration of Latin American mega-cities, in A. Gilbert (ed.) *The Mega-City in Latin America*, Tokyo: United Nations University Press.

Webb, B. and O'Keefe, J. (2002) *The case for global real estate*, working paper, UBS Global Asset Management.

Webb, B. and Rubens, J. H. (1989) *Diversification gains from including foreign real estate in a mixed asset portfolio*, paper presented at the *American Real Estate Society Meetings*, San Francisco.

Wheaton, W., Torto, R. and Evans P. (1997) The cyclic behavior of the Greater London office market, *Journal of Real Estate Finance and Economics*, 15(1), 77–92.

Whitaker, B. (2001) Why should investors consider international real estate investment?, *Global Real Estate Perspective*, June, 2–15.

Wilson, P. and Okunev, J. (1996) Evidence of segmentation in domestic and international property markets, *The Journal of Property Finance*, 7(4), 78–97.

Wilson, P. and Okunev, J. (1999) Special analysis of real estate and financial assets markets, *Journal of Property Investment and Finance*, 17(1), 61–74.

Winograd, B. (2004) US Pension Funds and Real Estate: Still Crazy After All These Years, in W. Seabrooke, P. Kent and H.H.H. How (eds) *International Real Estate: An Institutional Approach*, Oxford: Blackwell.

World Bank Data Statistics; http://siteresources.worldbank.org/DATASTATISTICS/Resources/table4_1.pdf; http://investintaiwan.nat.gov.tw/en/env/stats/gdp_growth.html

Worzala, E. (1992) *International direct real estate investments as alternative portfolio assets for institutional investors: an evaluation*, unpublished dissertation, University of Wisconsin-Madison.

Worzala, E. and Vandell, K. (1995) *International real estate investments as alternative portfolio assets for institutional investors: an evaluation*, paper presented at the *IRES/ERES Meetings*, Stockholm, Sweden.

Ziobrowski, A. and Boyd, J. (1991) Leverage and foreign investment in US real estate, *Journal of Real Estate Research*, 7(1), 33–58.

Ziobrowski, A.J. and Curcio, R.J. (1991) Diversification benefits of US real estate to foreign investors, *Journal of Real Estate Research*, 6(2), 119–42.

Index